China's State-Owned Enterprises

Why do Chinese state-owned enterprises (SOEs) routinely respond to central-level goals and policies in different ways, and why do their reform trajectories often vary significantly across firms and over time? This book introduces a leadership approach to studying the politics, processes, and outcomes of economic reform in China's public sector. Using a series of in-depth case studies, Wendy Leutert analyzes the exercise and effects of leadership in Chinese SOEs. She uncovers the "intra-organizational politics of reform," the daily dynamics of cooperation and conflict between leaders and their subordinates inside public-sector organizations. She also identifies common tactics that Chinese SOE leaders use to execute their agendas and ways in which their subordinates respond. Updating and expanding existing knowledge, this book highlights the growing global context and consequences of leadership in Chinese SOEs and why leadership remains vital for understanding China today.

WENDY LEUTERT is Assistant Professor and GLP-Ming Z. Mei Chair of Chinese Economics and Trade at Indiana University Bloomington. She has a PhD in government from Cornell University, an MA in international relations from Tsinghua University, and a BA in political science and philosophy from Wellesley College. In 2022, she was awarded the Emerging Scholars Policy Prize from University of Pennsylvania Perry World House and *Foreign Affairs*.

Business and Public Policy

Series Editor

ASEEM PRAKASH, University of Washington, Seattle

Series Board

This series aims to play a pioneering role in shaping the emerging field of business and public policy. *Business and Public Policy* focuses on two central questions. First, how does public policy influence business strategy, operations, organization, and governance, and with what consequences for both business and society? Second, how do businesses themselves influence policy institutions, policy processes, and other policy actors and with what outcomes?

Other books in the series

RICHARD W. CARNEY *China's Chance to Lead*

MANUEL P. TEODORO, SAMANTHA ZUHLKE and DAVID SWITZER *The Profits of Distrust: Citizens, Drinking Water, and the Crisis of Confidence in American Government*

JANE L. SUMNER *The Cost of Doing Politics: How Partisanship and Public Opinion Shape Corporate Influence*

KATHRYN HOCHSTETLER *Political Economies of Energy Transition: Wind and Solar Power in Brazil and South Africa*

PAASHA MAHDAVI *Power Grab: Political Survival through Extractive Resource Nationalization*

STEFAN RENCKENS *Private Governance and Public Authority: Regulating Sustainability in a Global Economy*

SARAH BAUERLE DANZMAN *Merging Interests: When Domestic Firms Shape FDI Policy*

(continued after index)

China's State-Owned Enterprises

Leadership, Reform, and Internationalization

WENDY LEUTERT
Indiana University Bloomington

CAMBRIDGE
UNIVERSITY PRESS

CAMBRIDGE
UNIVERSITY PRESS

Shaftesbury Road, Cambridge CB2 8EA, United Kingdom

One Liberty Plaza, 20th Floor, New York, NY 10006, USA

477 Williamstown Road, Port Melbourne, VIC 3207, Australia

314–321, 3rd Floor, Plot 3, Splendor Forum, Jasola District Centre, New Delhi – 110025, India

103 Penang Road, #05–06/07, Visioncrest Commercial, Singapore 238467

Cambridge University Press is part of Cambridge University Press & Assessment, a department of the University of Cambridge.

We share the University's mission to contribute to society through the pursuit of education, learning and research at the highest international levels of excellence.

www.cambridge.org
Information on this title: www.cambridge.org/9781009486521

DOI: 10.1017/9781009486576

When citing this work, please include a reference to the DOI 10.1017/9781009486576

First published 2024

A catalogue record for this publication is available from the British Library

Library of Congress Cataloging-in-Publication Data
Names: Leutert, Wendy Elizabeth, 1983– author.
Title: China's state-owned enterprises : leadership, reform, and internationalization / Wendy Elizabeth Leutert, Indiana University, Bloomington.
Other titles: Leadership, reform, and internationalization
Description: 1 edition. | New York, NY : Cambridge University Press, 2024. | Includes bibliographical references and index.
Identifiers: LCCN 2024009538 | ISBN 9781009486521 (hardback) | ISBN 9781009486576 (ebook)
Subjects: LCSH: Government business enterprises – China. | China – Economic policy. | China – Politics and government – 21st century. | China – Foreign relations.
Classification: LCC HD4318 .L4628 2024 | DDC 338.620951–dc23/eng/20240315
LC record available at https://lccn.loc.gov/2024009538

ISBN 978-1-009-48652-1 Hardback
ISBN 978-1-009-48654-5 Paperback

For Yingtao Guo

Contents

Figures

Tables

Acknowledgments

This book originated in my PhD research at Cornell University, where I had the privilege of working with four superlative scholars as my committee members: Peter Katzenstein, Andrew Mertha, Nicolas van de Walle, and Li-an Zhou. Peter Katzenstein urged me to read widely across disciplines, inspired creative thinking, and provided an unparalleled example of how to be a scholar, mentor, and teacher. Andrew Mertha encouraged me to delve into the weeds of Chinese politics and face fieldwork challenges with perseverance and humor. Nicolas van de Walle provided an invaluable comparative perspective throughout the project's development. Li-an Zhou shared his deep insights into China's political economy and generously hosted me several times as a visiting researcher at Peking University's Guanghua School of Management in Beijing.

Many others at Cornell were also instrumental to this study. Conversations with and the work of Allen Carlson, Xu Xin, Jeremy Wallace, and Jessica Chen Weiss deepened my knowledge of Chinese politics. Jonathan Kirshner challenged me to think unconventionally and shared writing advice. David Patel taught me how to conduct field research. Muna Ndulo shared his expertise in international investment and how to leverage scholarship for real-world impact. Henry Wan inspired me with his passion for research on industrial policy and East Asia's economic transformation. I gained new ways of thinking about institutions from Victor Nee. I also learned from classmates at Cornell who studied China, including Christopher Cairns, Amanda Cheney, Jack Meng-Tat Chia, Manfred Elfstrom, Matthew Erie, Lin Fu, Lauren Hansen, Isaac Kardon, Peter Lavelle, Ningzi Li, Elizabeth Plantan, Lesley Turnbull, Youyi Zhang, and Taomo Zhou. Sarah Maxey and Catherine Reyes-Housholder sustained the project from the start with their friendship. Toby Goldbach provided years of crucial solidarity, laughter, and writing company.

Numerous researchers generously assisted my research in China and beyond. They include Chen Qi, Chen Zhiwu, Fan Shitao, Gary Hua, Jia Qingguo, Li Wei, Tao Ran, Wang Haibin, Wu Jinglian, Wu Yongping, Xu Jin, Ye Jing, Zhang Chunlin, and Zhou Jingxin. The employees at the state-owned enterprise (SOE) in Beijing where I conducted research explained its organizational structure and operations, shared their experiences and knowledge, and provided companionship over many lunches in the cafeteria. I also thank Beth Bader for giving me a space to work at the University of Chicago Center in Beijing. During a research stay in Hong Kong at the Chinese University of Hong Kong, I benefited from the help of Gao Xin and Celia Wong at the University Services Centre, as well as from conversations with Li Chen and Leslie Zeng. Jack Kai Yui Wong assisted me to collect additional materials at the Centre. Ja Ian Chong, Bert Hofman, and James Tan welcomed me to the National University of Singapore and enabled me to access research materials at its East Asian Institute. Fiifi Bright made my fieldwork visits in Ghana both productive and fun.

A predoctoral fellowship with the Brookings Institution supported research in Beijing and Washington, DC. At the Brookings-Tsinghua Center for Public Policy, Li Yuan, Wang Mengni, Zhou Xuelian, and Zhu Mengye gave me a source of daily community in Beijing. In DC, I learned immensely from colleagues at the John L. Thornton China Center, especially David Dollar, Cheng Li, Kenneth Lieberthal, and Jonathan Pollack. Ryan McElveen, Vincent Wang, Wang Wei, Lucy Xu, and Zhai Xinhui welcomed me to Brookings and DC. Benjamin Wittes gave me wise writing and career advice. Several China experts kindly offered feedback on my research in progress in DC, including Pieter Bottelier, Donald Clarke, Erica Downs, Scott Kennedy, Nicholas Lardy, Philippe LeCorre, and Richard McGregor.

Postdoctoral fellowships at the University of Pennsylvania, Columbia University, and Harvard University enabled me to revise and improve this book. Avery Goldstein and Jacques de Lisle gave me the privilege of joining the close-knit community of Penn's Center for the Study of Contemporary China. Roselyn Hsueh, Yeling Tan, Michael Useem, and Lu Zhang provided invaluable feedback at my book workshop. I learned from and was helped by many at Penn, including Regina Abrami, Hanming Fang, Amy Gadsden, Yue Hou, Denise van der Kamp, Siyao Li, Neysun Mahboubi, Marshall Meyer, Seung-Youn Oh, Zoe (Zhe) Qiao, Scott Wingo, Guobin Yang, Zeng Yu, and Yuanyuan

Zeng. The Columbia-Harvard China and the World Program community offered new perspectives and insight. I especially thank Thomas Christensen, Andrew Chubb, Takako Hikotani, Iain Johnston, Tyler Jost, Benjamin Liebman, Lien-Hang Nguyen, and Daniel Suchenski. The Fairbank Center for Chinese Studies at Harvard University and the Fung Library became a second home. I am very grateful to Bill Alford, Christopher Carrothers, James Evans, Joseph Fewsmith, Josh Freedman, Julian Gewirtz, Arunabh Ghosh, Nancy Hearst, William Kirby, Daniel Koss, Meg Rithmire, Kyle Shernuk, Austin Strange, Katharin Tai, Yeling Tan, Kibrom Teweldebirhan, Ezra Vogel, Yuhua Wang, Saul Wilson, Mark Wu, and Xu Liang. Fan Shitao and He Wenkai gave tremendously helpful comments and advice during my first visit to the Fairbank Center.

I learned from many scholars of China while writing this book. I thank William Joseph for sparking and supporting my interest in Chinese politics. Barry Naughton has long been my role model for research on China's political economy. Kristen Looney generously shared advice and expertise in Chinese politics over many years. Samantha Vortherms was an amazing source of support and insight throughout the entire research and writing process. Abigail Coplin introduced me to new readings and ideas and helped make academic work more fun. Yufan Huang provided invaluable research assistance and input. I have also learned greatly from and been helped during this project by many researchers, including Kasper Ingeman Beck, Deborah Brautigam, Kjeld Erik Brødsgaard, Alvin Camba, Chelsea Chia-Chen Chou, Michael Davidson, Dominic DeSapio, Matthew Ferchen, Xue Gong, Nis Grünberg, Peng Hai, Koji Hirata, Kyle Jaros, Franziska Keller, Pierre Landry, Ching-Kwan Lee, Li-wen Lin, Chih-shian Liou, Melanie Manion, Curtis Milhaupt, Kacie Miura, Aldo Musacchio, Sara Newland, Tami Groswald Ozery, Margaret Pearson, Daniel Rosen, Dorothy Solinger, Joseph Torigian, Yuan Wang, and Stella Hong Zhang. I especially thank my current and former colleagues at Indiana University who work on China and East Asia and who supported this study: Hannah Airriess, Gardner Bovingdon, Yea-fen Chen, Hilary Holbrow, Adam Liff, Ethan Michelson, Shawn Reynolds, Jason Wu, Nick Vogt, John Yasuda, and Steven Yin.

Many people helped bring this book to press. Aseem Prakash and John Haslam at Cambridge University Press offered editorial advice and expertly guided the book throughout the review process. Roger

Haydon at Cornell University Press offered very helpful advice on an early iteration of the manuscript. Anonymous reviewers gave critical suggestions that significantly improved its content and quality. Fan Shitao, Toby Goldbach, Lauren Hansen, Nancy Hearst, Ethan Michelson, Joseph Torigian, Michael Useem, Samantha Vortherms, Andrew Walder, and others provided insightful written comments on various chapters. James Conran shared valuable suggestions on manuscript submission. Nancy Hearst skillfully copyedited the manuscript and references and enriched the project from its inception with her expertise and kindness. All remaining mistakes and typos are my own.

Multiple institutions and programs generously supported research and writing for this book. I thank the China-Africa Research Initiative of the Johns Hopkins School of Advanced and International Studies, the Chinese Scholarship Council, Columbia University, Cornell University, the Ford Foundation U.S.-China Exchange Fellowship Program, the Fulbright-Hays Doctoral Dissertation Research Abroad Program of the United States Department of Education, Harvard University, Indiana University, the Institute for Humane Studies, the Smith Richardson Foundation, and the University of Pennsylvania.

A wonderful group of people who I met in Beijing provided community and friendship, including Dai Shuping, Dong Zhixiong, Hao Qing, Mrs. Jiang, Mr. Jin and Mrs. Xia, Shang Yan, Tie Jiao, Wang Yang, Xia Dawei and Zhou Shanshan, and Xu Zhi and Wang Lin. Classmates from Tsinghua University, especially Cui Zhinan and Tang Tingting, provided fun and camaraderie during get-togethers in Beijing. Classmates and others from my time at the Inter-University Program for Chinese Language Studies became lifelong friends, including Joel Backaler, Sarah Eaton, Heather Hausladen, Andrew Herron, Peter Lavelle, Michael Martina, Brendan Mrosak and Gizelle Chavez, Claire Nelson, Evan Randall and G. P. Ooi, Peter Swartz, Lesley Turnbull, Shannon van Sant, Nicholas Wagner, Rhonda Wagner, Graham Webster, Gabriel Wildau, and Yuan Jing and Christina Yuan.

I relied on the kindness and hospitality of many friends around the world during this decade-long endeavor. I thank especially Anna Azaryeva and Rudy Valente, Cassie and Dan Barone, Evan and Brittany Barr, Ariel Diamond, Brinley and Jeff Esposito, Ursula Jessee and Alex Papo, Daniel Lambauer, Nhu Le, Sarah Ledbetter, Jessica Lipski, Sam Lockhart and Becky Depalma, Mike Razzano and Chantal

Berot, Meredith Riley, Phil and Colleen Sandick, Dorie Withey and Justin Perricone, and Alexandra Yannias-Walker.

My family is the foundation of my work and all that I do. My grandmother, Margrit Leutert, inspired me with her independent and international life. My parents, Werner and Christine Leutert, and my sisters, Pamela Lazarto and Stephanie Leutert, and their families supported my study of China even when it meant many years abroad. My son, Kai Guo Leutert, brought new joy to the final stages of the project. I could not have completed it without my husband, Yingtao Guo. I dedicate this book to him.

Abbreviations

BRI	Belt and Road Initiative
CCCC	China Construction Communications Corporation
CCDI	Central Commission for Discipline Inspection
CCP	Chinese Communist Party
CGN	China General Nuclear Power Group
CNPC	China National Petroleum Corporation
COD	Central Organization Department
COFCO	China National Cereals, Oils, and Foodstuffs Corporation
CREC	China Railway Engineering Corporation
CSRC	China Securities Regulatory Commission
EDF	Électricité de France
EVA	economic value added
GATT	General Agreement on Tariffs and Trade
IGO	intergovernmental organization
IMF	International Monetary Fund
INGO	international nongovernmental organization
IPO	initial public offering
MOU	memorandum of understanding
NDRC	National Development and Reform Commission
NPC	National People's Congress
PPP	public–private partnership
SAAB	State Assets Administration Bureau
SASAC	State-owned Assets Supervision and Administration Commission
SGIDC	State Grid International Development Company
SOE	state-owned enterprise
TVE	township and village enterprise
UHA	ultra-high-voltage
WTO	World Trade Organization

1 *Reform and Leadership*

"Prioritizing international business is of top importance." The chairman of China Infrastructure (CI) spoke slowly, sweat glistening on his brow as he surveyed the packed conference room in the firm's Beijing headquarters.[1] "We do not enjoy a natural monopoly," he emphasized. "Intense competition must make us become a company with competitive advantages."[2] Those of us in attendance knew all too well that he was right. Both the number and the contract value of CI's overseas projects had recently exceeded that of its domestic works. Yet further expanding the company's international business involved fierce contestation for market share with other Chinese state-owned enterprises (SOEs) as well as with foreign rivals, such as the American construction firm Bechtel and the South Korean contractor Hyundai Engineering and Construction.

Few might have anticipated such global, entrepreneurial ambitions for a SOE founded in the 1950s to advance the national industrialization efforts of the Communist Party of China (CCP). During the 1950s and 1960s, CI's nationwide network of construction bureaus built basic infrastructure projects across China, from Guizhou in the southwest to Jilin in the northeast. The government ministry to which CI belonged allocated it labor, capital, and projects. A patriotic commitment to industrializing the New China motivated the firm's activities, not profits or faraway markets. As verses from a 1965 company song exhorted workers: "Hardship is glorious and joyful, the spring of revolution is full of vigor. Resolve to strengthen one's skills, build a good start for the motherland."[3]

1 China Infrastructure (CI) is a pseudonym. The use of pseudonyms is a standard practice in similar studies using information gathered through participant observation and company documents that are not available publicly (Ding, 2022; Hanser, 2008; Lee, 1998; Raynard et al., 2020; Zhang, 2014). See Appendix A for a detailed discussion of the book's methodology and research design.

2 CI subsidiary annual shareholder meeting, June 2014, Beijing.

3 Construction bureau workers song, 1965, in CI Construction Bureau yearbook, 2008.

After China's reform and opening accelerated in the late 1970s, CI was formally reorganized as an enterprise owned and controlled by the central government. As the company's operations expanded rapidly, it began targeting international markets. China Infrastructure's earliest commercial forays overseas during the 1990s were highly centralized, reflecting the company's roots in the planned economy. Headquarters dispatched delegations to foreign governments to broker deals in an approach that CI leadership termed "direct line style." Later, CI also began to bid on international projects in Asia and Africa through a tightly centralized internal process. Employees referred to overseas projects by number, just as they had for domestic projects since the Mao Zedong era. Despite challenges and missteps, the firm's early overseas business grew swiftly. Contracts for international projects more than tripled from 47 in 2004 to 171 in 2009.[4]

As the 2010s continued, CI's construction bureaus, each with a distinctive provincial home base and identity, began to act less like builders and more like entrepreneurs. The construction bureaus courted potential clients – governments and private developers in now more than fifty countries in Asia, Africa, Latin America, and Europe – and scoured host country government planning documents and local media for business leads. The construction bureaus were especially interested in smaller projects, those with a contract value under USD 50 million, that they were authorized to bid on directly and execute more independently. For larger projects, the construction bureaus required approval and greater financing support from the firm leadership back in Beijing. Construction bureau staff visited headquarters to deliver PowerPoint pitches that mixed detailed engineering specifications with maps of foreign countries and photos of CI and host country leaders smiling and shaking hands.[5]

In the second half of the 2010s, another shift occurred. The construction bureaus hit the brakes on efforts to win new clients. Instead, representatives from company headquarters in Beijing reemerged on the front lines, touching down in host country capitals for short- and long-term visits to develop local markets and relationships. Company headquarters also began to dispatch engineering teams to tour the varied

[4] "CI International: 10 Years of Overseas Development," exhibition in company lobby, Beijing, June 2014.

[5] Headquarters meeting with construction bureau employees, Beijing, 2015.

terrains of client countries and to recommend infrastructure projects to their governments. This contrasted starkly with what had occurred in previous years, when actors based on the front lines enjoyed primary responsibility for identifying potential projects. In less than a decade, CI's mode of market expansion boomeranged from centralized to decentralized and back again. What explains these changes?

Answering this question requires opening up the black box of the firm. The heady days of CI's early commercial expansion unfolded under the leadership of Chairman Chen.[6] After unveiling a strategy prioritizing international markets, Chairman Chen eschewed a top-down design approach by instead authorizing construction bureaus to identify and develop market opportunities abroad. As the construction bureaus led the charge overseas, competing with other firms and even with one another for opportunities, a highly decentralized mode of market expansion emerged. This arrangement was like that of a large family, a CI employee explained, in which the company headquarters was the mother and the subsidiaries were the sons who competed freely and fiercely – including with one another – for the family's overall benefit.[7]

Midway through the 2010s, Chairman Chen retired on schedule and was succeeded by the second in command, Chairman Wu. Chairman Wu proposed a new strategy for CI that privileged engineering and technological expertise and emphasized top-down planning, standardization, and control. He envisioned a single chain of command – originating in the Beijing company headquarters – that directed international business, instead of "many guns firing at a single bird."[8] Under Chairman Wu, CI sent headquarters' representatives to work side by side with the construction bureaus abroad. The company also dispatched engineering teams to tour foreign countries and propose integrated infrastructure packages to their respective governments.

As CI's market expansion became increasingly centralized, the balance of influence among intra-firm actors began to shift. A construction bureau manager described the change from Chairman Chen to Chairman Wu as follows: "In the beginning, we found our own projects

[6] The names of the CI chairmen provided here are pseudonyms.

[7] Subsidiaries had to be sons in this familial metaphor, he explained, because "daughters will be married to somebody else." Conversation with Sino-Construction International employee, 2016. Sino-Construction International was a subsidiary of CI.

[8] Company annual work plan, 2016.

and made our own contacts. We could develop spontaneously. … Now our room for development is greatly limited. For everything, we must listen to the holding company [i.e., headquarters]. We are being controlled to death."[9]

From the outside, it is easy to overlook Chinese SOE leaders. News about their appointments and activities is typically buried in Chinese-language company or government websites and rarely receives media coverage. Even those who are aware of these executives might readily dismiss their significance. The concept of "China, Inc." that portrays the Chinese bureaucracy as a unified, hierarchical corporation has grown in popularity. The cover of *Newsweek* magazine, for example, once depicted the commercial reach of Chinese companies – and the CCP-dominated government's presumed control of them – by caricaturing China as an octopus with its tentacles wrapped firmly around the globe.[10] In this view, SOE leaders are simply extensions of the state, interchangeable agents who execute orders from above.[11]

Yet, in other national contexts, anyone who wants to understand how a company is organized and behaves looks naturally to the company leader. Volumes such as *Jack Welch and the GE Way: Management Insights and Leadership Secrets of the Legendary CEO* (Slater, 1999) and *Matsushita Leadership: Lessons from the 20th Century's Most Remarkable Entrepreneur*, about Panasonic founder Konosuke Matsushita, fill shelves on both sides of the Pacific (Kotter, 1997). Such books highlight how the choices and actions of executives affect corporate structure and performance. Yet, when analyzing SOEs, especially in an authoritarian political context such as China, even the names of their leaders rarely earn a mention. Why is this the case?

Put simply, SOE executives and other officials like them in China often are not considered "leaders." The conventional wisdom remains

9 Interview with construction bureau employee, 2016.

10 Cover of *Newsweek* magazine, September 3, 2001. See also Thomas J. Duesterberg, "There Is a Better Alternative to Huawei," *Wall Street Journal*, February 5, 2020, www.wsj.com/articles/there-is-a-better-alternative-to-huawei-11580947530, and the illustration by Michael Morgenstern in "Australia's Chinese Entanglement," *The Economist*, April 30, 2009, www.economist.com/asia/2009/04/30/australias-chinese-entanglement.

11 Vladimir Lenin previously termed such a concept a "state syndicate"; Eastern European Communists called it "Party State Incorporated" (Wu and Ma, 2016: 22–25).

that the top national politicians in Beijing make decisions; public-sector organizations and their heads simply carry them out. This reflects a common belief that leaders engage in experimental, visionary, flexible, and creative work, while managers carry out more structured, controlled, deliberate, and orderly activities (Hickman, 1990). In reality, however, the heads of Chinese SOEs and other public-sector organizations exercise leadership every day by experimenting, formulating strategies, restructuring their organizations, adjudicating conflict, leveraging expertise to influence others, imbuing their organizations with values, and persuading or coercing others to follow their lead (Aberbach, Putnam, and Rockman, 1981; Knight, 2009). Recognizing that political authority remains highly centralized in China and that the heads of public-sector organizations do engage in managerial and administrative work should not also preclude taking individuals such as Chairman Chen and Chairman Wu seriously as leaders.

This book introduces a leadership approach to studying China's politics and economy. Leadership, I argue, helps to explain variation in reform outcomes in China's public sector.[12] Specifically, a leadership approach involves analyzing a leader's decisions about strategy and structure and their execution – relative to that of their predecessors and controlling for other factors – on outcomes at the organization level. It proceeds in four steps: (1) identifying the leader – the top-ranked individual in a given public-sector organization; (2) examining if (and how) the leader responds to a particular government goal or policy; (3) studying what tactics the leader uses to execute their decisions about organizational strategy and structure and how their subordinates respond; and (4) assessing the effects of leader's choices and their execution on reform outcomes at the organization level.

[12] The public sector is a broad realm encompassing both elected and appointed officials and organizations, including government agencies, SOEs, utilities, universities, and hospitals. Public-sector organizations, as opposed to private-sector organizations, have two key characteristics: (1) the use of public funding and/or state-owned assets, which may be employed together with private capital, to provide government services and public goods; and governmental services or public goods; (2) the pursuit of multiple social and political objectives that may include, but are not limited to, profit maximization (Downs, 1967; Thompson, 1967). Finally, even though the public sector is termed "public," there may be both private and public users of the government services and public goods that public-sector organizations supply. Imagine the cases of a state-owned utility or a subway, for example, which may exclude non-payers from the goods and services they provide.

Leadership is an important driver of Chinese SOE reform and internationalization. Specifically, leadership helps to explain (1) variation in the degree to which SOE market expansion is decentralized; and (2) changes in the balance of influence among intra-firm actors, that is, who gains and who loses during reform. Conventional analyses of reform in China's state sector remain strongly domestic in orientation. They typically center on changes in the composition of formal ownership or shifts in authority relations among enterprises and the state over long periods of time. For example, one might assess the declining proportion of state ownership in a particular industry or firm, or the devolution of authority for commercial decision-making from government authorities to enterprises. In contrast, the two indicators used here extend the analysis of reform beyond changes in the enterprise's formal financial ties and relative autonomy vis-à-vis the state to investigate actors and activity at the firm level. Additionally, they illuminate the increasingly global context and content of reform by considering SOEs' business abroad. In the following section, I first introduce the presence and purpose of SOEs in China's economic and political system.

Chinese SOEs Today

The state sector remains a critical part of the Chinese economy. SOEs account for an estimated one-quarter of national GDP – and have done so for nearly twenty-five years.[13] State firms channel investment to critical industries, providing more than three-quarters of domestic investment in infrastructure and one-half of domestic investment in coal and oil.[14] They dominate Chinese equity markets, constituting approximately 40 percent of total market capitalization and 50 percent of company revenues for the Shanghai and Shenzhen stock exchanges (Rosen, Leutert, and Guo, 2018: 9). China leads the world with the highest share of SOEs among its biggest companies (Kowalski et al., 2013), and Chinese SOEs are now among the largest global firms by revenue (see Table 1.1).

13 Andrew Batson, "The State Never Retreats," Gavekal Dragonomics, October 2020. For another analysis of SOEs' contribution to China's GDP, see Zhang (2019).

14 "Fiscal Monitor – April 2020," Online Annex 3.1. "China: State-Owned Enterprises Remain Key Players," International Monetary Fund (IMF), April 2020, www.imf.org/-/media/Files/Publications/fiscal-monitor/2020/April/English/onlineannexes31to37.ashx.

Table 1.1 ***Largest Chinese SOEs by revenue***

Name	Level of state ownership	Industry	Revenue (USD million)	Number of employees
State Grid	Central	Electricity	$530,009	870,287
China National Petroleum	Central	Petroleum and petrochemicals	$483,019	1,087,049
Sinopec Group	Central	Petroleum and petrochemicals	$471,154	527,487
China State Construction Engineering	Central	Construction	$305,885	382,492
Sinochem	Central	Chemicals	$173,834	223,448
China Railway Engineering Group	Central	Construction	$171,669	314,792
China National Offshore Oil	Central	Petroleum and petrochemicals	$164,762	81,775
China Railway Construction	Central	Construction	$163,037	342,098
China Baowu Steel Group	Central	Steel	$161,698	245,675
China Mobile Communications	Central	Telecommunications	$139,597	452,202

Source: Fortune Global 500 (2023), https://fortune.com/ranking/global500/2023/search/.

On the 2023 *Fortune Global 500* list, 85 of the 135 companies from mainland China and Hong Kong are state-owned.[15]

Chinese SOE performance, however, continues to lag far behind that of private firms. While SOEs do seek to make profits, they do not necessarily aim to maximize them (Lee, 2017). They frequently behave as "asset maximizers" rather than as "profit maximizers" (Lardy, 2019).

15 For a list of these companies, see SASAC, 《2023年《财富》世界500强揭晓，国资监管系统85家企业榜上有名》 [2023 *Fortune Global 500* Announces 85 Companies in the State-Owned Assets Supervision System Make the List], 澎湃 [*The Paper*], August 2, 2023, https://m.thepaper.cn/newsDetail_forward_24085799.

Even though SOEs account for nearly one-third of China's industrial assets, they contribute less than one-fifth of total industrial profits. Returns on assets, a standard measure of how efficiently a company generates profits from its assets, was only 3.0 percent for SOEs compared with 6.7 percent for private firms in China as of the second quarter of 2020.[16] Approximately one-quarter (by assets) or more than one-third (by number) of Chinese SOEs are loss-making.[17] As a percentage of GDP, SOE debt soared to a record high of more than 142 percent in 2020.[18] As lockdowns to contain the COVID-19 virus spread in China between 2020 and 2022, SOEs – already hit harder by the pandemic than privately owned firms – faced renewed economic difficulties (Wu and Xu, 2021).

Yet the Chinese leadership remains materially and ideologically committed to SOEs because they serve crucial functions for the state. They support stability by providing employment opportunities and by maintaining low prices for key inputs. They also serve a subnational redistributive function by expending most of their investment on infrastructure in poorer interior provinces.[19] The Chinese government routinely leverages SOEs to respond to economic, political, and social crises.[20] In addition, SOEs advance Chinese industrial policy by channeling capital to develop targeted technologies and sectors, such as nuclear power, aerospace, and artificial intelligence. They also play a leading role in domestic and international initiatives, such as the Xi Jinping

[16] Rhodium Group and Asia Society Policy Institute, "China Dashboard: State-Owned Enterprise Policy Reform," Winter 2021, https://chinadashboard.gist.asiasociety.org/winter-2021/page/state-owned-enterprise.

[17] "Fiscal Monitor – April 2020," Online Annex 3.1. "China: State-Owned Enterprises Remain Key Players," International Monetary Fund (IMF), April 2020, www.imf.org/-/media/Files/Publications/fiscal-monitor/2020/April/English/onlineannexes31to37.ashx.

[18] Karen Yeung, "China Debt: Highly Leveraged State Firms Could Threaten 'Efficient Growth,' Private Investment Post-Pandemic," *South China Morning Post*, February 8, 2021, www.scmp.com/economy/china-economy/article/3121039/china-debt-highly-leveraged-state-firms-could-threaten.

[19] Andrew Batson, "The State of the State Sector," Gavekal Dragonomics, March 2017.

[20] 《国资委采取有力措施维护股票市场稳定》 [SASAC Takes Effective Measures to Safeguard Stock Market Stability], SASAC, July 10, 2015, www.ccpnt.org/article/3763.html; Keith Zhai, "Exclusive: China Prods State Firms to Boost Investment in Crisis-Hit Hong Kong – Sources," *Reuters*, September 12, 2019, www.reuters.com/article/us-hongkong-protests-soe-exclusive/exclusive-china-prods-state-firms-to-boost-investment-in-crisis-hit-hong-kong-sources-

administration's poverty alleviation campaign, the Belt and Road Initiative (BRI), and Made in China 2025.

Strong state influence in the Chinese economy blurs the boundary between SOEs and private firms. Like SOEs, private companies today are expected rhetorically and materially to support government policies and priorities, ranging from the BRI to rural development and pandemic control (Coplin, 2019; Li, 2017). Similarly, private companies benefit from access to government subsidies and discounted factors of production, especially in sectors targeted for state promotion such as electric vehicles and biotechnology. During the reform era, private-company executives have become more embedded politically through their membership in bodies such as local legislatures and the National People's Congress (NPC) (Hou, 2019; Truex, 2016). Inside private firms, Party committees and employees who are Party members serve this embedding function (Koss, 2021). Some private entrepreneurs may attempt to evade top-down political control by engaging in behaviors including obfuscation, mutual endangerment, and financial manipulation (Rithmire, 2023; Rithmire and Chen, 2021). However, they remain subject to state oversight and discipline through regulatory actions, inspections, fines, and even arrests.

Nevertheless, overall, the Party-state controls SOEs more tightly than it controls private companies. It assigns SOEs explicit targets and tasks, directly evaluates company and leader performance, and determines executive salaries and career trajectories. Leaders of SOEs serve much shorter average terms than private-company executives, many of whom are company founders with long tenures and disproportionate influence.[21] The heads of SOEs are thus not as well-positioned as private-company executives to develop deep internal networks to obscure company affairs from external scrutiny, or to push back against administrative superiors. SOEs also assume greater responsibility for political directives and priorities than private firms (Li and Zeng, 2019). Their greater embeddedness in the Chinese bureaucracy is further evident in their highly regimented systems of internal

idUSKCN1VY08C; 《央企战疫图鉴》 [Illustrated Compendium of Central SOEs' War Against the Epidemic], SASAC, April 24, 2020, www.sasac.gov.cn/n4470048/n13461446/n14326116/index.html.

21 For example, sixty of the seventy-two interviewed executives in private Chinese companies were company founders who were still leading their companies as of 2015 (Useem et al., 2017).

approvals and rank-based promotions, with some state firms having as many as fifty different levels of employee rank.

China's largest and best-known state firms are central SOEs (中央国有企业). Central SOEs refer to companies operating in nonfinancial sectors that are owned by the central government and administered by the State-owned Assets Supervision and Administration Commission (SASAC), a special commission of the State Council.[22] Central SOEs are concentrated in industries with high strategic value and barriers to entry, such as defense, electricity, petroleum, and telecommunications (Hsueh, 2011). They also operate in more commercially oriented and competitive sectors, ranging from automobiles to metals and electronics. Local SOEs owned by governments at the provincial level and below are much more numerous than central SOEs, but they are also much smaller.

The Chinese government formally separates central SOEs into two groups based on their size and strategic importance.[23] The first group is a batch of "core" firms termed "important backbone SOEs" (重要骨干国有企业). This group includes China's largest and best-known state firms, such as China Mobile, State Grid, and Sinopec. The second group, which includes the remaining central SOEs, is more diverse, with a mix of global industry leaders like Sinosteel and China Railway Engineering Corporation, lesser-known companies like China National Salt Industry Corporation, and state-run research and design institutes like the General Research Institute for Nonferrous Metals.

Central SOEs are typically structured as enterprise groups (企业集团). At the top of each enterprise group is a holding company, an administrative entity wholly owned by SASAC. Below the holding company is a multilayered pyramidal constellation of as many as 100 to 200 or more subsidiaries, including joint venture firms, research institutes, finance companies, and other bodies. Each member entity

[22] SASAC administered 97 central SOEs as of November 23, 2023, down from 189 at SASAC's establishment in 2003. For a list of these firms (in Chinese), see http://wap.sasac.gov.cn/n2588045/n27271785/n27271792/c14159097/content.html.

[23] 《一文看懂138家央企级别和管理》 [Understand the Level and Management of 138 Central SOEs in One Article], 澎湃新闻 [*The Paper*], May 3, 2016, www.thepaper.cn/newsDetail_forward_1464250;《解析央企一把手：前54家多为副部级 中国新闻周刊》[Analysis of the Top Leaders of Central SOEs: Most of the Top 54 are at the Vice–Ministerial Level], 中国新闻周刊 [*China Newsweek*], June 3, 2013, https://m.huanqiu.com/article/9CaKrnJALKI.

may itself have subsidiary companies or hold stakes in numerous other enterprises (Lin and Milhaupt, 2013). As Child and Warner (2003: 35) describe the typical top-down organization and operation of Chinese SOEs, "[a] large 'power distance' tends to be maintained between top managers and other members of the organization, with relatively little delegation of authority and a strong emphasis on vertical links within hierarchies."

Central SOEs are subject to both government and Party authority. All central SOEs are formally under SASAC's administration; however, the Central Organization Department (COD), the CCP's powerful personnel affairs agency, appoints and assesses the leaders of the core central SOEs. Given their differences in size and strategic importance, central SOEs and their leaders have varying formal administrative standings. The standing of core firms and their executives is equivalent to a vice-ministerial (副部级) rank; the remaining central SOEs and their heads have a department-level (正厅级) rank equivalence.[24] Figure 1.1 depicts the administrative hierarchy and organizational structure of Chinese central SOEs.

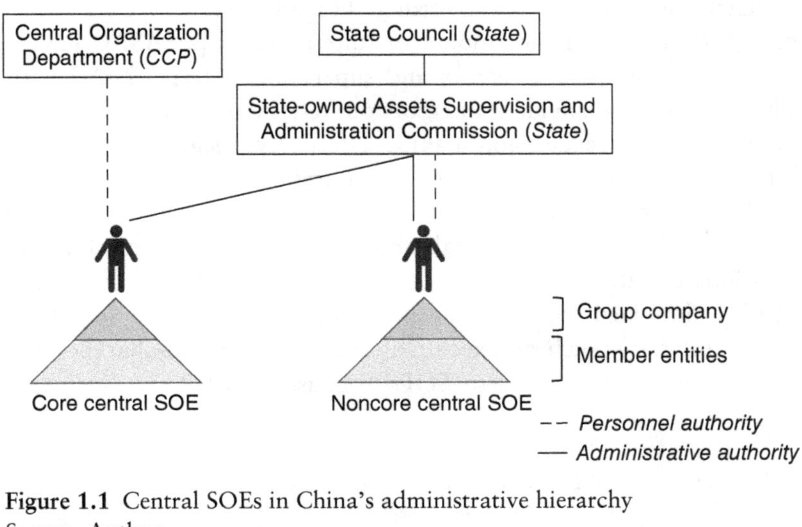

Figure 1.1 Central SOEs in China's administrative hierarchy
Source: Author.

[24] Central SOE heads are not civil servants (公务员), but they do have formal administrative rank equivalence.

Central SOE Leaders

This book focuses on central SOEs and their leaders. Like other high-ranking officials in China, almost all central SOE leaders are ethnically Han men in their fifties.[25] Today, nearly all of them are college graduates, and many also hold advanced degrees in science, education, or management (Leutert, 2018a). They meet routinely with foreign dignitaries and international executives, and some are fluent in at least one or more foreign languages. From the perspective of the Chinese bureaucracy, however, central SOE leaders remain a somewhat insular group. Most have spent their entire careers in the state sector, and some have worked in local or central government. However, virtually none have private-sector experience. Central SOE leaders also move around less within the Chinese bureaucracy compared to their same-ranked peers, although the rotation of leaders among core central SOEs has occurred more frequently under Xi (Leutert, 2018a, 2018b).

Boards of directors exist formally in Chinese SOEs, but they have little ability to check executive authority. Importantly, this is because SOE boards lack the critical powers of executive selection, assessment, compensation, and standard-setting. For any "state-invested enterprise," regardless of the amount of state ownership, SASAC has the authority to propose directors and supervisors (Ozery, 2021: 950). There are few independent directors on SOE boards, and they cannot monitor executive decision-making effectively because the controlling state shareholder nominates and appoints them (Jiang and Kim, 2015).[26] Furthermore, many nominally independent directors have ties with SOE insiders that fall short of formal standards for relationships of interest and that formal standards fail to capture (Lin, 2013b). Standard economic incentives to align executive and shareholder interests, such as executive compensation and shareholding, are absent in most Chinese SOEs because of CCP-imposed curbs

[25] Between 2003 and 2017, only 2 out of 243 – less than 1 percent – of central SOE leaders with vice-ministerial rank equivalence were women: Wang Yinxiang of China Aviation Group Corporation and Xie Qihua of Baosteel (now Baowu Steel) (Leutert and Vortherms, 2021).

[26] In theory, independent directors are able to monitor executive leadership more effectively because their lack of overlapping interests makes them more likely to report abuses.

(Jiang and Kim, 2020).[27] Most central SOE leaders concurrently also serve as chairmen of the holding company or as chairmen of a key subsidiary, thereby further strengthening their internal authority.

The Party-state governs central SOE leaders primarily through its executive appointment authority and target-setting. As discussed in the previous section, the COD, in conjunction with the higher Party authorities, appoints the leaders of the core central SOEs; SASAC appoints the leaders of noncore central SOEs. It also sets yearly targets for certain metrics, such as operating revenue, profits, economic value added (EVA), and total new contract value. Every year, SASAC evaluates all central SOEs and their leaders based on these targets and assigns them a grade from A to E.[28] Target fulfillment determines the compensation of the SOE leaders relative to a fixed baseline and affects their professional advancement. Political considerations likely also factor into SOE executive performance assessments; however, information about this is not publicly available.

Extant research explicitly addressing leadership in Chinese SOEs focuses primarily on smaller, local SOEs. Jing and McDermott (2013), for example, in an examination of three SOEs in Sichuan in the 1990s, find that top managers could generate institutional change through negotiation, manipulation, and coercion. Ma (2011) shows that managers of SOEs owned by the Chinese Academy of Sciences during the 1990s and 2000s who had closer authority relations to their superiors were less likely to be demoted or laid off, and their firms were less likely to be divested or dissolved. Buckley, Clegg, and Tan (2005) highlight the importance of managerial initiative during the transformation of

27 In 2015, the Politburo cut SOE leaders' pay by up to 50 percent in a policy dubbed the "pay ceiling order" (限薪令). Since then, boards of directors have not gained authority to determine top executives' compensation. Senior government or Party agencies continue to set and approve the salaries of SOE leaders. 中央管理企业负责人薪酬制度改革方案 [SOE Executive Compensation Reform Plan], January 1, 2015 (Politburo. CCP Central Committee, 2015); 国务院关于改革国有企业工资决定机制的意见 [State Council Opinions on Reforming SOE Salary Decision Mechanisms], May 25, 2018, www.gov.cn/zhengce/content/2018-05/25/content_5293656.htm.

28 The SASAC's widely known system of annual grades discloses a list of the highest performing firms; however, the grades for all firms and executives are not publicly available. For a recent list of A-rated firms, see SASAC 《2019年度央企企业负责人经营业绩考核A级企业名单》 [List of Central Enterprise Business Leaders' A-Level Performance Assessments for 2019], July 20, 2020, www.sasac.gov.cn/n2588030/n2588954/c15165394/content.html.

Sinotrans, a central SOE, into an integrated logistics service operator in the 1990s. Raynard, Lu, and Jing (2020), in an analysis of a small state-run Chinese factory between 1996 and 2016, explain how the leaders' "values work" overcame their subordinates' initial ideological opposition to corporate restructuring.[29]

This book advances existing scholarship in several ways. Its focus on central SOEs broadens the substantive scope of previous work, which mainly analyzed local SOEs (Bai et al., 2016; Jing and McDermott, 2013; Lee, 2007; Nolan, 1998). To my knowledge, it is also the first published research to employ data gathered through long-term participant observation in a Chinese central SOE.[30] This book's examination of SOEs during the 2010s extends the time span of previous studies, which mostly address the 1980s and 1990s and less frequently the 2000s (Ma, 2011; Raynard et al., 2020; Steinfeld, 1998). It further complements extant longitudinal studies spanning multiple decades by tracing fine-grained organizational change occurring during a period of years and within the tenure of a single national leader (Bai et al., 2016; Ma, 2011; Raynard et al., 2020). In addition, it investigates interactions among different intra-firm entities as well as leader–subordinate relations (Ma, 2011; Raynard et al., 2020).

Multiple factors make central SOEs and their leaders a least-likely case for the argument that leadership affects reform outcomes (Eckstein, 1975; George and Bennett, 2005).[31] First, central SOEs are embedded in the administrative hierarchy of the Chinese state at the highest levels. Unlike local officials, who are distant from the center of political power in Beijing, most central SOEs are headquartered in the capital and their leaders interact regularly with central-level government and Party authorities. Central SOE heads are CCP- and government-appointed officials with formal administrative rank

[29] The authors define "values work" as "a category of actions directed at (re) articulating what is right or wrong, good or bad, in the design and operation of an organization" (Raynard et al., 2020: 1301).

[30] Other studies involve only short-term participant observation in Chinese central SOEs. For example, Zhang Lu conducted participant observation for two months in a central state-owned automobile company in June 2004 and September 2006 (Zhang, 2014); Raynard et al. (2020) observed eleven executive meetings in a central SOE between March 2001 and October 2015.

[31] Extending the logic of "crucial" cases, a least-likely case is one in which a theory fits a case in which it is least likely to be true, thereby providing strong evidence in support of the theory.

equivalence. As such, they are subject to CCP personnel control and its strong emphasis on hierarchy, authority, and conformity. For all of these reasons, if leadership is found to influence reform outcomes for central SOEs, it may also be an important factor affecting reform outcomes in other parts of the Chinese bureaucracy that are subject to less centralized control.

Moreover, widespread entrepreneurialism among leaders in China's public sector may make central SOEs more representative of other public-sector organizations than one might initially expect. In education, for example, Ang (2016: 103–4) describes the case of "Principal Zhou," the head of a public school in China who raised funds exceeding a million dollars in value by borrowing from teachers and taking out bank loans using the teachers' property as collateral. As Ang observes: "Notably, such behavioral norms are not exclusive to top leaders in the political hierarchy like party secretaries and mayors." At lower levels of government, local leaders' entrepreneurial initiative is well-documented (Blecher and Shue, 2001; Duckett, 1998; Oi, 1992, 1999). Although additional investigation is needed to assess whether this book's findings about leadership can be extended beyond central SOEs, widespread entrepreneurialism in China's public sector suggests there are plausible grounds for further research.

Argument, Overview, and Contributions

This book's core argument is that leadership helps to explain variation in reform outcomes at the organization level. Empirically, I analyze the effects of Chinese central SOE leaders' decisions about strategy and structure and their execution on company reform during the 2010s. I examine two specific reform outcomes: (1) the degree to which a company's market expansion is decentralized; and (2) changes in the balance of influence among intra-firm actors – who gains and who loses during reform. A leadership approach highlights the elite agency linking broad government goals with these reform outcomes at the organization level.

Chapter 2 outlines a leadership approach to studying China's politics and economy. It explains how the autonomy of Chinese public-sector leaders originates from multiple sources: the discretion built into the CCP's cadre management system, *guanxi* (关系) with superiors and allies, decentralization of authority in the Chinese bureaucracy, and policy ambiguity and uncertainty. It critically reviews recent studies of China's politics and economy to uncover the importance and influence of leadership. It concludes by discussing how a leadership approach also helps to account for divergence, inaction, and subversion.

Chapter 3 surveys enterprise reforms in China since the late 1970s to highlight evolving constraints and space for leadership in SOEs. It examines five periods: emergence and decline of "dual track" economic reform (1978–91), establishment of a socialist market economy (1992–4), retrenchment of state ownership in the "commanding heights" (1995–2001), internationalization and consolidation of the state sector (2002–12), and combination of limited economic liberalization with increased political control (2013 to present). Since the late 1970s, SOE leaders have transitioned from managing production to determining how to restructure their firms, managing state-owned capital, and expanding in both domestic and international markets. Although the overall trend has been toward expanded space for leadership, the current Xi administration has significantly tightened political and commercial control.

Chapter 4 opens up the black box of the firm to assess the effects of leadership on reform outcomes in CI, a central SOE in the construction industry. I conducted paired comparisons of the consecutive tenures of chairmen and process tracing of original data gathered during fifteen months of fieldwork inside the company, primarily in its Beijing headquarters. I carried out this fieldwork between January 2014 and June 2016, with follow-up visits in June 2018, December 2019, and December 2023. I find evidence that the chairman's leadership generated variation in the degree to which market expansion was decentralized and shifts in the balance of influence among intra-firm actors. I also evaluate and rule out alternative explanations: *guanxi* with and intervention by higher-level officials, shifts in policy by administrative superiors, and changes in industry competition in domestic and international markets.

Chapter 5 extends the analysis beyond CI to examine the effects of leadership on reform outcomes in four other central SOEs: State Grid, China General Nuclear Power Group, Sinochem, and China Railway Engineering Corporation.[32] I select these companies to

[32] These company names are not pseudonyms because the analysis for these cases does not involve data collected through participant observation or from internal company documents.

capture full variation along two key dimensions: industry strategic importance and firm type. For each, I compare the consecutive tenures of their chairmen to assess the effects of leadership on reform at the company level. This survey provides additional evidence that successive leaders' decisions about organizational strategy and structure are an important driver of variation in reform outcomes. Cross-firm analysis further suggests that the effects of leadership on reform are a matter of degree and are conditioned by existing institutions, policies, and economic factors.

Chapter 6 develops an integrated framework of leader–subordinate dynamics in Chinese SOEs. How do leaders interact with subordinates to execute their agendas, and how do subordinates respond? Grounded in reward, coercion, and legitimate bases of power, I identify a set of SOE leader tactics: leveraging position authority, conducting personnel ploys, emphasizing material and status gains, invoking external threats, underscoring superiors' directives and policies, and appealing to subordinates' personal duty and morality. Subordinates may react by praising and supporting the leader or by expressing alternative views, delaying or subverting implementation, shirking, engaging in critical expression, or quitting. Leader–subordinate interactions are iterative and evolve over time.

Chapter 7 concludes by summarizing what a leadership approach contributes to the analysis of China's politics and economy. I introduce what I term the "intra-organizational politics of reform": the daily dynamics of cooperation and conflict between leaders and their subordinates inside public-sector organizations. While elite politics and bargaining among different parts and levels of the Chinese bureaucracy have received much attention, the internal world of public-sector organizations is also a crucial arena for reform politics. Such intra-organizational politics both constitute the everyday substance of reform and shape its ultimate course. Next, I discuss the increasingly global context and consequences of leadership in Chinese SOEs. Finally, I explain why leadership continues to matter despite the ongoing centralization of political authority under Xi, and I outline several directions for future research on leadership in China's public sector during the Xi era.

By developing and applying a leadership approach, this book makes three contributions to existing research about economic reform in China. First, it identifies leadership as a key variable and shows how to analyze its effects by linking individual leaders' decisions about organizational strategy and structure and their execution with differences in reform outcomes. Second, it provides empirical evidence that leadership helps to explain variation in contemporary reform outcomes in Chinese central SOEs. Third, it illuminates and foregrounds the "intra-organizational politics of reform": the daily dynamics of cooperation and conflict between leaders and their subordinates inside public-sector organizations such as SOEs.

2 *A Leadership Approach*

Most observers of China are well-acquainted with its top national leaders – Xi Jinping, Hu Jintao, Jiang Zemin, and Deng Xiaoping – and their respective roles in shaping politics and the economy during the reform era. A wealth of scholarship and media explores their lives and legacies. Images of the top national leaders are ubiquitous in China – on subway television screens, magazine covers, and commemorative pins, plates, and stamps. However, few observers may be familiar with other public-sector leaders, such as Tang Renjian, the minister of agriculture and rural affairs (2020–), Xin Changxin, the Party secretary of Jiangsu (2023–), or Wang Tongzhou, the chairman of China Communications Construction Corporation (2020–).

At first glance, it seems unlikely that such individuals would matter much at all in a high-capacity authoritarian state such as China. Indeed, political authority in China remains firmly centralized in the hands of the ruling CCP. The CCP cadre management system decides who holds the leading positions in politics, the economy, and society. The Party-state delineates common goals for public-sector organizations – growth, stability, and innovation. It tasks SOEs, ministries, and local governments with implementing the same policies, from Xi's poverty alleviation campaign to the BRI. Why then do SOEs, ministries, and local governments routinely respond to these goals and policies in different ways and with divergent results?

A "leadership approach" helps to answer this question. Leaders' decisions about whether, how, and when to alter the strategy and structure of public-sector organizations seem mundane, but this is how reform actually occurs. Violent clashes between petitioners and local officials at the grassroots or contests between dueling elite factions in Beijing are understandably more dramatic and visible than exchanges occurring in SOE boardrooms. However, the wheels of the Chinese bureaucracy – and with it the trajectory of reform – turn daily through public-sector leaders' decisions and interactions with subordinates inside the guarded perimeters and nondescript concrete buildings where they work across China. Leadership and organizational "elbow politics" are especially important at the central level, where autonomy and influence are just as much the goals and currency of politics as is control over tangible resources such as money and land.[1]

A leadership approach foregrounds individual agency within institutional constraints. Prevailing modes of institutional analysis posit that the "rules of the game" direct behavior in uniform and predictable ways (Elster, 1993; Lijphart, 1992; North, 1990; Steinmo, Thelen, and Longstreth, 1992; Thelen and Conran, 2016). Firms such as SOEs, in this view, are unitary actors with similar responses to external institutional incentives, and their leaders are passive recipients with homogeneous preferences (Prakash, 2000). Even within the same institutional environment, however, leaders' decisions and actions vary widely – and these differences have real-world effects. Change in heads of state, for example, is associated with divergent outcomes across a range of domains, including economic growth, democratization, and the use of force (Jones and Olken, 2009; Saunders, 2011).

This chapter proceeds as follows. First, I define leadership and outline the main ways through which individuals exercise it. Next, I identify and discuss the sources of leaders' autonomy in China's public sector and the situational and paternalistic leadership styles that these leaders exhibit. I review recent studies of China's politics and economy to provide evidence that leadership is already a crucial yet underappreciated factor in current analyses. Finally, I discuss how a leadership approach helps to explain variation in reform outcomes by accounting for divergent responses, inaction, and informal experimentation.

Leadership

I define leadership as a process of choice and influence through which individuals seek to maintain or alter the strategy and structure of the organizations they lead, relative to their predecessors. I deliberately use the term "leadership" to draw attention to leading officials' decisions and actions as well as their efforts to influence others – not

[1] "Elbow politics" refers to the informal strategies and tactics that individuals use to gain influence or advantage within an organization or group, often through personal relationships, networking, or behind-the-scenes maneuvering.

simply leaders' individual characteristics or past experiences. This differs from upper echelons theory in management studies and political science research that examines correlations between leaders' individual-level attributes and economic and political outcomes, such as financial performance or military conflict (Carpenter, Geletkanycz, and Sanders, 2004; Hambrick and Mason, 1984; Horowitz, Stam, and Ellis, 2015). Such studies examine "leaders" but not "leadership," that is, what leaders actually do.

Leadership can be operationalized for analysis in two main ways. One way is to study leadership as a dependent variable: Why do leaders make the choices and take the actions they do with respect to organizational strategy and structure? Another way is to study leadership as an explanatory variable: What are the effects of leaders' particular decisions and actions on outcomes in a particular policy domain? This book treats leadership as an explanatory variable. It focuses on the effects of leaders' decisions and actions on an outcome of interest – reform in SOEs. It does not investigate the factors that motivate leaders to make particular decisions and actions.

Execution – leaders' efforts to implement their decisions regarding strategy and structure – is a core part of the exercise of leadership. Execution involves ongoing interactions between leaders and their subordinates within a particular public-sector organization. Leaders must mobilize others to carry out their leadership agendas while simultaneously satisfying their supporters and dealing with their critics and challengers. To do this, they employ varied tactics, including appointing allies to key posts, invoking external threats, and appealing to subordinates' personal duty and morality.[2] Subordinates respond to these tactics in a variety of ways, ranging from support to inaction to critical expression to exit.

Instead of strategy dictating the type of leadership an organization needs, organization leaders may redefine strategy. It is typically assumed that leaders are selected based on their "strategic fit" with an organization's needs (Andrews, 1971; Chandler, 1962; Useem, 2022; Useem et al., 2017). However, leaders may also redefine organizational strategy through learning, adaptation, and invention. This is especially true in post-socialist settings and emerging economies,

[2] Tactics refer to the actual means that powerholders use to direct or change the behavior of target persons (Kipnis, 1984: 179).

where rapid, far-reaching socioeconomic change is the norm. In these contexts, public-sector leaders must continually adjust their strategies to contend with political and market volatility, demographic transformation, uneven state regulatory capacity, and shifting alliances with foreign capital (Appel and Orenstein, 2018). However, leaders cannot act entirely separately from the strategies they create. Once articulated, strategies can constrain even their creators by narrowing the range of compatible choices and actions.

Individuals also exercise leadership by maintaining or altering the structure of their organizations. Specifically, this may include creating, eliminating, or modifying existing departments or production facilities; altering hierarchical authority relationships among subordinate units; or reallocating assets, capital, and personnel internally. Numerous aims may motivate such efforts, from improving overall operational efficiency to politically driven ambitions such as distinguishing oneself from one's predecessor or channeling resources to supporters in a particular part of the organization. Modifications to an organization's structure may also originate from the directions of administrative superiors.[3]

However, the exercise of leadership is not limited to enacting change. It also entails choices about whether to continue predecessors' policies, to not act at all, or to delay, subvert, or even oppose implementation of the directives from administrative superiors. Bias for organization heads to maintain the status quo may be powerful because of the costs and risks that change entails. As Fligstein (1993: 9) observes: "Those who are in control generally base that control on existing organizational strategy and structure." Decisions about organizational strategy and structure thus reflect both leader preferences and strategic assessments about which course of action (or inaction) is feasible and desirable in particular organizational or institutional settings.

In summary, leadership is exercised through a multistage process. Given a particular institutional environment, the leaders of

[3] For example, Premier Li Keqiang announced in May 2016 that SOE leaders should pursue the reform goal of a "lean and healthy body" (瘦身健体) by decreasing the layers of management and the numbers of subsidiaries by at least 20 percent. However, SOE leaders, not the State Council, were responsible for determining how to alter SOEs' organizational structures to achieve this aim. Wang Nianzi [王念兹]: 《李克强为央企"瘦身健体"列出时间表》 [Li Keqiang Sets Timetable for Central SOEs to "Get Lean and Healthy"], 人民日报 [*People's Daily*], May 19, 2016.

Figure 2.1 Exercise of leadership
Source: Author.

public-sector organizations determine whether, how, and when to respond to government goals. They make specific decisions about either changing or maintaining organizational strategy and structure. Next, the leaders attempt – sometimes unsuccessfully and with a significant time lag – to mobilize subordinate support to implement these decisions. Implementation efforts by leaders may ultimately be successful or unsuccessful. Figure 2.1 summarizes this process.

Of course, leadership may also have a dark side. Some public-sector leaders engage in rent-seeking, asset stripping, embezzlement, bribery, or trading of political favors. The same autonomy for the exercise of leadership also creates leeway for illicit activity when monitoring and control by administrative superiors or shareholders are weak or absent. As Klitgaard's (1988: 75) well-known formula puts it: "corruption = monopoly + discretion – accountability." The large size, complexity, and opacity of public-sector organizations provide conditions that facilitate graft. The possibility of corrupt activities may be greater in authoritarian states due to weak rule of law, less independent monitoring by media and civil society organizations, and decreased or no possibility of punishment by an independent judiciary, special investigatory body, or electoral defeat (Brunetti and Weder, 2003; Lindstedt and Naurin, 2010; Rose-Ackerman, 1999; Rotberg, 2017).

Constraints, Autonomy, and Leadership Styles

Constraints

Leaders in China's public sector have constrained yet still significant autonomy. Even in an authoritarian political context, state designs do not translate automatically or immediately into particular outcomes.

Leaders at all levels possess meaningful if bounded autonomy, creating the conditions for "layered leadership," from the apex of China's political system down to the grassroots (Singh and Useem, 2016). They exercise leadership by interpreting government policies and economic conditions, making decisions about their organizations' strategies and structures, and then attempting – sometimes unsuccessfully and with a significant time lag – to mobilize resources and support to carry them out. Subordinates may support a leader's agenda and endeavor to implement it – or they may stall, subvert, or reject it entirely.

Leaders act within the constraints that existing institutional, political, and economic conditions impose. Institutional rules and norms narrow the repertoires of permissible, feasible, or desirable decisions and behavior. Executives in China, as elsewhere, negotiate strategic decisions within their domestic institutional contexts (Child and Rodrigues, 2005). Government policies also incentivize or discourage certain decisions about organizational strategy and structure. But because policies vary significantly in scope and clarity, the extent to which they constrain leadership also depends on how leaders assess their applicability and interpret their content.[4] Economic factors, such as a domestic economic slowdown, excess industrial capacity, or shifting commodity prices, may also prompt leaders to revise organizational structures or to formulate new expansion or diversification strategies.

Cadre Management System

The autonomy of public-sector leaders in China originates from multiple sources. The first is the CCP cadre management system, which governs leading officials in all areas of the Chinese bureaucracy. The Party center has long used this system as an institutional mechanism to guide official behavior and integrate its governance of localities and SOEs (Brødsgaard, 2012; Brødsgaard and Beck, 2021; Burns, 1989;

[4] Policies may range in scope from local or national guidance focused on a particular set of actors or issue areas to broad, seemingly all-encompassing dictates, such as the Hu Jintao administration's "harmonious society." Policies also differ in clarity. For example, Ang (2023) distinguishes among three varieties of policies: "red" policies that explicitly forbid a particular course of action, "gray" policies that allow limited experimentation, and "black" policies that clearly authorize a specific course of action.

Huang, 2003; Landry, 2008; Li, 2016; Li and Zhou, 2005; Manion, 1985). Officials are tasked with fulfilling an array of performance targets, the most important of which is economic growth, while simultaneously avoiding other targets that would damage their career prospects, such as major industrial accidents (Leng and Zuo, 2022).[5] In theory, the cadre management system aligns Chinese officials' individual career incentives with the Party center's priorities using a combination of carrots (political advancement) and sticks (sanctions). By establishing the standards used to assess Chinese officials in disparate posts and localities, the cadre management system incentivizes their behavior and directs it toward particular goals.[6]

However, these "rules of the game" for officials in the CCP's internal labor market do not come with a playbook prescribing how individuals must act to realize government objectives. The cadre management system neither specifies nor determines the decisions that leaders make during policy experimentation and implementation. As a Chinese think-tank researcher put it: "The CCP decides major policies. But each leader operates in different times and circumstances. Given this, different people have different ideas about what should be done."[7] Built-in institutional ambiguity, which in theory facilitates local adaptation and innovation, is in practice an important source of autonomy for public-sector leaders to exercise leadership.

Moreover, not all public-sector leaders in China are compliant policy implementers jockeying for promotion. Some are content to remain in their current positions until retirement. Growth in SOE revenue and the large size of many local economies after decades of rapid economic growth have made local rent extraction more lucrative, thereby weakening the relative material incentives to climb the administrative ladder. Furthermore, those who assume leadership positions after decades in their industries or localities possess deep networks and specialized expertise that cannot be easily exported elsewhere.

5 For a discussion of targets in China's cadre evaluation system and how officials navigate and can sometimes even shape targets in practice, see Leng and Zuo (2022).

6 Each official signs an individual responsibility contract identifying the goals that they are responsible for achieving within their unit and particular functional domain.

7 Interview with retired think-tank researcher (Chinese Academy of Social Sciences), Beijing, April 2016.

Mandatory retirement ages may also foster inaction, noncompliance, or even illicit behavior if older officials know their current position is probably their last.[8] Even those eager to advance politically may engage in "selective implementation" or seek quick returns through risky or unnecessary investments (O'Brien and Li, 1999).[9] Both types of officials – those seeking to stay and those attempting to move – may choose to ignore, delay, or subvert government policies. This is especially likely if the goals are unclear, if they cannot be easily measured, or if implementation will harm existing interests.

Guanxi

Guanxi is another potential source of leader autonomy. *Guanxi*, an indigenous Chinese construct, refers to informal connections among individuals that involve implicit expectations of long-term relations, mutual commitment, loyalty, and obligation (Chen and Chen, 2004: 306). Relational dyads between two people are the basic building blocks of larger *guanxi* networks, which spread out from each individual's personal connections (Fei, 1992 [1947]). Ties may be based on multiple and potentially overlapping factors, such as shared work or educational experiences, regional identities, profession, gender, or family background. In practice, *guanxi* encompasses overt and covert as well as formal and informal interactions of an ongoing nature, governed by social norms of interdependence and reciprocity (Boisoit and Child, 1988; Wilpert and Scharpf, 1990). *Guanxi* relationships may be either hierarchical (patron–client) or horizontal (allies) in orientation.

Leaders in China's public sector engage in the practice of *guanxi* – deliberately cultivating and using these social relations – to advance their agendas and overall careers (Yang, 1994). *Guanxi* with higher-ranking officials may provide leaders with valuable political and material support to implement their decisions about organizational strategy and

[8] China's 1982 Constitution established the first mandatory official retirement ages corresponding to administrative ranks. The tendency of officials approaching retirement age to engage in risky behavior with short-term time horizons is known colloquially in China as the "59 phenomenon" (59现象) or "58 phenomenon" (58现象) (SASAC Research Office, 2012).

[9] "Selective implementation" refers to when officials endeavor to carry out some state goals (such as urbanization) while superficially implementing or even ignoring others (such as environmental protection).

structure. Close ties with superiors can increase leaders' autonomy and enable them to act more innovatively, opportunistically, and strategically (Marinova, Child, and Marinov, 2011). Having strong relations and support from state actors, while simultaneously negotiating a degree of freedom from them, is itself an important entrepreneurial competency (Child and Rodrigues, 2005). *Guanxi* can also benefit leaders' career advancement. As Xi Chen (2020: 560) observes: "The formal procedure of performance measurement provides a common standard by which to evaluate individual performance, but it may require supervisor evaluation and still leave room for individuals to pursue competitive advantage through *guanxi.*" *Guanxi* with peers of similar rank also helps leaders because it generates an ally network facilitating their preferential access to information, resources, and opportunities.

Guanxi can augment SOE leaders' autonomy in multiple ways. Informal, personal connections aid executives and their firms in managing crises and accessing valuable resources, for instance loans, subsidies, tax breaks, land grants, and other forms of material support (Wang and Laufer, 2020). Trust developed through particularistic social relations involving mutual commitment facilitates commercial activity, especially under conditions of uncertainty (Kollock, 1994; McMillan and Woodruff, 1999). *Guanxi* can thus help SOE leaders expand their firms' business or even secure particular projects over which a patron or an ally has influence. In addition, *guanxi* can further assist SOE leaders in obtaining or expediting regulatory approvals. For instance, Yi-chong Xu (2018) describes how State Grid's chairman Liu Zhenya personally gained the support of high-ranking officials, including National Development and Reform Commission (NDRC) Minister Ma Kai and Vice Premier Zeng Peiyan, thereby enabling the company to develop the world's first commercially operational ultra-high-voltage (UHV) power grid.

However, *guanxi* can also constrain leaders' autonomy. These social networks inevitably involve unequal power relationships and exclusion (Gold, Guthrie, and Wank, 2002). Powerful patrons may attempt to control or coerce those with whom they have *guanxi* at lower levels of the Chinese bureaucracy. This can restrict public-sector leaders' freedom to make decisions about organizational strategy and structure – or it can make their decisions more difficult and costly to implement. Ambiguous or fluctuating patron preferences may discourage leaders from acting entrepreneurially and instead incentivize conservatism or even inaction. Since *guanxi* can draw individuals into larger competitions among political groups, in extreme cases clientelism and factionalism risk reducing public-sector leaders to becoming merely actors in a game directed from Beijing rather than autonomous actors in their own right (Cai and Treisman, 2006).

For SOE executives specifically, *guanxi* can be a burden. Domestic reform of Chinese SOEs – and now their global expansion – forces their executives to navigate dual market and political logics. This is because "the shift to market allocation causes changes in relative rewards that reduce the payoffs of network advantages based on political position and offer incentives and opportunities for economic actors to engage in productivity-enhancing entrepreneurial activity" (Nee and Opper, 2012: 235). However, the Chinese government still relies on state firms to support employment levels, keep prices for key inputs low, respond to economic crises or natural disasters, and in some cases supply rents directly. Fulfilling such strategic tasks for political superiors can aid SOE leaders professionally because the cadre management system rewards stability (Leutert and Vortherms, 2021). However, the economic cost of these activities can negatively affect company performance, thereby impeding SOE executives' career advancement outside the context of patron–client relationships.

Decentralization

Decentralization of authority between central and subnational governments is another institutional factor giving public-sector leaders limited autonomy for choice and action. As Heilmann and Perry (2011: 13) observe: "Strategic decisions are the preserve of the top leadership; yet operationalization and implementation require substantial latitude for initiative and independence." The process of decentralization began with sharing authority (分权), for example permitting provinces to participate in decisions about economic planning and materials distribution later in the Mao era. It subsequently expanded to devolving authority (放权) to enterprises and localities (especially special economic zones and coastal regions), allowing them to make decisions about production, operations, and profit allocations.[10]

[10] Some economic functions of government remain centralized, such as taxation, banking, and customs.

Emergent local corporatism during the reform era further strengthened subnational governments' capacity and influence in economic decision-making vis-à-vis the central government (Oi, 1992, 1999; Walder, 1995).

Decision-making authority at and below the central level is increasingly fragmented among a larger and more diverse set of actors – each with their own interests and agency (Brødsgaard, 2016; Lieberthal and Oksenberg, 1988; Mertha, 2009). In today's China, as Lampton (2013: 70) puts it: "Pluralism is everywhere. It is present in the conflicting ambitions of powerful individuals and evident within and among China's bureaucracies, economic sectors, localities, and social groups." Fragmentation of authority facilitates individuals' ability to engage in "policy entrepreneurship" by framing or "repackaging" policy problems and outlining possible alternative solutions (Kingdon, 1984; Mertha, 2008, 2009). SOE leaders also engage in policy entrepreneurship to garner top-level support for policies or regulatory approvals that benefit their firms (Xu, 2017, 2018).

Widespread "administrative subcontracting" (行政分包) in the context of decentralization generates space for leadership. In this practice, the central government delegates responsibility for government functions, such as budget-making, personnel selection, and public-service provision, to subordinate organizations or levels of government, which in turn reassign it to those below them, all the way down to the bottom level (Zhou, 2008, 2014). Similar discretion was built into particularistic contracting between levels of government and between government and enterprises during the early reform period; this incentivized officials to deliver on central goals while simultaneously enabling them to assign their own contracts and benefit personally (Shirk, 1993: 16).

Decentralization thus creates significant leeway for leaders of SOEs and other public-sector organizations to make decisions autonomously. Take for instance the case of central SOE Shenhua and its leader Ye Qing. As chairman between 1998 and 2003, Ye charted Shenhua's reform path as the company faced a slew of challenges: insufficient expertise, difficulty introducing modern corporate governance techniques, responsibility for loss-making state-owned mines, and stiff competition from local township and village enterprise (TVE) mines (Rui, 2005). Throughout his tenure, Chairman Ye enjoyed a surprising degree of autonomy:

> Before leaving his post [as chairman of Shenhua Group], Ye confessed to the vice-premier in charge of energy, Zeng Peiyan: "I have to apologise [*sic*] that I have not reported to you earlier or received permissions on many decisions. I did what I thought was best for the company without going through the formal procedures. Fortunately, everything turned out alright; we succeeded and made huge profits." (Zhao and Xu, 2012: 36)

As this quotation indicates, administrative superiors did not dictate how Chairman Ye should interpret or respond to the challenges that Shenhua faced. Decentralization gives Chinese public-sector leaders such as Chairman Ye much more discretion than one might expect to make and execute decisions about organizational strategy and structure during the reform process.

Ambiguity and Uncertainty

Deliberate ambiguity of government policies and goals also creates autonomy for leaders in China's public sector. In what Ang (2016) terms "directed improvisation," official directives are deliberately broad in scope to enable subordinates to interpret, experiment, and implement them in accordance with local conditions. Zhi and Pearson (2017: 407) conceptualize this dynamic as a "signal-response mechanism." They write: "This mechanism creates an uncertainty that hangs over the bureaucratic environment, yet also provides some flexibility (and negotiating space) as to how subordinate officials may respond." Some scholars suggest that such "structured uncertainty" about the means and ends of policy is not only a defining feature of China's political system but also a necessary condition for its functioning (Breznitz and Murphree, 2011).

The autonomy of public-sector leaders may be even greater under conditions of uncertainty. The uncertainty associated with rapid political, economic, and social transformation or crisis expands possibilities for "protean power" (Katzenstein and Seybert, 2018: 25). Actors respond to uncertainty – and may even amplify it – by reinterpreting existing rules and their meanings, or by innovating and improvising in the absence of rules. Discretion for interpretation and action increases when organizational forms and institutional rules and norms are in flux. Altered chains of command or personnel turnover can further open up space for leadership by changing authority relations among leaders, their superiors and subordinates, and business and social groups. Public-sector leaders in China have consistently experienced high levels of uncertainty during the reform era because of rapid economic growth, profound social transformation, and acute crises ranging from the Tiananmen upheaval to the COVID-19 pandemic.

Leadership Styles

The exercise and effects of leadership in China's public sector also depend on situational factors. Each leader faces variation in the tasks at hand and their subordinates' ability, willingness, and readiness to execute them (Hersey, Blanchard, and Johnson, 1996; Jago, 1982). However, the Chinese bureaucracy has limited between-leader variability, whereby specific situational needs can be addressed simply by changing the leader. The cadre exchange system (干部交流制度) aims primarily to develop officials' comprehensive knowledge and abilities for future office, not to match particular leaders with immediate needs in any given position or locale.[11] Chinese officials typically assume leadership posts after decades of climbing up the bureaucratic ladder; once in office, some serve until retirement. Regardless of a leader's particular abilities or career stage, they must adapt to dynamic, demanding, and often uncertain organizational and external environments. Adaptive leaders approach their daily work by considering "the task to be done, the situation in which the task is to be accomplished, and the readiness of their employees to accomplish the task" (Silverthorne and Wang, 2001: 401). While institutional factors generate autonomy for leaders, situational factors affect their decisions about organizational strategy and structure and their implementation.

Situational leadership involves both directive and supportive elements. Directive leadership entails a leader defining roles, determining evaluation goals and methods, issuing explicit orders, setting timelines, and closely monitoring their subordinates' progress (Northouse, 2019: 168). In theory, subordinates might participate in making decisions, even if a leader closely directs their implementation (Muczyk and Reimann, 1987). In practice, however, the highly hierarchical nature of the Chinese workplace leaves few, if any, mechanisms for subordinates to participate in high-level decision-making. But this does

11 This mechanism of CCP personnel control involves the routine rotation of officials between different posts and/or different localities within the country.

not mean that leaders in China's public sector do not exercise any supportive leadership. Leaders commonly consider their subordinates in day-to-day ways, such as acting approachable, looking out for others' welfare, or encouraging on-the-job learning (House, 1996). Leaders in China exercise both directive and supportive leadership depending on situational needs.[12]

Through paternalistic leadership, Chinese public-sector leaders further blend authoritarianism and benevolence with moral authority (Farh and Cheng, 2000). Paternalistic leaders support and guide their subordinates' professional and personal lives in material and immaterial ways, with the moral authority of a father who knows what is best for his children (Pellegrini and Scandura, 2008). Chinese public-sector leaders can draw upon "a deep respect for age and for the father figure within a tradition of paternalistic authority" (Child, 1994: 188). The reform-era shift away from Mao-era asceticism gave SOE leaders greater material resources for paternal care in the form of salaries, subsidies, and fringe benefits (Walder, 1991). Confucian philosophy underpins paternal leadership through its emphasis on hierarchy, authority, and conformity (Child, 1994).[13] As Bedi (2020) writes: "In the workplace, the Confucius philosophy shapes the role of the leader as a father or a close friend who cares genuinely about the well-being of their followers. The role of the follower is to reciprocate through appreciation and obedience the leader's care and support." However, paternalism is not always harmonious – it may involve punishment and even exploitation if paternal care is provided solely to elicit compliance (Aycan, 2006).

Research on leadership styles provides an important context for the analysis of leadership in China's public sector. Leaders must adapt their decisions about organizational strategy and structure to task requirements and to their subordinates' ability, willingness, and readiness to implement them. Strict hierarchies of management in the Chinese

[12] For example, Zheng et al. (2021) find that company leaders in China's primarily state-owned construction sector routinely combine directive and supportive leadership styles.

[13] Confucian philosophy posits hierarchies among individuals based on morality, kindness, and deference to authority (Aycan, 2006). Redding (2002: 234–35) identifies numerous Confucian values relevant to leadership in China: societal order, hierarchy, reciprocity and personalism, control, insecurity, family-based collectivism, and knowledge.

workplace support a predominantly directive leadership style; however, leaders also exercise varying levels of supportive leadership. Combining authoritarianism with benevolence, Chinese leaders – who are almost uniformly men – gain additional moral authority by dispensing paternal care and punishment to subordinates. Using original data on leadership in Chinese SOEs, this book investigates how leaders and subordinates interact beyond a "directive" and "supportive" behavioral dichotomy. It also grounds studies of leadership styles in the intra-organizational politics of reform by examining the effects of leadership on the balance of influence among actors inside Chinese SOEs.

Uncovering Leadership

Ultimately, perception may be the most fundamental obstacle to studying leadership in China. Large-N quantitative analyses typically treat Chinese officials as interchangeable observations, except for their variation along a fixed set of individual-level attributes. Even if such studies do include leadership tenures as a variable, in practice this frequently aims to measure the power of political incentives from the center, not what individual leaders themselves actually do. Some qualitative work does examine individual leaders but often subsequently downplays their role to make broader generalizations about collective actors, such as "local governments" or "local officials" writ large.[14] A closer look at recent scholarship on China's politics and economy, however, reveals both the presence and the importance of leadership.

Multiple works report on evidence of a relationship between leadership and variation in economic outcomes. At the county level, for example, Bulman (2016) finds that leadership helps to explain differences in economic growth. Analyzing Party secretaries and per capita GDP growth in six neighboring counties of Jiangsu and Anhui, Bulman concludes that differences in the leaders' capabilities and incentives best account for any divergence in growth outcomes. Through additional analysis of forty-three counties in Jiangsu and Anhui that have

[14] An illustrative example is the study by Blecher and Shue (2001: 372) on how Xinji municipality adhered to the local developmental state model by establishing a fur and leather trading center. Although the authors describe how Mayor Bian Qunyou convened multiple meetings and forums to push for the trading center's creation, they consistently refer to the "Xinji authorities" or the "municipal officials" as the main protagonist.

leaders who have served in multiple counties, Bulman (2016: 121, 118) reports that leader effects explain 19.2 percent of the variance in GDP growth.[15] He contends: "Given the high degree of personalized leader control in China, leaders should have systematic personal effects on growth, assuming that their ability and incentives differ."

Leadership also helps to account for differences in development at the city level. Using a paired comparison of Qingdao and Dalian, Chung (2005) identifies leadership – that of Yu Zhengsheng in Qingdao and Wei Fuhai and Bo Xilai in Dalian – as a key factor explaining why Dalian's economic growth increased during the 1980s while Qingdao's did not pick up until the early 1990s.[16] In Chung's analysis, the central government's appointment of Yu as mayor of Qingdao in 1989 and as Party secretary in 1992 catalyzed the laggard locality's economy. "Given the central role Yu Zhengsheng performed in Qingdao," Chung (2005: 129) concludes, "leadership really counts." Leadership was not the only ingredient in Qingdao's and Dalian's "recipe of coastal development," but it was a crucial one (Chung, 1999).

"Agent-centric" factors were a key factor in the economic divergence among Suzhou, Wenzhou, and Dongguan after the 2008 global financial crisis. As these model municipalities faced the financial downturn, Shen and Tsai (2016) find that institutional adaptability was proactive in Suzhou, delayed in Dongguan, and reactive in Wenzhou. The authors acknowledge the relevance of structural factors, such as natural resource endowments, historical legacies, external resources, and fiscal conditions. However, they also find that "agent-centric factors," including mayors' and the Party secretaries' leadership and openness to new policy ideas, were the strongest determinants of the observed variation. Moreover, such agency is proactive, not merely reactive,

15 Bulman uses a sample of leaders who serve in multiple counties in the same roles to separate county and leader effects. Xu, Wang, and Shu (2007) employ a similar research design to assess the effect of governor transfers on provincial economic growth.

16 Chung (2005: 106) conceptualizes leadership as both decision and execution, calling attention to "concrete strategies devised and adopted by local leaders in their pursuit of growth" and their ability to bargain with higher-level governments and cultivate linkages with foreign capital. Yu Zhengsheng was Qingdao mayor (1989–94) and Party secretary (1992–97). Wei Fuhai served as Dalian mayor (1983–92). Bo Xilai served as Dalian mayor (1993–2000) and Party secretary (1999–2000).

creating "the possibility that local agents could introduce policies that lead a region to diverge from an apparently self-reinforcing developmental trajectory, even before a crisis demands a policy reaction" (Shen and Tsai, 2016: 109).

Leadership also affects economic reform and growth in smaller Chinese cities. In *How China Escaped the Poverty Trap*, Ang (2016: 146–80) analyzes an underdeveloped, hill-locked city in Fujian she calls "Forest Hill" to show how states harness weak institutions to build markets, emerging markets then stimulate strong institutions, and strong institutions ultimately preserve markets. However, leadership also forged Forest Hill's developmental trajectory. Ang attributes the locality's early push for infrastructure development to Party Secretary Chen, dubbed "The Builder," who prioritized infrastructure expansion and won central government approval for a new regional railway (Ang, 2016: 173). Forest Hill's subsequent shift to seeking investment capital appears inseparable from Mayor and subsequent Party Secretary Yang, termed "The Recruiter." His successor, Mayor Lin, emphasized both "quality" and "development" instead of merely economic growth, thereby representing a "turning point" (Ang, 2016: 176). The transitions and characteristics of the three development stages that Ang identifies coincide exactly with changes in the local leaders' tenures and differences in their individual priorities. Leadership motivates the coevolution of markets and institutions; this process does not occur automatically or without direction.

Provincial leaders, too, influence development outcomes. For example, Jaros (2019: 205–8) describes how Jiangsu Party Secretary Li Yuanchao (2002–7) replaced his predecessor's approach with a "Riverside Development" strategy prioritizing development of a Yangtze River corridor across the provincial heartland. Li lobbied for this strategy at public meetings and political events despite skepticism and opposition; he also sought support from top national leaders and local networks that he had developed as a Jiangsu native and as a former mayor of Nanjing. The "Riverside Development" strategy successfully boosted economic development in Nanjing and Suzhou as well as smaller river cities. It ended in 2007 when a new provincial Party secretary, Liang Baohua, replaced it with his own "Coastal Development" strategy, shifting the locus of development toward Jiangsu's less-developed coastal city regions. Jaros finds that provincial leadership's effects on development outcomes are greatest when the leaders enjoy connections to central-level officials who can facilitate access to financing and when impending retirement does not disincentivize bold policies.

Competition and compromise among national leaders in China also shape political and economic outcomes. A rich literature addresses the importance of central-level leadership during key historical episodes, such as the Great Leap Forward (1958–62), the Cultural Revolution (1966–76), the post-Mao leadership transition (1976–78), and the Tiananmen Square upheaval (1989) (Fewsmith, 1988; Lee, 1978; Teiwes and Sun, 1999, 2016; Torigian, 2022; Yang, 1996). Other studies probe the networks among top Chinese leaders and local leaders, using factional politics to explain patterns in economic policymaking (Heilmann and Shih, 2013; Shih, 2008). However, research on Chinese officials at the central level still focuses primarily on top national leaders; it has yet to fully engage a broader set of individuals – such as ministers or directors of national commissions – or to consider how they exercise leadership and its effects.

Moving from a study of "leaders" to "leadership" in China's politics and economy demands critically reexamining existing studies to theorize a factor that has been there all along. It requires recasting arguments about "agents" and "agent-centric factors" in terms of "actors" and "agency." It means not only coding leaders' tenures and individual-level attributes based on their CVs but also examining what they actually do while in office. This can be done by applying a leadership approach to investigate leaders' decisions about organizational strategy and structure, their success or failure in carrying them out, and their effects. Only by studying the origins, limits, and exercise of leadership in the public sector can the politics of reform – and the variation in reform outcomes – be fully understood.

Conclusion

This chapter introduces a leadership approach to analyzing reform in China, centering on the top-ranked individuals in public-sector organizations. A leadership approach foregrounds such leaders' decisions and actions within institutional constraints instead of assuming that these constraints axiomatically determine outcomes. In China's public sector, leaders' autonomy originates in the cadre management system, *guanxi*, bureaucratic decentralization, and policy ambiguity and uncertainty. This bounded autonomy enables leaders to make and attempt to execute decisions about organizational strategy and structure. A leadership approach thus illuminates why public-sector organizations such as SOEs routinely respond to the same state goals and policies in divergent ways.

Studying leadership also helps to explain inaction and subversion. Some scholars suggest that the essence of governance in China is "integrated fragmentation," whereby the CCP uses mechanisms such as the cadre management system or leading small groups to achieve central goals despite confronting segregated *xitong* (系统, vertically organized administrative hierarchies focused on particular issue areas), multiple layers of subnational government, and competing interest groups (Brødsgaard, 2012; Li, 2016). But these integrative mechanisms do not necessarily motivate action – some organizations may still ignore, delay, or distort policy implementation. Especially when uncertainty is high, organizational forms and practices are in flux, and rules are not yet firmly established, leaders enjoy significant leeway for interpretation and behavior. Inaction and subversion may be even more likely under these conditions because they decrease the political risks of such behavior.

Chinese officials below or even at the ministerial level are rarely seriously analyzed as "leaders." Instead, public-sector leaders are often considered to be agents of the CCP-dominated authoritarian state, not political actors in their own right, or their individual agency is downplayed in order to make broader inferences. Yet "leadership" describes much of the work that leaders of Chinese public-sector organizations do every day: experimenting, formulating strategies, restructuring organizations, adjudicating conflict, and influencing others to follow the directions they set. Indeed, a closer look at existing research reveals the presence and influence of leadership in China's politics and economy at all levels. Chapter 3 traces how space for leadership has emerged and evolved in China's state-owned economy since 1978 and the continued limits leadership now faces.

3 *Enterprise Reforms since 1978*
Evolving Constraints and Space for Leadership

Analysis of enterprise reforms in China's state-owned economy since 1978 reveals both growing space for leadership and enduring constraints. State-owned enterprises (SOEs) have been transformed from administrative appendages into increasingly market-oriented actors, remaking their relationship with the state from one of bureaucratic command to one of strategic bargaining. Heads of SOEs have transitioned from managing production in line with top-down commands to restructuring their firms, managing state-owned capital, and expanding into domestic and international markets. Today, SOE leaders play a key role in a dynamic reform process that is unfolding on a global stage.

Leaders of SOEs must continually navigate shifting political and economic constraints. The rules and norms at any given point in time render some decisions more feasible and desirable than others while tacitly or explicitly restricting others. For example, partial privatization through issuances of shares was deemed incompatible with state ownership during the 1980s, but it became ideologically acceptable – and even encouraged – in the 1990s. Economic challenges such as increased competition, industrial overcapacity, or tariffs may force SOE leaders to modify their corporate strategies and structures. Taken together, such constraints affect SOE leaders' decisions and actions, even if they do not determine their individual behavior.

This chapter reviews the reform-era policies behind the emergence of China's "national champions": large, centrally controlled SOEs. Initial attempts to create big, multi-region corporations began in the early 1980s when the State Council established "general companies" under the central ministries. These efforts gained momentum with national pilots to develop large SOE groups and Jiang Zemin's reform strategy of "grasping the large and releasing the small." Throughout the 1990s, the central government built internationally competitive SOEs by supporting their "going out" abroad and partial public listings. While the overall trend during the reform era has been expanded space for SOE leadership, the Xi Jinping administration has significantly tightened economic and especially political control.

Enterprise reforms in China's state-owned economy since 1978 can be divided into five periods. These periods encompass the emergence and decline of "dual track" economic reform (1978–91), establishment of a socialist market economy (1992–94), retrenchment of state ownership in the "commanding heights" (1995–2001), internationalization and consolidation of the state sector (2002–12), and combination of limited economic liberalization with increased political control (2013 to present) (see Table 3.1). For each period, this chapter summarizes the key enterprise reforms – their content, implementation, and results. It then discusses the evolving constraints and space for leadership.

Table 3.1 ***Key enterprise reforms in China's state-owned economy since 1978***

Period	Enterprise reform (starting date)
Emergence and decline of "dual track" economic reform (1978–91)	Expanding enterprise autonomy (1978) Economic responsibility system (1981) General companies (1981) Tax-for-profit (1983) Contract responsibility system (1987) Enterprise groups (1991)
Establishment of a socialist market economy (1992–94)	Shareholding-system restructuring (1992) Separating government from enterprises (1992)
Retrenchment of state ownership in the "commanding heights" (1995–2001)	Grasping the large and releasing the small (1995) Partial public listings of large industrial SOE assets (1997) Corporate governance (1999)
Internationalization and consolidation of the state sector (2002–12)	"Going out" (2002) Creation of SASAC and central SOEs (2003)
Limited economic liberalization combined with increased political control (2013 to present)	Mixed ownership (2013) State capital management (2014)

This analysis extends existing accounts of post-1978 enterprise reforms in China by examining developments since the 2000s and incorporating original data and new sources.[1] It draws upon elite interviews conducted primarily in Beijing between 2013 and 2019 and an extensive body of sources, including official policy documents, government yearbooks, internal government journals, writings and memoirs by Chinese officials and economists, US State Department cables declassified at my request, and secondary sources.[2]

Emergence and Decline of "Dual Track" Reform (1978–1991)

Enterprise Reforms

At the end of the 1970s, China's state-owned economy consisted of wholly state-owned and state-run factories embedded in industrial bureaus (see Figure 3.1). These factories were in essence production units. They had little authority over operational decision-making or responsibility for performance. Industrial bureaus oversaw the factories' daily operations and determined their production methods, inventory levels, and product distribution. The bureaus also participated in employee recruitment, training, discipline, and housing allocations (Keister, 2000). If a factory did not meet its production quota, the bureau could make up for it by drawing from other factories under its supervision. Although factories were formally subject to both ministry and local-government control, the ministries directly controlled only a small number of key factories and the local governments controlled

[1] Seminal works on China's state-owned economy examine enterprise reforms but their analysis ends in 1993 (Naughton, 1995; Shirk, 1993). Two more recent studies examine SOE reforms during the following decade from the perspectives of ideational and bureaucratic contestation, respectively (Eaton, 2016; Li, 2014).

[2] I collected these sources in Hong Kong and Beijing between 2013 and 2019 from the Universities Services Centre of the Chinese University of Hong Kong, National Library of China, Peking University Library, and materials purchased online. I incorporated additional sources gathered in the United States between 2016 and 2022 from the Fairbank Center Collection of the Fung Library and the Harvard-Yenching Library at Harvard University as well as the East Asia Collection of the Kroch Library at Cornell University. I further supplemented them in Singapore in 2023 with sources from the East Asian Institute Library at National Singapore University.

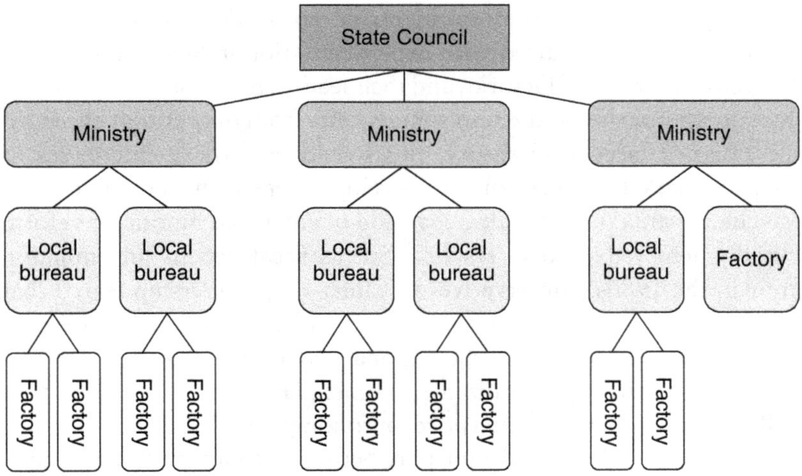

Figure 3.1 Organization of state-owned industry in China at the start of reform
Source: Author.

the rest. Horizontal links across factories and localities did exist, but they were limited and frequently informal in nature (Lyons, 1990). Only with the advent of market-oriented reforms did state-owned factories begin the long journey to becoming first "state-run" enterprises (国营企业) and then "state-owned" enterprises (国有企业).

Early reforms upheld the dominance of state ownership and the planning system while simultaneously introducing market mechanisms and limited operational autonomy. This combination of plan and market is popularly known as China's "dual track" approach to economic reform. However, the plan itself changed too. Central planning evolved from top-down mandates and administrative compulsion to bargaining between planning authorities and enterprises about production targets. Enterprises signed contracts with the state and gradually assumed responsibility for profits and losses. Direct administrative commands gave way to indirect guidance using macroeconomic instruments such as taxes, interest rates, and credit allocations (Hay et al., 1994: 19). These ideas resonated with earlier economic governance proposals in China, such as Xue Muqiao's advocacy of "indirect planning" in the 1950s as a way of indirectly shaping economic activity (Fan and Xue, 2022).

Enterprise autonomy reform involving power delegation and profit sharing (放权让利) started with experimentation in Sichuan in 1978.[3] The reform permitted factories and their leaders to devise their own production approaches and retain some profits from output that exceeded the assigned targets. In theory, this would incentivize enterprises to adapt to market competition and develop independent economic interests. Incremental nationwide expansion of enterprise autonomy reform initially achieved positive results.[4] But as fiscal deficits and inflation grew in the 1980s, conservatives in China's top leadership feared that the economy was out of control.[5] Party elder Chen Yun (1980) successfully led calls to "adjust the national economy" (调整国民经济) by temporarily reviving centralized economic planning.

Reforms to expand enterprise autonomy (扩大企业自主权) ultimately succeeded in important part because of factory leaders' decisions about organizational strategy and structure. Historical accounts of enterprise autonomy reform typically credit Zhao Ziyang, who was then serving as Sichuan Party Secretary, but the leadership in state-owned factories also played a crucial role (Gewirtz, 2017). Consider, for instance, Ningjiang Machine Tool Plant, one of the first six factories in Sichuan to pilot the reform, and its manager Liu Lunbao. As market demand for boring machines and high-precision machine tools plummeted, the factory's leadership revamped organizational strategy and structure to focus on the more profitable parts processing and automatic lathe production (Lin, 1984: 84). Most importantly,

[3] Enterprises gained limited authority over input sourcing, production, sales, investment, and compensation. They could sell goods produced in excess of the central plan and retain a fixed percentage of the additional earned profits. Enterprises could reinvest the retained profits into infrastructure or employee bonuses and services (Shao, 2014: 10–11).

[4] The Sichuan government repeatedly expanded reform pilots until they encompassed 417 industrial enterprises and 250 commercial enterprises in 1980. In addition, six central ministries and commissions – including the Ministry of Finance and the State Economic Commission – selected eight enterprises in Beijing, Tianjin, and Shanghai to pilot enterprise autonomy reforms starting in 1979. By 1980, 5,777 pilot enterprises from 28 provinces, municipalities, and autonomous regions reported increases of 6.9 percent in the value of state-owned assets, 11.8 percent in profits, and 7.4 percent in remitted profits compared to that in the previous year (Wang, 1986: 438).

[5] China experienced unprecedented fiscal deficits of RMB 17 billion in 1979 and RMB 12.1 billion in 1980, while the consumer price index rose 1.9 percent in 1979 and then soared 6 percent in 1980 (Zhang, 2006: 61).

Manager Liu executed a pivotal decision to make Ningjiang Machine Tool Plant the first Chinese enterprise to publicly advertise the sale of production equipment (Chen, 2008). As Manager Liu recalled:

> It is very difficult to find things in the world that are 100 percent conservative. When taking a plane, it can fall down; when taking a train, it may go off the rails; even if you are on the road, you may be hit by others. One can only blame Marx for dying too early; he did not specifically say how socialism should be implemented! So I stood up and said loudly: "Comrades, I have heard everyone's opinions and have thought them over. My opinion is: We will not only publish an advertisement, we will publish it in *People's Daily*! Since that was the Party newspaper, it had credibility." (Chen, 2008: 43)

Ningjiang Machine Tool Plant's advertisement ran on June 25, 1979, on the fourth page of *People's Daily*. Its effects on the business were immediate. Within two months, Ningjiang Machine Tool Plant signed sales contracts for 1,300 machine tools with clients from across China, equivalent to four times the factory's state-allotted output (Li, 2009: 415).

State-owned enterprise leaders such as Liu took bold and calculated action during the early reform period, despite facing opposition and political risks. In the past, Ningjiang Machine Tool Plant had been investigated by the government for "disposing of state-allocated products without permission" because it had sold surplus products (Li, 2009: 415). A number of economists and officials harshly criticized Ningjiang Machine Tool Plant's advertisement, arguing that machine tools were a means of production and therefore should not be commercially advertised and sold on the market as commodities. *People's Daily* even ran a special column on the topic featuring different views. Bo Yibo, a Party elder and one of the contributors to the column, ultimately concluded: "The advertisement for the machine tools has performed a meritorious deed for the economic restructuring of China" (Li, 2009: 416). However, SOE leaders still faced significant limits on their autonomy, because they had to deal with various administrative principals and had little independent authority over hiring (Yuan, 2019).

Efforts to increase enterprise autonomy resurfaced in the 1980s under the label of economic responsibility system reform (企业责任制改革). This reform reaffirmed enterprise autonomy while additionally imposing contractual limits on it. It required enterprises to negotiate annually with government bureaus to establish specific targets, profit retention rates, and responsibility for shortfalls or losses.[6] While this incentivized more market-oriented enterprise behavior, it also motivated enterprise heads to lobby for lower targets and higher output prices.[7] The nationwide rollout of economic responsibility system reform initially reduced debt and increased productivity; however, the state's fiscal revenue grew slowly despite rising enterprise profit retention rates.[8] Enterprise heads exploited information asymmetries to negotiate lower production targets, for example by underreporting profits and concealing enterprise capabilities. Significant latitude for central adjustments also weakened the reform's intended incentive effects.

Policy experimentation continued with the tax-for-profit reform (利改税改革) in the early 1980s, which substituted an income tax for the SOEs' profit remittances.[9] The goal was to legalize the firms' economic responsibility to the state while making them more accountable for their losses.[10] However, clashes among political elites weakened the tax-for-profit reform and its hasty introduction yielded disappointing results: SOE profits declined for twenty-two consecutive months after implementation.[11] Substituting taxes for profits was unworkable

[6] For details about the three main types of power delegation and profit-sharing arrangements between the state and enterprises during this period, see Shao (2014: 14–15).

[7] The two-tiered system of market and plan also incentivized agents to divert goods from plan to market to obtain the "rents" embodied in the goods due to administrative control (Byrd, 1987: 432).

[8] Between 1981 and 1982, more than 30,000 state-owned industrial enterprises across China, constituting approximately 80 percent of all such firms, implemented enterprise responsibility reforms (Wang, 1986: 442). The national fiscal deficit decreased from RMB 12.7 billion in 1980 to RMB 2.5 billion in 1981. Fiscal revenue (enterprise revenue plus tax revenue) increased from RMB 1.16 billion in 1980 to RMB 1.18 billion in 1981 and to RMB 1.21 billion in 1982 (Zhang, 2006: 63; also *China Statistical Yearbook*, multiple years, as cited in Jing 2017: 56–58).

[9] The earliest efforts began in 1980 with 10 SOE pilots (later expanded to 400) in Shanghai, Sichuan, and Guangxi. The first phase in April 1983 mandated that state-owned enterprises pay a flat income tax of approximately 55 percent of their profit target. The second stage began in September 1984 when the State Council called for nationwide implementation.

[10] A small number of more profitable state firms were also required to pay an additional "adjustment tax" (调节税), an additional variable percentage of their after-tax profits (State Council, 1983).

[11] The struggle to formulate tax-for-profit reforms reflected the top-level split between Zhao Ziyang (who advocated for tax-for-profit reform) and CCP General Secretary Hu Yaobang (who favored a contracting approach). More

without price reform because enterprise profitability derived from pricing, not only efficiency gains.[12]

After the tax-for-profit reform failed, Chinese policymakers turned back to profit contracting. Their new approach, contract responsibility system reform (承包制改革), differed from previous economic responsibility system reform because it involved long-term agreements. Instead of annual negotiations on specific tax rates and profit-sharing arrangements, the reform introduced long-term contracts of three to five years or longer. By the end of 1987, more than 78 percent of all industrial enterprises in the central plan had implemented the contract responsibility system, including 82 percent of all medium and large SOEs (Zhang, 2006: 177). The reform achieved initial success, but Chinese leaders realized that the rosy performance figures masked serious issues.[13] The government was losing out on revenue because enterprise managers' information advantages and the low baselines locked in at contract signing ultimately made many contracts highly favorable for the enterprises. Problems of moral hazard and soft budget constraints persisted because enterprise managers assumed responsibility for gains but not for losses (Bai and Wang, 1998). The core idea of the reform – that SOEs could succeed economically without privatization if the right incentives were in place – appeared increasingly faulty.

During the 1980s, the central government also began to develop massive industrial conglomerates – the predecessors of today's central SOEs. Chinese leaders envisioned that "general companies" (总公司) – large corporate entities linking multiple factories across provincial lines – would amalgamate assets, employees, supply networks, training facilities, and research and design institutes of production units. By the end of 1982, the State Council had established approximately 120 nationwide industrial general companies under the authority of thirty-eight ministerial agencies (Li, 2014: 50). However, fledgling

than twenty draft plans for the second stage of reform were prepared in 1984, reflecting intense bargaining. Some opposed increasing the enterprises' economic burdens (State Economic Commission, local officials); others wanted to shore up central government revenue (the Ministry of Finance) (Naughton, 1995: 184; Shirk, 1993: 246; Zhang, 2006: 110).

12 On price reform in the 1980s' Chinese market reform debates, see Weber (2021).

13 Combined profits and taxes for industrial enterprises in the national budget were RMB 36.9 billion at the end of 1988, equal to the total amount of their profits and taxes for the six years from 1981 to 1986 (Zhang, 2006: 177).

general companies faced resistance on multiple fronts. Local governments were loath to relinquish control of and revenue from the local production units that were combined to form the new general companies. Additionally, local production units themselves, which had distinct interests and geographically based identities, did not want to be integrated into a unitary general company and subject to the authority of a distant headquarters.

By the 1990s, Chinese leaders had embraced enterprise groups (企业集团) as a way to improve SOE performance and the economy while simultaneously maintaining social stability and state control (Eaton, 2016; Hong, 1999; Keister, 2000).[14] In 1998, Vice-Premier Wu Bangguo stated: "Now and in the next century our nation's position in the international economic order will be to a large extent determined by the position of our nation's largest enterprises and groups" (Nolan, 2001: 17). Like general companies, enterprise groups were large multi-region corporations.[15] However, their organization started from large production units (their "core enterprises") at a lower level of the production system and under the central ministries, rather than originating from the central ministries or even directly from the State Council (Li, 2014: 64). In December 1991, reform of the enterprise groups gained momentum with a national-level pilot that was expanded throughout the decade.[16] Yet multiple challenges also beset the pilot enterprise groups: weak performance, lack of cohesion between the holding company and subsidiaries, and continued government interference (Chen, 1995: 12).

[14] The goals for the enterprise groups included improving state-sector and enterprise performance through specialization and creating economies of scale; pooling scarce labor and capital resources among member enterprises to develop new technologies and products; insulation from competition by creating larger industrial players; reducing pressure on state banks and potential employee layoffs by merging struggling SOEs with stronger performers; and facilitating coordination to make government macroeconomic adjustments more effective.

[15] An enterprise group comprises multiple separate enterprise units, each an independent legal entity, connected through varying legal, economic, and social ties and typically spanning multiple industries (Keister, 2000: 26–29).

[16] In December 1991, the State Council's "Announcement of Guidance on the Selection of a Batch of Large Enterprise Groups for Experimental Pilots" named fifty-five pilot enterprises under twelve different industrial ministries. The State Council later expanded the number of pilot enterprises to fifty-six.

Constraints and Space for Leadership

Taken together, the early reforms created new yet limited space for SOE heads to exercise leadership. For the first time, they could influence reform implementation by bargaining directly with the industrial bureaus on production targets and profit-sharing agreements. Heads of SOEs actively exploited information asymmetries to their advantage (Chen, 1994). They also assumed greater responsibility for decisions about strategy, operations, personnel matters, employee remuneration, and retained profit allocations. In addition, leaders revamped enterprise organizational structures by creating positions and departments to carry out new tasks, such as budget-making, marketing, distribution, and strategic planning. The degree of delegation to SOE bosses varied across enterprises and was greater in some areas than others, such as quality control, which remained subject to greater oversight by external bodies (Child and Lu, 1990). Inside their firms, SOE leaders also gained influence relative to subordinates. As Child (1994: 87) writes of this period: "Under the new conditions, directors have more opportunities to centralize decisions to themselves, perhaps in the desire to secure a more unified approach, or because they may not trust the capabilities of subordinates, or simply due to the fact that they now bear a more exposed personal responsibility for their enterprise's performance."

However, continued government interference constrained SOE heads' nascent space for leadership. Bureaus continued to control access to financing, markets, and material inputs, perpetuating enterprise dependence on higher administrative authorities despite the formal expansion of autonomy (Child, 1994). Bureaus also influenced enterprise affairs through their authority to regulate operations, assess product quality, grant administrative approvals, and provide what was in effect obligatory guidance on production matters and organizational restructuring. "Industrial feudalism" aptly characterizes the high degree of the provincial and municipal authorities' control over SOEs during the early reform period (Boisot, 1987). According to a World Bank enterprise survey conducted between 1991 and 1992, only 29 percent of the Chinese SOEs polled reported having complete autonomy to set their own production plans (Jefferson and Singh, 1999: 44). Many SOE leaders struggled to rid themselves of government influence because the bureaus controlled their salaries and had appointed them to their positions.[17] Although SOE leaders' decision-making authority increased during this period, government interference still limited their execution ability.

Establishment of a Socialist Market Economy (1992–1994)

Enterprise Reforms

In his "Report to the 14th Party Congress" in October 1992, Jiang announced that the development of a "socialist market economy" (社会主义市场经济) would be the official goal of China's reform efforts. This concept endorsed the coexistence of diverse economic elements while simultaneously upholding the continued dominance of state ownership. This was a major ideological shift because it legitimized the diversification of SOE ownership rights and implied that state ownership could be embodied in a variety of corporate forms, ranging from wholly state-owned limited liability companies to majority state-owned joint-stock shareholding companies.

Enterprise reforms during this period aimed to establish a "modern enterprise system" (现代企业制度) through a restructuring of the shareholding system and separating government from enterprises.[18] In theory, partial public listings of SOE assets could check multiple boxes on Chinese leaders' reform wish list: limiting government intervention, improving performance, reducing the debt burdens of state-owned banks by creating new channels to raise capital, and converting the government's previously unlimited liability into limited liability (Peng, 1993). Separation of government from enterprises formally detached ownership from control rights, but in reality government and Party influence on the largest industrial enterprises remained significant.

Specifically, the shareholding-system reform (股份制改革) involved reorganizing SOEs into limited liability companies or shareholding

[17] According to this survey, 92.8 percent of the heads of the 889 SOEs in the sample were appointed by their supervisory agency (Jefferson and Singh, 1999: 49).

[18] Commentary, "Unswervingly Deepening SOE Reform," 人民日报 [*People's Daily*], December 13, 2001, http://en.people.cn/200112/13/eng20011213_86546.shtml.

companies.[19] Unlike earlier efforts in which SOEs issued stock to employees and other enterprises, the new reform encouraged some SOEs to publicly issue shares on equity markets (Wang and Xing, 1987).[20] After the State Council outlined the relevant procedures in 1992, there were nearly 3,700 pilot shareholding-system reform enterprises by year's end, including 69 publicly listed enterprises (State Economic System Restructuring Commission, 1992; State Economic System Restructuring Commission et al., 1992; Zhang, 2006: 305). The number of enterprises listed on the Shanghai and Shenzhen stock exchanges rose steadily in the following years.[21] In addition, the State Council acted to diversify ownership rights for the largest industrial enterprises by selecting three firms in 1994 to pilot restructuring as state holding companies, thereby enabling the partial public listings of their subsidiaries' assets.[22]

State-owned enterprise leaders again played key roles in the process and outcomes of the shareholding-system reform. Take, for instance, the case of Yuchai Diesel Engine Company, once China's largest diesel engine manufacturer. Its head since the mid-1980s, Wang Jianming, successfully led the firm to restructure and access international capital through a public listing as well as foreign investment. Nolan (2001: 58) describes the importance of his leadership to the company's reform:

> Wang Jianming was crucial to Yuchai's success. ... When Wang Jianming took over the plant in the mid-1980s it was deeply indebted. From early on Wang Jianming drove Yuchai to "look towards the market," and change its traditional pattern of behaviour. He was directly responsible for the huge change in Yuchai's institutional structure, for mapping out its course of becoming a Joint-Stock Company, a Sino-foreign joint venture, and its flotation on the New York Stock Market.

[19] For an explanation of the differences between the capital registration requirements, authority structures, and share liquidity of limited liability companies and shareholding companies, see Lin and Zhu (2001: 310–11).

[20] Of the 3,800 enterprises that had issued stocks as of 1988, 85 percent issued stock to their own employees, 13.5 percent sold stock to other enterprises, and 1.5 percent sold stock on the open market (Naughton, 1995: 219).

[21] It reached 185 at the end of 1993, 291 at the end of 1994, and 334 at the end of 1995 (Zhang, 2006: 371, 406).

[22] These companies were China Petrochemical Corporation (Sinopec), Aviation Industry Corporation of China (AVIC), and China Nonferrous Metals Industry Group (Zhang, 2006: 371, 430).

Manager Wang was indisputably the driving force behind Yuchai's initial transformation from a low-ranking producer to a top industry player, even though his ambitious plans to create China's flagship diesel producer ultimately foundered amid intense competition from other central SOEs (Nolan, 2001).

State-owned enterprise leaders who undertook shareholding-system reform confronted multiple practical problems. These challenges ranged from determining the market value of assets, to securing professional services in China's fledgling accounting and legal sectors, and to mounting speculation and weak government oversight of domestic stock exchanges.[23] Moreover, much shareholding-system restructuring occurred in name only. Many enterprises reported that they had reorganized to fulfill requirements, without fundamentally changing their management or operations. Such enterprises were popularly known as "turn-card enterprises" (翻牌公司) for their superficial adoption of the new organizational forms. Experimentation with large-scale state holding companies also floundered, because the central ministries persisted in using administrative methods to control the pilot enterprises.[24]

Separating government from enterprises (政企分开) was the other core element of the modern enterprise system. In theory, this involved removing enterprise functions from the government and curbing administrative interference in enterprise affairs. Initial efforts focused on adopting new forms of corporate organization rather than developing corporate governance.[25] However, the first national pilot scheme employing this approach

[23] As the senior economist Wu Jinglian writes: "In the initial period, accounting firms, law firms and other organizations are not yet sound, rules for stock issuance and circulation are incomplete, and supervision and management are not strict, causing China's shareholding reform pilots to fail to achieve the desired results. ... They have for some time caused a speculative atmosphere in financial markets and the occurrence of an economic 'bubble'" (Wu, 1993).

[24] In 1996, the State Council tried to revive the lagging reforms by reaffirming the autonomy of the three pilot enterprises' holding companies to manage and delegate authority to member enterprises; establishing procedures safeguarding their ability to reinvest their operational income without administrative interference; and granting them greater control rights with regard to investment, raising capital, and other matters (Zhang, 2006: 430–31).

[25] Initially, the Chinese leadership did not equate the separation of government from enterprises with corporate governance (公司治理), although an influential 1993 article by the economists Wu Jinglian and Qian Yingyi had explicitly linked the two concepts. Neither Jiang Zemin's 1992 Report nor the 1993 Decisions mentioned corporate governance, expressed then by the

in 1994 ended in failure.[26] Most of the 100 pilot enterprises were reorganized as wholly state-owned enterprise groups, but they retained the "factory system" (工厂制) method of enterprise governance, in which the state rather than the enterprise and its head directed planning, production, and sales (State Economic and Trade Commission, 2000: 24).[27] Enterprise heads proved reluctant to adopt new governance mechanisms that would formally transfer decision-making authority from the state to the enterprise and thereby increase their personal responsibility for losses. An internal review conducted one year later concluded that not a single pilot enterprise met the assessment standards. "It was a change of form but not of substance," recalled a retired official who personally participated in the pilot enterprise assessment.[28] The State Economic and Trade Commission ultimately attributed the pilot's failure to a host of political and economic factors.[29]

Constraints and Space for Leadership

The space for leadership that SOE heads had during this period expanded from production decisions to management of state-owned assets – their sale, lease, and transfer – in an increasingly competitive

Chinese terms "法人治理结构," "公司治理制度," and "公司制度." Early drafts of the 1993 Decisions and the 1997 15th National Party Congress Report originally included corporate governance; however, it was ultimately omitted from the final version due to concerns that officials lacked familiarity with and understanding of the concept (Wu and Qian, 1993). Interview with participant in the drafting process, retired government official (State Council), Beijing, June 2016.

26 Zhu Rongji outlined plans for this pilot at the "National Working Conference for Experiments on Establishing a Modern Enterprise System" in November 1994. The State Economic and Trade Commission led the pilots; the State Economic System Restructuring Commission was responsible for 30 of the 100 pilot enterprises.

27 The remaining firms restructured as stock companies (股份有限公司) or limited liability companies (有限责任公司).

28 Interview, retired government official (National Resource and Development Commission), Beijing, June 2016.

29 These included the absence of a central-level system for managing state-owned assets; lack of diversified channels to raise capital; contradictions between the cadre management system and a modern enterprise system; limited public listings of state-owned assets; a nascent social welfare system; and limited fiscal resources to support the costs of reform (State Economic and Trade Commission, 2000: 31–32). For the State Economic System Restructuring Commission's assessment, see Zou and Zhang (1998: 15–17).

market environment.[30] In particular, the 1992 "Regulations on the Transformation of Operational Mechanisms of Industrial Enterprises Owned by the Whole People" were a milestone in expanding space for leadership. The regulations granted SOE heads legal decision-making authority across fourteen areas, including production, product and labor pricing, imports and exports, investments, asset allocations (sales, mortgages, and transfers), and joint ventures and mergers (State Council, 1992).[31] At the same time, the 1994 fiscal reform and new, standardized taxes created harder budget constraints and a more even playing field for Chinese enterprises (Wang, 1997). Increasing market competition further impelled SOE leaders to restructure and formulate new development strategies. As Keister and Hodson (2009: 136) observe: "Managers were aware that enterprise closures were likely to become more common with time, and many responded by ascertaining firm strengths and adopting appropriate, but limited, innovations."

The ability of enterprise heads to resist or delay reform implementation also indicates their growing space for leadership. One example is the emergence of "turn-card enterprises" after 1992. Leaders of SOEs responded to the central government's shareholding-system reforms by reporting that their enterprises had restructured as limited liability companies or shareholding companies – without in fact fundamentally changing firm management or operations. This was in part because firms lacked knowledge and experience concerning shareholding-system restructuring and many SOE leaders simply shied away from assuming the economic and political risks of these novel organizational forms. The result was formal compliance coupled with substantive inaction.

Retrenchment of State Ownership in the "Commanding Heights" (1995–2001)

Enterprise Reforms

Beginning in the mid-1990s, the Jiang administration's strategy of "grasping the large and releasing the small" (抓大放小) concentrated

[30] See, for example, the granting of greater asset management autonomy to seven pilot enterprises in 1992 (an eighth pilot enterprise was later added) (State-owned Assets Administration Bureau et al., 1992).

[31] For a summary of the internal debates during the process of drafting this document, see State Economic System Restructuring Commission Policy and Regulation Division (1992).

state ownership in the "commanding heights" of the economy. Premier Zhu Rongji (1998–2003) "released the small" by allowing thousands of small and medium-sized SOEs to be bought up or to go bankrupt. According to official statistics, the number of workers in SOEs fell from 112 million in 1996 to 86 million in 2000, a 23 percent decrease in less than five years.[32] State sector downsizing severed the implicit social contract and neo-traditionalist ties previously binding labor to SOEs (Chen, 2000; Hurst, 2009; Lee, 2007; Walder, 1986, 1991).[33] Those seen as "too old, too weak, or too ignorant" became destitute (Solinger, 2009: 308). Many experienced profound dislocation and disillusionment: "All that workers had been raised and propagandized to take for granted as part of their leading role was snatched away or torn asunder" (Gold et al., 2009: 5–6). Corruption ran rampant as insiders stripped state-owned assets, sold them below market prices, or even borrowed against state-owned assets to reinvest in them under employee shareholding schemes (Lü, 2000).[34]

The state simultaneously "grasped the large" by fostering a core group of large SOEs in strategically important industries that it designated as the "commanding heights." The set of companies selected to participate in enterprise group pilots in the 1990s suggests that these industries included electricity, defense, basic materials, heavy industry, airlines, steel, automobiles, chemicals, and electronics (Sutherland, 2003: 50–51). The 1999 Fourth Plenum of the 15th Central Committee stated that state ownership should remain dominant in "important industries and key areas" (重要行业和关键领域) and in "backbone enterprises in important industries" (重要产业中的骨干企业) (Central Committee of the CCP, 1999).[35] Major restructuring

32 *China Statistical Yearbook*, as cited in Fewsmith (2001: 579). The actual number of workers laid off from SOEs during this period likely exceeds these official numbers.

33 Lee (2007: 12) describes this "socialist social contract" as "an implicit state guarantee of employment security and welfare in exchange for the workers' political acquiescence."

34 Estimates of the loss of state-owned assets during this period are contested and vary; one researcher estimates the loss of investment in the state-owned economy at RMB 180–230 billion (USD 26–34 billion today) between 1995 and 1999, equivalent to 2.4–3.1 percent of China's GDP at the time (Hu, 2001).

35 "Important industries" refers to sectors relating to national security, natural monopolies, and public goods or services provision; "key areas" refers to high and emerging technology industries.

of the State Council in 1998 augmented the incipient national team with a new batch of "centrally controlled enterprises" (中管企业). The Chinese leadership ordered these large industrial SOEs to help China "catch up," and it urged them to publicly list assets on domestic and overseas stock exchanges (Zhou, 1998).

Building national champions assumed new urgency as China continued negotiations to join the World Trade Organization (WTO).[36] Chinese leaders wanted to strengthen the biggest industrial firms to prepare them for greater domestic competition, especially in sectors slated for significant short-term liberalization such as automobiles. The Chinese leadership also wanted to build large industrial conglomerates with the market share, technology, and capital necessary to go head-to-head with foreign multinationals abroad. In 2000, Vice-Minister Jian Qiangui described the "imperative to develop a number of large enterprise groups to make up the backbone of the national economy and the country's main force to participate in international competition" (Nolan, 2001: 17). While observers often cite how Zhu leveraged China's WTO commitments to drastically downsize the state-owned economy, Chinese leaders only intended to "release the small" and never to "release the large" (Bajona and Chu, 2004; Lardy, 2001). As the strategy of "grasping the large and releasing the small" suggests, they viewed these two objectives as complementary.

The domestic economic slowdown in China, worsened by the 1997 Asian financial crisis, prompted Chinese leaders to intensify their support for public listings of large industrial SOEs.[37] In March 1999, the State Economic and Trade Commission reported that 30 percent of 7,680 large and medium SOEs and one-third of the 512 key large SOEs were in the red during the first half of 1998. State-owned companies accounted for 90 percent of all nonperforming loans held by state-owned banks by 1999 (*China Statistical Yearbook*, cited in US Embassy in Beijing, Cable, 1999). Jiang and Zhu sprang into action

[36] China requested a resumption of its status as a contracting party to the General Agreement on Tariffs and Trade (GATT) in July 1986; it formally requested WTO accession in November 1995.

[37] The China Securities Regulatory Commission began to review and approve central SOEs as listing candidates for overseas IPOs in 1993, with twenty-three firms approved by December 1996; however, actual public listings lagged because few were attractive candidates for investment (Walter and Howie, 2012: 177).

to avert an economic crisis: Jiang personally chaired meetings on SOE reform across the country, while Zhu privately ordered the leaders of China's largest SOEs to "restructure and go to market at any cost" (US Embassy in Beijing, Cable, 1999).[38]

Large industrial SOEs heeded the Chinese leadership's call and rapidly repackaged assets for public listings in the early 2000s. The preparatory process involved carving out the SOEs' core production assets from noncore businesses and welfare entities, then putting them into a subsidiary entity organized as a joint-stock company for public listing. As a foreign lawyer who participated in the restructuring of PetroChina, Sinopec, and other large industrial SOEs for their initial public offerings (IPOs) recalled:

> You have to spin off the hospitals, roads, schools, etc. and put them in another vehicle. Then they entered into a contract between what would become the public company and the others, where the public company had to pay a fee to receive the services. That was the basic methodology adopted. ... How you took a state-owned enterprise which geographically was actually more like a city than it was like a company, and divided it into two parts, one the municipal and the other the corporate business part. And it was that framework that was then followed in all of the 1990s to 2000 or so public offerings.[39]

During this restructuring process, SOE leaders dealt with intense internal competition over resources, jobs, and autonomy. This included navigating the relationship between the "parent" holding company and its newly listed subsidiary "children" (Zhang, 2004). Efforts to carry out

[38] 《江泽民主持召开华东七省市国有企业改革和发展座谈会》 [Jiang Zemin Holds a Symposium on the Reform and Development of SOEs in Seven Provinces and Cities in East China], 人民日报 [*People's Daily*], June 27, 1999; 《江泽民主持召开西北五省区国有企业改革和发展座谈会》 [Jiang Zemin Holds a Symposium on the Reform and Development of SOEs in Five Provinces and Autonomous Regions in Northwest China], 人民日报 [*People's Daily*], June 18, 1999; 《江泽民在成都主持召开四省市国有企业改革和发展座谈会》[Jiang Zemin Holds a Symposium in Chengdu on Reform and Development of SOEs in Four Provinces and Cities], 人民日报 [*People's Daily*], April 23, 1999; 《江泽民在武汉主持召开六省区国有企业改革和发展座谈会》 [Jiang Zemin Holds a Symposium in Wuhan on Reform and Development of SOEs in Six Provinces and Autonomous Regions], 人民日报 [*People's Daily*], May 31, 1999; 《江泽民主持八省区市国企改革和发展座谈会》[Jiang Zemin Holds a Symposium on the Reform and Development of SOEs in Eight Provinces and Cities], 人民日报 [*People's Daily*], August 13, 1999.

[39] Interview, foreign lawyer, Beijing (by telephone), May 2019.

public listings were contentious and complex, but ultimately successful. By the end of 2000, China National Petroleum Corporation (CNPC) subsidiary PetroChina executed a dual IPO on the Hong Kong and New York stock markets, and Sinopec completed a triple IPO on the Hong Kong, New York, and London stock markets. Other national champions followed suit, including China Unicom, China National Offshore Oil, and Aluminum Corporation of China (Walter and Howie, 2012).

The Jiang administration also revived the concept of corporate governance (公司治理制度), mentioning it in an official document for the first time in 1999. A State Economic and Trade Commission study stated: "Only on the basis of standardized corporate governance and genuine transformation of operational mechanisms can a modern enterprise system truly be built and real reform results achieved" (State Economic and Trade Commission, 2000: 32–33). That year, the "Decision of the CCP Central Committee on Several Major Issues Concerning the Reform and Development of SOEs" mandated that all restructured SOEs "clarify the responsibilities of the shareholders' meeting, the board of directors, the board of supervisors, and the management to form a corporate governance structure, with each assuming responsibility, coordinated operations, and effective checks and balances" (Central Committee of the CCP, 1999).[40]

Yet early corporate governance reforms had a limited impact because they frequently altered form but not function. As Zhang Delin (2008: 147) describes this phenomenon: "It was rather like drawing a tiger with a cat as a model; they [Chinese policymakers] were not able to fathom the true meaning of the principle and structure of corporate governance – that is, the principle of separation and balance of power – or to adapt it to the enterprises that they were reforming." Moreover, in most large SOE groups, only publicly listed subsidiaries established boards of directors – not the unlisted holding companies that controlled them and administered the bulk of (unlisted) state-owned assets (Rosen, Leutert, and Guo, 2018). The role of the Party also complicated meaningful change. As a former senior State Council official underscored this paradox: "The roles of the Party committee

[40] Corporate governance in China is synonymous with the "three new committees" (新三会): the board of directors, the supervisory committee, and the shareholders meeting. The "old three committees" (老三会) refers to the Party committee, the workers representative assembly, and the workers union.

and the board of directors are not clear, and they may be contradictory. When the Party controls everything, then how can corporate governance be meaningful? If the Party leads all, then corporate governance cannot have space to develop."[41]

Constraints and Space for Leadership

Space for leadership in SOEs expanded during this period, but it did not exhibit uniform growth. Overall, SOE leaders continued to gain autonomy through the restructuring of the state-owned economy and individual firms. The massive downsizing of the state sector under Zhu was a central-level strategy, but much of the decision-making that drove it occurred at the firm level. Enterprise heads decided how many employees to lay off and when, which assets to lease or to sell, and which firms to acquire. In Chongqing SOE Jialing Chemical Plant, for example, head Li Shouchuang initiated property estimates, planned a restructuring, and led negotiations with the local government to reorganize the firm as a joint-stock company with an employee stock ownership plan (Jing and McDermott, 2013). Enterprise heads could pursue partial public listings under state supervision and determine how to invest the raised capital. Leaders of SOEs pushed eagerly for expanded rights to access and manage capital, despite practical constraints (Zhou, 1998).

The State Council explicitly urged SOE leaders to formulate new strategies and restructure their firms. In a 1995 speech, Vice-Premier Wu Bangguo explained that these strategies "should be realistic, accurately identifying one's own position in both domestic and international markets, getting clear about one's advantages – a realistic development strategy is particularly important for enterprise groups. It must solve internal stock adjustment, enabling resources to flow in the direction of development and good efficiency" (Wu, 1995: 5). Leaders now navigated between the state and markets to chart comprehensive, long-term paths forward for their enterprises, moving beyond the bargaining with bureaus and short-term responses to market shifts that had characterized the earlier reform period.

For heads of the largest SOEs, space for leadership expanded but not unequivocally. On the one hand, they gained autonomy within the overall administrative hierarchy. The restructuring of the State Council

41 Retired senior government official (State Council), Beijing, April 2016.

in 1998 abolished the State Assets Administration Bureau (SAAB), the former central-level overseer of state-owned assets, thereby freeing some SOEs from ministerial ownership and control.[42] As the former director of SAAB's Research Institute recalled: "When SAAB was abolished, all of its work units and personnel were eliminated. It was abolished very cleanly. Afterward, the situation returned to management [of state-owned assets] by multiple actors."[43] This ushered in a phase of "nine dragons ruling the waters" (九龙治水), in which multiple government and Party organizations were responsible for SOE affairs.

Moreover, some SOE heads struggled to exercise leadership despite the greater space to do so. A then classified US government report about a World Bank training project in China observed that SOE managers found it difficult to delegate authority, make strategic rather than tactical decisions, and use inductive reasoning to flexibly respond to rapidly changing market conditions.[44] It cites enterprise managers' fear of losing their authority and the resources for patronage it conferred, as well as the perceived risks of accountability for decisions delegated to subordinates (US Department of State, 1999). These observations underscore that enterprise heads did not always lead by making and implementing decisions about strategy and structure – even if they had greater autonomy to do so.

Internationalization and Consolidation of the State Sector (2002–2012)

Enterprise Reforms

Two interrelated trends distinguish developments during the Hu Jintao administration between 2002 and 2012. The first is the internationalization of SOE operations, assets, and capital. After officially adopting the "going out" (走出去) policy in 2002, the Chinese government provided

[42] The SAAB was set up in 1988 under the Ministry of Finance. Similar agencies were established earlier at the provincial and municipal levels.
[43] Lecture by former government official (SAAB), Beijing, April 2016.
[44] The report attributes this to SOE managers' education and practices during the planned economy. During that period, they strictly adhered to standard operating procedures, followed hierarchical commands, and used deductive rather than inductive reasoning to respond to plan directives and expected performance criteria (US Department of State, 1999).

economic, political, and administrative support for the overseas expansion of SOEs. The second is the formal consolidation of state-owned assets and administrative authority. The Hu administration's creation of SASAC in 2003 ended the fragmentation of government authority for state-owned asset management.[45] The establishment of SASAC also set the stage for further consolidation of state-owned assets through government-directed mergers among central SOEs.

The 16th National Party Congress Report in November 2002 officially adopted "going out" as a "major measure taken in a new stage of China's reform and opening movement."[46] This differed from earlier statements because it proposed a comprehensive, long-term global expansion strategy and a fundamental shift in economic orientation – from the internationalizing domestic economy toward world markets – for all Chinese enterprises.[47] The state encouraged companies to pursue international investments, cross-border mergers and acquisitions, joint ventures with foreign firms abroad, and overseas-registered subsidiaries.[48] It did so using measures such as targeted loans, regulatory liberalization, and a loosening of administrative rules. At the firm level, the going-out policy impelled leaders of large SOEs to develop international expansion strategies and adapt their organizational structures both at home and abroad.

The Hu administration established SASAC in 2003 as a state ownership agency to administer 189 central SOEs (State Council, 2003).[49]

45 The present study focuses on the central-level SASAC, a special commission of the State Council charged with representing state ownership rights and administering a portfolio of central SOEs.

46 Jiang Zemin, "Full Text of Report at the 16th Party Congress," November 8, 2002, www.china.org.cn/english/2002/Nov/49107.htm.

47 As early as 1998, top Chinese leaders had urged high-performing SOEs to "go out" and set up factories in Africa, Central Asia, the Middle East, Eastern Europe, and Latin America. Jiang Zemin, 《讲好国内经济工作 增强承受地域风险 江泽民 国内经济》 [Doing Domestic Economic Work Well, Strengthening the Ability to Withstand and Resist Risks], February 26, 1998, www.reformdata.org/1998/0226/4537.shtml.

48 The state's previous efforts to foster cross-border economic activities primarily involved foreign direct investment into China, domestic joint ventures, collaborative research and development initiatives between Chinese and foreign firms, public listings on stock exchanges in China and abroad, and support for Chinese firms' exports.

49 Central SOEs are called "中央国有企业" and are commonly abbreviated as "央企." They include both the former general companies, which were set up under central ministries and later broken up by the 1998 State Council

As a former National Development and Reform Commission official explained the rationale: "The ownership problem existed at the company level and the national level. The [1993] Company Law was intended to solve the ownership issue at the company level, but it did not create an institutional framework at the national level for SOE management."[50] The mission of SASAC was therefore twofold: (1) to represent the state as shareholder; and (2) to formulate and approve a SOE reform program in accordance with State Council policies. The Hu administration granted SASAC full ministerial rank and a comparatively large allocation of 555 staff (Brødsgaard, 2012: 630). Its mandate to "manage assets, people, and affairs" (管资产，管人，管事) gave SASAC significant authority over enterprises, although it was not authorized to intervene in their daily operations.

In the years after SASAC's establishment, however, initial regulatory ambitions confronted the realities of oversight. The SASAC relied primarily on personnel appointments, administrative guidance, information reporting, and periodic on-site inspections by its supervisory board members to monitor and manage central SOEs; however, these proved to be indirect and incomplete methods of control (Leutert and Eaton, 2021). Rapid growth in the size, organizational complexity, and global operations of central SOEs steadily outstripped SASAC's supervisory capacity. The average size of central SOE enterprise groups more than doubled from 82 member entities in 2003 to 191 in 2010 (Hsieh and Zheng, 2015). In addition, China's RMB 4 trillion (USD 586 billion) stimulus package after the global financial crisis gave many central SOEs a massive capital injection. Together, these factors weakened SASAC's ability to rein in SOE empire building at home and to monitor SOE activities and investments abroad.

Constraints and Space for Leadership

Space for leadership by SOE heads grew significantly during the decade-long Hu administration (2002–12). Compared to the previous period, state interference in the affairs of individual enterprises declined.

restructuring, and the former large enterprise group pilots that originated at lower levels of the former ministry-coordinated production system.

50 Interview with retired government official (National Development and Reform Commission), Beijing, March 2016.

Despite SASAC's ministerial rank and large allocation of personnel, it lacked the mandate and operational capacity for routine interventions in company decision-making. The rapid expansion and internationalization of the assets and revenues of the central SOEs further weakened SASAC's regulatory capability. In addition, China's fiscal stimulus during the global financial crisis boosted both the resources and influence of central SOEs. As Wang, Xiao, and Tang (2008: 57) describe the difficulty of regulating increasingly large and politically powerful SOEs: "the cat wants to catch the mouse, but the mouse is bigger than the cat."

As their assets and autonomy increased, central SOEs became like small individual kingdoms. As a former government official described these developments: "The positive results of Zhu Rongji's reforms began to appear around this time. His reforms got rid of many burdens and cleared the way for foreign investment. SOE performance began to improve. This was the golden age for SOEs."[51] Enterprise leaders leveraged increased SOE autonomy and resources to carve out greater room for maneuver vis-à-vis administrative superiors and subordinates. In some central SOEs, leaders also used their positions and their firms' vast resources for political patronage and personal enrichment.[52]

Yet central SOE heads still faced constraints on their leadership. Party organs and SASAC retained key levers of influence through their continued authority over executive selection, assessment, and compensation. Between 2004 and 2009, SASAC experimented with establishing boards of directors in central SOEs at the holding company level. In theory, this move would increase external monitoring and impose checks and balances on leaders' decision-making.[53] However, these boards of directors have yet to genuinely constrain executive and corporate behavior (Rosen, Leutert, and Guo, 2018).

[51] Interview with retired government official (National Development and Reform Commission), Beijing, April 2016.

[52] One such high-profile case involved Jiang Jiemin, the former chairman of CNPC and director of SASAC, who was sentenced to sixteen years in prison in 2014 for bribery and abuse of power.

[53] In 2004, SASAC and the COD selected seven central SOEs to establish boards of directors at the holding-company level with a minimum of two external directors. By 2009, this scheme expanded to twenty-four central SOEs. By the beginning of 2008, seventeen of the pilot enterprises had established boards composed of more than 50 percent external directors. In 2009, SASAC also issued provisional regulations to standardize the operations of the pilot enterprises' boards and to enshrine their powers in the companies' articles of

Limited Economic Liberalization with Increased Political Control (2013 to Present)

Enterprise Reforms

Xi Jinping initially raised hopes for ambitious market reform of the state-owned economy. The Decision of the Third Plenum of the 18th Central Committee in November 2013 repeatedly pledged a "decisive role" for the market in resource allocation. The Decision stated: "We must deepen reform of the economic system by focusing firmly on the decisive role of the market in allocating resources, adhering to and improving the basic economic system, and accelerating improvements to the modern market system, macro-control system, and open economic system."[54] Overseas observers initially heralded the new leadership's reform plan, viewing it as "a wonderful opportunity" and "the beginning of another wave of private-sector development."[55] They expected that Xi would initiate transformative economic change, marking "a turning point in China's modern history" (Rosen, 2014).

However, the Xi administration subsequently changed course. Stock market turbulence in 2015 underscored the risks of freer markets – and the utility of SOEs as a lever of economic control.[56] Rising concerns about the domestic security implications of reliance on foreign technology also deepened the commitment to state ownership. The new administration's SOE reform roadmap, released in September 2015

association. SASAC, 《关于中央企业建立和完善国有独资公司董事会试点工作的通知》 [Notice on the Establishment and Improvement of the Board of Directors Pilot Program for State-Owned Sole Proprietorship Companies in Central Enterprises], June 9, 2004; SASAC, 《董事会试点中央企业董事会规范运作暂行办法的通知》 [Temporary Regulations for Standardizing Board of Directors Operations in Central SOE Pilot Enterprises' Boards of Directors], March 20, 2009; Shao (2014: 542).

[54] CCP Central Committee, 《中共中央关于全面深化改革若干重大问题的决定》 [Decisions of the Central Committee of the CCP on Several Major Issues Concerning Comprehensively Deepening Reform], November 12, 2013, www.gov.cn/jrzg/2013-11/15/content_2528179.htm.

[55] Cheng Li, "Hailing Success of China's Third Plenum," *Brookings*, November 14, 2013, www.brookings.edu/articles/hailing-success-of-chinas-third-plenum/.

[56] The SASAC directed publicly listed SOE subsidiaries to halt share sales and to buy more shares to "safeguard market stability." SASAC, 《国资委采取有力措施维护股票市场稳定》 [SASAC Takes Effective Measures to Safeguard Stock Market Stability], July 8, 2015.

after delays, did not once mention a decisive role for the market.[57] By the early 2020s, stricter foreign government reviews of Chinese overseas investments, the US–China trade war, and the COVID-19 pandemic further confirmed the Xi administration's conviction that SOEs are essential to economic and technological self-reliance.[58] The Xi administration appears to have abandoned any intention of conducting a market-oriented overhaul of the state sector.

However, limited economic liberalization is nevertheless still occurring at the firm level. One such move is mixed ownership reform (混合所有制改革). This concept, which dates back to the 1980s, refers to the blending of public and private ownership in industrial firms. For SOEs, in practice this involves the diversification of their shareholding structures via partial public listing of assets, selling a portion of state shares to the private sector, and/or granting employees stock ownership. The Xi Jinping administration initially revived this concept in the Decision of the 2013 Third Plenum of the 18th Central Committee, which called for "enabling capital of all kinds of ownership to draw on one another's strong points to offset weaknesses, stimulate one another, and develop jointly."[59] Since then, the Chinese leadership has continued to promote this concept as a strategy to inject private capital and expertise into SOEs, thereby making their decision-making and resource allocation more responsive to market conditions.

Mixed ownership reform remains on the agenda, but its implementation has been slow and enthusiasm has waned. In 2014, SASAC launched national-level pilots for mixed ownership reforms, but the results were uneven and progress limited.[60] The government intended

57 CCP Central Committee and State Council, 《中共中央、国务院关于深化国有企业改革的指导意见》 [Guiding Opinions of the CCP Central Committee and the State Council on Deepening the Reform of SOEs], September 13, 2015, www.gov.cn/zhengce/2015-09/13/content_2930440.htm.

58 Huang Yue and Wang Zihui, 《在东北，习近平关注了这些事》 [In the Northeast, Xi Jinping Pays Attention to These Matters], *Xinhua News*, September 29, 2018, www.xinhuanet.com/politics/xxjxs/2018-09/29/c_1123505377.htm.

59 CCP Central Committee, 《中共中央关于全面深化改革若干重大问题的决定》 [Decision of the Central Committee of the CCP on Several Major Issues Concerning Comprehensively Deepening the Reform], November 12, 2013, www.gov.cn/jrzg/2013-11/15/content_2528179.htm.

60 Five years after the national pilots for mixed ownership reforms were launched and after a fourth expansion of the scheme in April 2019, there were only

for the 2017 restructuring of China Unicom's publicly listed flagship subsidiary to establish a "Unicom model" for mixed ownership reform.[61] However, the role that high-level leaders played in Unicom's restructuring suggests that private-investor reticence remains a major reform obstacle, and today a "Unicom model" is no longer discussed. According to the State Council, subsidiaries at the second and lower levels of SOE enterprise groups were ready to implement mixed ownership, while introduction of mixed ownership at the group company level remained at an exploratory stage.[62] Despite a November 2017 directive urging central SOEs to implement mixed ownership reforms at the group company level, no companies have done so yet.[63] Some private investors are concerned that state control will persist after the mixed ownership reforms are implemented, despite new corporate structures (Beck, 2022: 12). Government departments, local SASACs, and SOEs themselves also worry about the risks of losing state-owned assets through corruption and bribery during any mixed ownership reforms (Yue, 2018: 15).

State capital management reforms (国有资本管理改革) are another way in which the Xi Jinping administration is taking limited steps toward economic liberalization at the company level. State capital management encompasses two reform approaches. One involves

about 100 pilot enterprises. 《我国拟启动第四批混合所有制改革试点工作》 [China Plans to Launch Work on a Fourth Batch of Mixed Ownership Reform Pilots], *Xinhua News*, April 18, 2019, www.gov.cn/xinwen/2019-04/18/content_5384263.htm.

61 《BAT等14家入局联通混改，腾讯或入联通A股公司董事会》 [14 Companies Including BAT Have Joined Unicom Mixed Ownership Reform, Tencent May Enter Unicom's A-share Company Board of Directors], *Caixin*, August 16, 2017, https://tech.sina.cn/t/2017-08-16/detail-ifyixtym6064877.d.html.

62 State Council, 《国务院关于国有企业发展混合所有制经济的意见》 [Opinions of the State Council on SOEs Developing a Mixed Ownership Economy], September 23, 2015, www.gov.cn/zhengce/content/2015-09/24/content_10177.htm.

63 National Development and Reform Commission, Ministry of Finance, Ministry of Human Resources and Social Security, Ministry of Land and Resources, State Resources Commission, Tax Administration, China Securities Regulatory Commission (CSRC), National Defense Science and Technology Bureau, 《关于深化混合所有制改革试点若干政策的意见》 [Opinions on Deepening Certain Policies for Mixed Ownership Reform Pilots], November 29, 2017, www.ndrc.gov.cn/xxgk/zcfb/tz/201809/t20180918_962278_ext.html.

giving some SOEs and their leaders greater autonomy to make capital management decisions. In theory, letting state firms make their own decisions based on company circumstances and changing market conditions will improve performance and the efficiency of resource allocation. The second involves permitting selected SOEs with cross-industry holdings to act like asset management companies, managing state-owned assets and capital on behalf of government owners. In 2014, SASAC initiated experimental schemes for both approaches.[64]

Implementation of state capital management reform has been gradual and its results uneven. More experimentation and progress is occurring at the provincial and municipal levels than at the central level.[65] The government tapped ten central SOEs as state capital investment company pilots; local SASACs in Shandong and other provinces and major municipalities had established eighty-nine state capital investment companies and state capital operations companies as of July 2018.[66] Some SOEs have exploited increased autonomy to engage in empire building through commercially questionable acquisitions in noncore business areas.[67] Yet state capital management reforms do not mean that leaders are free to cast off the state's developmental goals. In contrast, increased financialization of the state sector is both a policy end and a means of continued bureaucratic economic coordination (Naughton, 2019).

[64] SASAC, 《国务院国资委举办"四项改革"试点新闻发布会》 [SASAC Holds a Press Conference on the "Four Reforms" Pilots], July 15, 2014.

[65] After SASAC's second expansion of the state capital management reform pilots for central SOEs in December 2018, there were only nineteen state-owned capital investment company pilots and two asset management company pilots. Wang Xueqing [王雪青], 《国有资本投资公司试点扩容 11家央企入围》 [Eleven SOEs Shortlisted for Expansion of State-Owned Capital Investment Companies], 上海证券报 [Shanghai Securities News], December 29, 2018.

[66] Gao Jianghong [高江虹] and Hou Yuechan [侯悦婵]: 《国企国资改革深入推进："两类公司"第二批试点名单将出》 [The Reform of SOEs and State-Owned Assets Is Further Advanced: The Second Batch of Lists of Pilots for "Two Types of Companies" Will Be Released], 21世纪经济报道 [*21st Century Business Herald*], August 30, 2018, https://m.21jingji.com/article/20180830/dc5c7d276073dd3791c1ae7ea868b2aa.html.

[67] Yanmei Xie, "The Next Wave of SOE Consolidation," Gavekal Dragonomics, November 2018.

The Xi administration is combining these steps toward limited economic liberalization with increased political control. Anti-corruption efforts are central to this push (Carothers, 2022). Xi launched a far-reaching anti-corruption campaign in 2013 that quickly put state firms in its crosshairs. Central SOEs had long been notorious for weak accounting and a lack of internal oversight. The anti-corruption investigations uncovered executive embezzlement, bribes, and lavish perks, such as RMB 25,000 (USD 3,600) lunches.[68] The Central Commission for Discipline Inspection (CCDI) launched multiple rounds of anti-graft inspections targeting central SOEs – at two firms in 2013, ten firms in 2014, forty-three firms in 2015, forty-two firms plus SASAC in 2019, and twenty-seven firms in 2023.[69] At the end of Xi's first five years in office in 2017 alone, twelve top executives of core central SOEs had been removed on corruption charges, far more than the two taken out under Hu (Leutert, 2018b: 32).

The Xi administration also tightened political control by specifying and institutionalizing the Party's "leadership function" (领导作用) in SOEs. Early on, it directed SOEs to make the Party the "political core" (政治核心) of their governance structures.[70] The Chinese leadership under Xi also revised the Party constitution to confirm the Party committee should "exercise leadership" (发挥领导作用) in SOE decision-making. In addition, SASAC ordered central SOEs to modify their articles of association to formalize Party building requirements and the leadership role of Party committees

[68] Laura Zhou, "Senior Executives of Power Utility State Grid Punished Over Lavish Lunch," *South China Morning Post*, March 25, 2015, www.scmp.com/news/china/article/1746941/senior-executives-power-utility-state-grid-punished-over-lavish-lunch.

[69] 《中央纪委监察部网站已发布央企被查领导64人》 [CCDI Inspection Department Website Announces 64 Central SOE Leaders Have Been Investigated], *Xinhua News*, January 4, 2016, www.xinhuanet.com//politics/2016-01/04/c_1117665184.htm; CCDI, 《十九届中央第三轮巡视整改进展情况全部公布》 [Situation of the Third Round of Inspection and Rectification of the 19th Central Committee], March 23, 2020, www.gov.cn/xinwen/2020-03/23/content_5494367.htm; CCDI, 《二十届中央第一轮巡视对象公布》 [Announcement of the Targets of the First Round of Inspections of the 20th Central Committee of the CCP], March 23, 2023, www.mem.gov.cn/dj/xsdt/202303/t20230328_445953.shtml.

[70] CCP Central Committee, 《关于在深化国有企业改革中坚持党的领导加强党的建设的若干意见》 [Several Opinions on Adhering to Party Leadership and Strengthening Party Building in Deepening the Reform of SOEs], September 25, 2015, www.gqhgyjy.com/portal/policy/detail/id/286.html.

in corporate governance.[71] Together, these developments have deepened political control over SOEs.

Constraints and Space for Leadership

The Xi administration's combination of limited economic liberalization with increased political control has had varied effects on the space for leadership in SOEs. On the one hand, the mixed ownership and state capital management reforms give SOE leaders new resources and greater autonomy for commercial decision-making. Mixed ownership reform enables leaders to harness private capital while ceding little authority to new shareholders. State capital management reform means less direct state interference in firm activities, particularly decisions about investments and resource allocation. The State Council has continued to formally devolve new powers to SOEs, explicitly confirming their leaders' autonomy to set strategies and to restructure their companies.[72]

Yet company leaders have also become subject to greater oversight. The Fourth Plenum of the 18th Central Committee in 2014 announced the concept of "lifelong accountability" (终身责任) for major investment and operational decisions made by leading officials in the public sector.[73] The State Council formally established a lifelong accountability system for SOE leaders in 2016. Any SOE leader who violates regulations, or who causes the loss of state-owned assets or other "serious adverse consequences" because of decisions made during their tenure, can be held legally liable until death.[74] While there are no publicly

71 SASAC, 《关于加快推进中央企业党建工作总体要求纳入公司章程有关事项的通知》 [Notice on Matters Regarding Speeding Up and Advancing Inclusion of the Overall Requirements for Central SOEs' Party-Building Work in Their Articles of Association], January 3, 2017.

72 State Council, 《国务院办公厅关于公布国务院国有资产监督管理委员会履行出资人职责企业名单的通知》 [Notice from the General Office of the State Council on the Publication of the List of Enterprises in which SASAC Performs the Role of Investor], October 21, 2003, www.gov.cn/gongbao/content/2003/content_52517.htm.

73 《中共十八届四中全会公报(全文)》 [Communiqué of the Fourth Plenary Session of the Eighteenth CCP Central Committee (Full Text)], *Xinhua News*, October 23, 2014, http://news.sohu.com/20141023/n405406666.shtml.

74 State Council, 《国务院办公厅关于建立国有企业违规经营投资责任追究制度的意见》 [Opinions of the General Office of the State Council on Establishing an Accountability System for SOE Violations of Business Operations and Investment Regulations], August 2, 2016, www.gov.cn/zhengce/content/2016-08/23/content_5101590.htm.

Table 3.2 *Evolving constraints and space for leadership in China's state sector since 1978*

Period	Constraints and space for leadership
Emergence and decline of "dual track" economic reform (1978–91)	Relationship between the state and SOEs (and their leaders) is transformed from bureaucratic command to strategic bargaining SOE leaders transition from managing production to participating in reform experimentation and implementation, bounded by greater accountability for performance
Establishment of a socialist market economy (1992–94)	SOE leaders exercise new decision-making rights regarding production, operations, and restructuring against the backdrop of the goal of developing a "modern enterprise system"
Retrenchment of state ownership in the "commanding heights" (1995–2001)	SOE leaders determine how to restructure their firms under the "grasping the large and releasing the small" strategy SOE leaders begin to manage state-owned capital as well as state-owned assets both in China and overseas through public listings and overseas expansion
Internationalization and consolidation of the state sector (2002–12)	Overall reduction in state interference and limited monitoring by SASAC, together with asset growth and increased access to capital, loosens constraints and boosts autonomy for SOE leaders Under the "going out" policy, SOE leaders gain new space to develop strategies for overseas expansion
Limited economic liberalization with increased political control (2013 to present)	New autonomy and resources for commercial decision-making come with greater political control SOE leaders manage both state-owned capital and assets in an increasingly global context

known prosecutions of central SOE leaders to date, this policy has had a chilling effect in corporate headquarters in the state sector.

Xi's anti-corruption campaign and increased Party-building have put SOEs and their leaders under a political microscope. Discoveries of widespread graft and reports of lavish spending have motivated additional inspections. Corruption inspection findings have also prompted SASAC to strengthen information reporting requirements for SOEs' overseas investments.[75] However, such heightened political oversight under Xi does not necessarily equate with top-down control over SOE leaders' decision-making. Tightened political control can also be interpreted as a deliberate counterweight to expanded commercial autonomy. Table 3.2 summarizes the constraints and space for leadership in China's state sector from 1978 to the present.

Conclusion

A review of the post-1978 enterprise reforms reveals significantly expanded albeit still constrained space for leadership in Chinese SOEs. During "dual track" economic reform, company leaders played an important role in reform experimentation and implementation. They could negotiate with administrative superiors on production targets, determine the specific means by which to achieve them, and modify their organizations to carry out new tasks such as budget-making, strategic planning, marketing, and distribution. However, the continued involvement of government bureaus in enterprise affairs – together with their control over access to financing, markets, and material inputs – constrained this nascent space for leadership.

After formal establishment of a "socialist market economy" in 1992, the autonomy of enterprise heads over production matters expanded to encompass management of state-owned assets and state-owned capital. They exercised leadership by restructuring their firms as limited liability companies or shareholding companies, and they formulated development strategies for domestic and global markets. The growing influence of SOE leaders is evident in their implementation of new enterprise reforms – and also in their attempts to resist or delay them.

With the downsizing of the state sector and retrenchment of state ownership in the commanding heights beginning in 1995, enterprise heads exercised leadership by determining how specifically to restructure their organizations. The State Council moved large SOE groups in and out of national pilots and official groupings of "important

[75] SASAC, 《中央企业境外投资监督管理办法》 [Measures for the Supervision and Administration of Overseas Investments by Central SOEs], January 18, 2017, www.gov.cn/xinwen/2017-01/18/content_5160911.htm#1.

enterprises" and in some cases even combined them at will. However, enterprise leaders, not the State Council, determined their firms' strategies and structures as they expanded domestically and internationally. Yet the government continued to interfere in enterprise affairs, especially after the 1998 State Council restructuring granted multiple state and Party agencies regulatory authority over SOEs.

Between 2002 and 2012, administrative restructuring created a portfolio of central SOEs under the authority of SASAC. The Hu administration sought to recentralize state authority, but central SOEs' growing size, organizational complexity, and global operations steadily outstripped SASAC's monitoring capacity. At the same time, China's 2008–12 fiscal stimulus package expanded central SOEs' access to capital and fueled empire building at home and overseas. Executives gained new resources and latitude for decision-making regarding organizational strategy and structure on a global stage.

Since 2013, limited economic liberalization has come with greater political control. Mixed ownership reform and state capital management reforms have given SOE heads more autonomy for commercial decision-making. At the same time, the anti-corruption campaign plus stronger Party institutions and accountability mechanisms have made some SOE leaders more cautious and responsive to the state's strategic priorities. However, SOE leaders continue to make and execute decisions about organizational strategy and structure, maintaining and increasing state-owned asset value, and building globally competitive firms.

4 *Reform through Leadership in China Infrastructure (CI)*

From the outside, the headquarters of China Infrastructure (CI) in Beijing looks just like that of any other Chinese multinational corporation. Two glass and steel office buildings tower above the adjacent restaurants, shops, and low-rise brick apartment buildings. Security guards monitor the flow of vehicles and people through automatic gates as they enter the office compound. Two flagpoles flying the company and national flags frame the entrance while a long line of expensive foreign cars – Audis, Mercedes, and the occasional Maserati – wait for executives and visiting senior dignitaries. Once through the revolving doors, more security guards and reception staff dot a massive lobby featuring outsized works of art – carved jade, sculptures, and paintings. A throng of employees fills the lobby at the start of the workday; they stand watching news and commercials on television screens while waiting for the elevator. After exiting on the appropriate floor, employees walk to their departments down long marble hallways. The rankings of the departments' progress in achieving annual performance targets flicker on electronic signboards, interspersed with definitions of terms such as "money market" and "IPO," excerpts from a new speech by Xi Jinping, and a quote by the American writer Dale Carnegie about the importance of "horse sense."

Employees begin their workday by changing into the work uniform that is mandatory for most: a navy business suit with a white collared shirt and formal shoes. Some also wear a gold lapel pin featuring the CI logo. Many arrive before the official start of the workday at 8:30 a.m. to eat breakfast in the company cafeteria and prepare tea or coffee at their desks. They work in large open rooms, accented with potted plants, in cubicles just tall enough to look over while sitting. Glassed-in offices for department heads anchor the corners of the rooms. Each desk has its own company-issued computer and telephone. Employees talk on the phone with overseas clients in English, French, Spanish, and other languages. Others use the Chinese instant messaging program QQ to chat virtually with colleagues about internal approvals for an upcoming tender. There are always several vacant desks in each office, left empty by staff traveling for days or even weeks at a time.

Workdays at CI follow a predictable routine. At 10:00 a.m. – and again later in the day at 3:00 p.m. – several minutes of calisthenics set to up-tempo brass band music blare automatically through the loudspeakers. Most people ignore it, although a few go out to the hallway for some light aerobic exercise and stretching. Before the cafeteria opens for lunch at 11:30 a.m., employees take the stairs to line up early. They wind their way down the stairwell past scattered cigarette butts and a lingering odor of smoke that silently mock the "no smoking" signs on the walls. In the cafeteria, employees sit together at long tables and eat buffet-style meals from metal trays as large television screens broadcast the latest news. After lunch it is time for the "midday rest." Employees return to their offices carrying fruit and boxed yogurt drinks left over from lunch, turn off the overhead lights, and nap with their heads down on their desks; some even recline fully on company-issued folding cots. The lights are switched back on at around 1:00 p.m., and it is back to work. Around 4:50 p.m., those with newborn or young children are already trickling out of the office. At 5:00 p.m., the workday formally ends. By 6:00 p.m., only the company leaders, ambitious junior employees, and a handful of those living in on-site company housing remain.

Strict workplace hierarchies underpin the bustle of daily work at CI. Employees address anyone holding a position of department deputy manager and above by combining their name with their official title, a common practice in China when speaking to higher-ranking individuals. For example, a manager surnamed "Zhang" should be addressed as "Manager Zhang," not by his given name. An employee explained that, in a telephone call with a higher-ranked superior, the lower-ranked person must never first hang up the phone. In meetings, one is to refrain from speaking unless a superior solicits views from the attendees. "I have learned to say less unless I am invited to speak," an employee confided, adding: "Leaders don't like talk and no action."[1]

[1] Conversation with Sino-Construction International employee, 2014.

In Sino-Construction International, a CI subsidiary, every work cubicle was adorned with telephone trees printed on oversized pieces of paper. These telephone trees presented the names and contact information for key personnel in all departments; they also indicated how department employees were organized and ranked relative to one another by listing the names of work-group members and leaders.

A system of internal approvals structures workplace hierarchies and daily work at CI. From the chairman down to the lowest-ranking employees, internal approvals are the everyday substance of the authority relationships in Chinese SOEs. This practice, known as "signature and reporting" (签报) involves "seeking the leaders' guidance and reporting on work, updating on the situation, answering queries, and solving problems".[2] In CI, internal approvals ranged from informal oral approvals by a single individual to formal written approvals requiring the signatures of as many as six people, and they were requisite for company matters both large and small. Company leaders signed off on everything from multimillion-dollar investments to travel plans for senior staff. In the absence of explicit approvals from superiors, following standard operating procedures is a primary method of risk avoidance in Chinese SOEs. Employees shy away from acting without clear guidelines or explicit authorization, as this would entail their taking responsibility and subsequently being held accountable for the outcomes in their own performance assessments.

The issuing of "official documents" (公文) also reinforces the hierarchical authority relationships within Chinese SOEs. Intra-firm entities at all levels regularly issue directives addressing matters ranging from work plan implementation to safety guidelines to company vehicle use. Once an intra-firm entity obtains approval from superiors, it issues an official document and circulates it internally. Each CI official document is ranked on a three-level scale of importance – ordinary, urgent, and extremely urgent – with a corresponding processing time (company document).[3] Leaders in CI and other Chinese SOEs use these official documents to promote compliance by requiring each receiving department to sign each document and attest that they had implemented its directives. Sanctions back official document flows and

[2] Company document, 2016.

[3] Processing times were ten days for official documents designated as "ordinary," five days for those designated as "urgent," and three days for those designated as "extremely urgent."

their compliance function. Leaders at CI evaluate intra-firm entities on the basis of their official document management and quality in annual performance assessments. They even threaten to give lower evaluations and carry out criticism by public circular (通报批评) of any entities with poor performance and any individuals who held up compliance.[4]

As these glimpses inside CI suggest, Chinese central SOE work life today combines long-standing practices, such as mandatory employee uniforms and top-down approval systems, with increasingly global operations. Enterprise leaders' decisions about organizational strategies and structures and their execution involve personnel, assets, and capital around the world. Top executives must pay as much attention to their companies' performance in international markets as they do to the latest official documents from SASAC and the State Council. Leaders' speeches blend policy buzzwords like "innovation" and mentions of the BRI with discussions of the company's latest *Fortune Global 500* rankings and warnings about overseas political turmoil and trade protectionism. Preserving and increasing the value of state-owned assets depends more and more on company leaders' abilities to expand business beyond China's borders.

At the same time, Chinese SOE leaders must navigate the domestic incentives and constraints imposed by existing institutions, policies, and economic factors. The Chinese leadership sets two main objectives for SOEs and their leaders: (1) preserving and increasing the value of state-owned assets; and (2) building internationally competitive firms. The government and CCP authorities incentivize SOE leaders by making their career advancement contingent on achieving these objectives. Since state ownership now involves the management of capital as well as assets, SOE leaders' decision-making must take efficiency and profits into greater account. Some actions, however, remain off-limits for leaders, such as declaring bankruptcy or laying off large numbers of employees. Domestic economic factors, such as industrial overcapacity or changes in access to financing from state-owned development banks, may also limit SOE leaders' decisions about organizational strategy and structure and their ability to execute them.

[4] Company document, 2016.

In this chapter, I assess the effects of leadership on reform by analyzing the consecutive tenures of two chairmen in CI.[5] The chairman determines the specific strategies the company will employ to respond to the central authorities' objectives of preserving and increasing state-owned asset value and building internationally competitive firms. The chairman also makes decisions about whether to maintain or to modify the company's organizational structure by (1) creating, modifying, or eliminating intra-company entities like departments or subsidiaries; (2) changing existing authority relations among them; and (3) reallocating assets, personnel, and capital internally. In short, SOE leaders must determine whether, how, and when to react to central goals, make specific decisions about organizational strategy and structure, and then attempt – sometimes unsuccessfully and with a significant time lag – to mobilize subordinates to carry them out.

Introducing CI

The Chinese government formed CI in the early 2010s by merging two existing central SOEs: Sino-Construction and Sino-Engineering.[6] The main objectives of the merger were twofold: (1) to achieve vertical industrial integration by combining Sino-Construction's construction capacity with Sino-Engineering's engineering expertise; and (2) to build a global industry leader by increasing the new company's assets, capital, employees, and client networks. The newly created CI was a multilayered enterprise group with approximately 100 subsidiaries. The following analysis centers on the successive chairmen of CI and involves five main entities within the firm: the holding company, Sino-Construction International, the construction bureaus, Sino-Engineering (and Sino-Engineering International), and the design institutes. Table 4.1 briefly introduces these key players; Figure 4.1 presents a simplified depiction of CI's organizational structure focusing on them.

[5] The position of chairman (董事长) has the greatest authority in central SOEs. A single individual typically holds the positions of chairman and Party secretary simultaneously (Leutert, 2018b).

[6] "Sino-Construction" and "Sino-Engineering" are pseudonyms.

Table 4.1 *China Infrastructure (CI): key intra-firm entities*

Intra-firm entity	Description
Holding company	The administrative body at the apex of the enterprise group. It supervises the management and commercial operations of the subsidiaries through methods such as approvals for administrative and commercial matters and personnel control, for example by dispatching its employees to overseas offices.
Sino-Construction	The first of the two central state-owned companies that were merged to create CI in the early 2010s.
Sino-Construction International	Established in the early 2000s as a marketing, investment, and management platform for the company's overseas business. Its main business lines include energy and transportation infrastructure and municipal works.
Construction bureaus	CI has multiple construction bureaus located across China that execute domestic and international projects.
Sino-Engineering	The second of the two central state-owned companies that were merged to create CI in the early 2010s.
Sino-Engineering International	Established in the early 2000s to expand and manage Sino-Engineering's overseas business in renewables and clean energy, such as solar and wind power.
Design institutes	CI has multiple design institutes located across China that engage in project engineering design and planning. Design institutes also develop new engineering technologies, set national industrial standards, and conduct macro-level policy research.

First Leader of CI: Chairman Chen

Chairman Chen was the first leader of CI. Since Sino-Construction was the larger of the two firms merged to create CI in the early 2010s, its leader – Chairman Chen – became the new company's chairman. Born in the early 1950s, Chen did not have an engineering background; he held a graduate degree from the Central Party School and later earned an executive MBA degree from a leading Chinese university. He built his career in one of the company's construction bureaus

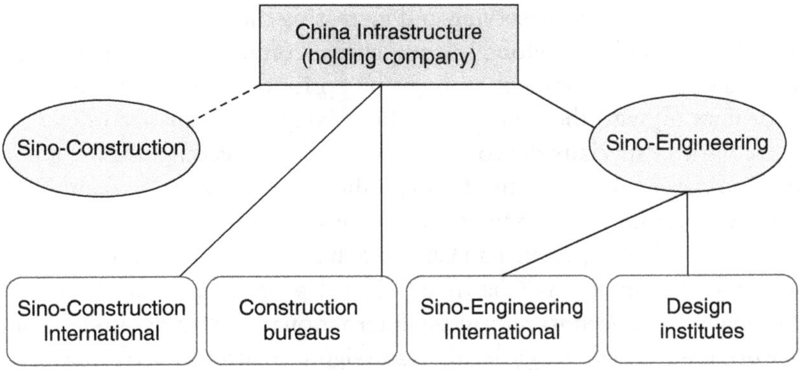

Figure 4.1 China Infrastructure (CI): organizational structure at establishment
The dotted line indicates that Sino-Construction was retained in name only after the merger in the early 2010s.
Source: Author.

over a period of decades, advancing from technician to deputy chief, to deputy director, to assistant director and deputy chief economist, and finally to deputy director and chief economist.

Chairman Chen was known for being direct, down-to-earth, and occasionally temperamental. As Chairman Chen once described his way of doing things:

> Before making a decision, I like to see the front and the back. After I make a decision, I dare to be determined, to strongly promote my decisions, and to persevere. To put it frankly, my thinking is clear, my target is accurate, and my actions are quick and ruthless. Outsiders assess me as being at the forefront, strong, and powerful.[7]

Chairman Chen also impressed employees for being down-to-earth. He regularly ate in the cafeteria for general employees, not in the separate dining area reserved for company leaders. However, Chairman Chen also had a reputation for sometimes being temperamental. For example, he personally ordered that the elevators in CI's headquarters building in Beijing be adjusted to no longer stop at the first through fourth floors, after he became irritated when he observed employees riding the elevator between adjacent lower-level floors.[8]

[7] Chinese media magazine interview, 2009.
[8] Conversation with Sino-Construction International employee, 2014.

Given the goals of preserving and increasing the value of state-owned assets and building a globally competitive company, Chairman Chen formulated a development strategy of "prioritizing the international, coordinating with the domestic." This strategy formally accorded CI's subsidiaries, especially the construction bureaus, a leading role in "going out" to develop overseas markets and thereby strengthening themselves through international competition. Instead of viewing subsidiaries as subservient entities, Chairman Chen emphasized their autonomy, rights, and responsibilities. As Chairman Chen described his strategy and its rationale: "We need to reform the international marketing model from the original way of a single legal person signing contracts and centralized marketing to a new system, a new model that organically combines … conducting centralized marketing together with subsidiaries that meet conditions engaging in autonomous marketing."[9]

For Chairman Chen, it was imperative that organizational strategy and structure respond to the market. At CI's first firm-wide meeting in 2011, he asserted: "The main task of subsidiaries is to respond to market demands and, in expressing their function as market actors, to do everything possible to guarantee markets, guarantee contracts, and guarantee development."[10] Chairman Chen put this even more bluntly the following year when he said: "We should recognize that market demand decides strategy, strategy decides organizational structure, resource allocation, management models, operational mechanisms, and business procedures." He called for "the devolution of international business management and daily operations to the front," with the headquarters retaining authority over major operational decisions and major risk control, encouraging "those [subsidiary] companies to autonomously develop international business" and serve as "model vanguard troops."[11]

Chairman Chen modified CI's organizational structure by altering the existing authority relations and reallocating assets and personnel. His most significant change was to increase the administrative rank of the construction bureaus. The construction bureaus moved up from being Sino-Construction International subsidiaries to becoming CI subsidiaries directly under the authority of the holding company (see Figure 4.1). For the first time, Chairman Chen granted the construction bureaus

[9] Speech at Sino-Construction International 2013 work meeting, February 2013.
[10] Speech at CI's first meeting of cadres, September 2011.
[11] Speech at the CI 2012 mid-year work meeting, July 2012.

authority to carry out "autonomous marketing" (自主营销) in most overseas markets, with the ultimate goal of engaging in "autonomous operations" (自主经营). He assigned fourteen of the company's sixteen construction bureaus country markets abroad; Sino-Construction International retained centralized marketing authority only for a single region. Chairman Chen also confirmed the construction bureaus' market autonomy by authorizing them to sign contracts in their own name for projects with a contract value of USD 50 million or less.

During the following years, Chairman Chen's leadership resulted in a highly decentralized mode of market expansion. Construction bureaus led the expansion of international business, with financial, administrative, and personnel support from the holding company.[12] The First Construction Bureau, for example, went from having one international project under construction in 2011 to having five international projects under construction in 2013, while the Eighth Construction Bureau more than doubled its newly signed international contracts from nine in 2012 to twenty-two in 2013.[13]

Global expansion might have been imperative for CI, but its decentralized nature was not inevitable. For instance, CI could have retained the original division of labor between Sino-Construction International and the construction bureaus, in which the former led international business development and the latter carried out project construction with minimal market autonomy. Or it might have supported the largest and most internationally experienced construction bureaus to specialize in overseas markets instead of authorizing all construction bureaus, including those with little experience operating abroad, to "go out."

Chairman Chen's leadership gradually transformed the balance of influence among intra-firm entities. As the holding company stepped back to a supporting rather than a directing role, the construction bureaus emerged as winners at the expense of Sino-Construction International. Empowered strategically to "go out" and no longer subsidiaries of Sino-Construction International, the construction

[12] Some construction bureaus had previous experience with international assistance projects as early as the 1960s and began to participate in overseas commercial projects beginning in the late 1980s. However, up until CI was created and Chairman Chen became its leader in the early 2010s, the construction bureaus had little autonomy for commercial infrastructure development abroad.

[13] Sino-Engineering Company Yearbook, 2012 and 2014.

bureaus increasingly felt that relations with the holding company were all that mattered. As a construction bureau manager related with pride:

> Before Sino-Construction International had a lot of power. It was they who issued official seals and signatures and who had capital. Everything they said went. ... But now we don't need them anymore. ... With regard to ability, we have no lack of it. If there were no Sino-Construction International, then it would have very little effect on us. If I were to put it more directly, we have no need of them at all.[14]

Sino-Construction International felt its decreased influence keenly. For example, a Sino-Construction International employee described with irritation how some construction bureaus now gave prospective overseas clients introductory pamphlets about their own respective bureaus rather than information about Sino-Construction International or CI as a whole, thereby giving the impression that they were operationally independent.[15]

Leadership Change: Chairman Wu

Halfway through the 2010s, Chairman Wu became the new chairman of CI. Chairman Chen reached the mandatory retirement age of sixty for Chinese officials of his administrative rank and was therefore required to step down.[16] Chairman Wu's appointment was expected; he was already second in command at CI. Moreover, Chairman Wu was the former chairman of Sino-Engineering – the other central SOE that merged with Sino-Construction in the early 2010s to create CI. This leadership succession triggered by fixed bureaucratic rules creates the requisite conditions to test a leadership explanation, because it ensures that the change of chairmen was not the product of outside intervention and was exogenous to any organization-level factors.

Born in the late 1950s, Chairman Wu held a master's degree in engineering from a leading government research institution. Before joining

[14] Interview with construction bureau employee, 2015.
[15] Conversation with Sino-Construction International employee, 2014.
[16] The mandatory retirement age for Chinese officials holding positions of vice-ministerial or department-level rank is sixty. The chairmanship of CI is a position with department-level rank equivalence.

Sino-Engineering, he served in multiple roles, conducting surveying, engineering design, and planning for a government ministry, working at both the provincial and central levels. He also served as vice-president of one of the most prestigious engineering design institutes in China. Beyond CI, he regularly published articles in industry journals on topics such as engineering technologies, infrastructure development, and resettlement of populations away from project areas.

Employees viewed Chairman Wu as reserved, intellectual, and principled. He impressed them by frequently embellishing his speeches with literary sayings and even reciting lengthy Chinese poems at company meetings.[17] Planning and principle trumped all else for Chairman Wu. When a foreign government once asked CI to speed up a project in that country in order to complete construction prior to an important national election, Chairman Wu replied:

> From a politician's point of view, I understand this request very well. But from the perspective of an engineer and the chairman of a Chinese central enterprise and *Fortune Global 500* company, I must tell you responsibly that this requirement is impossible to achieve. ... As an engineer, my professional ethics do not allow me to make this decision.[18]

Chairman Wu exercised leadership in the same ways as Chairman Chen: by making and executing decisions about organizational strategy and structure. But he chose not to continue his predecessor's approach: "prioritize the international, coordinate with the domestic." Instead, Chairman Wu proposed a new strategy for CI's development: "planning and design come first, technology leads." This strategy reflected Chairman Wu's ambition to sequence, standardize, and control the company's development while at the same time increasing the prioritization of engineering and technological expertise.

Chairman Wu also made major changes to CI's organizational structure shortly after becoming chairman – but not without internal opposition. In 2016, he presided over the largest internal restructuring of CI since its establishment: the creation of CI International. This new subsidiary amalgamated three entities: Sino-Construction International, Sino-Engineering International, and the Overseas Business Department

17 Conversation with CI International employee (former Sino-Engineering employee), 2016.
18 Chinese media magazine article, 2017.

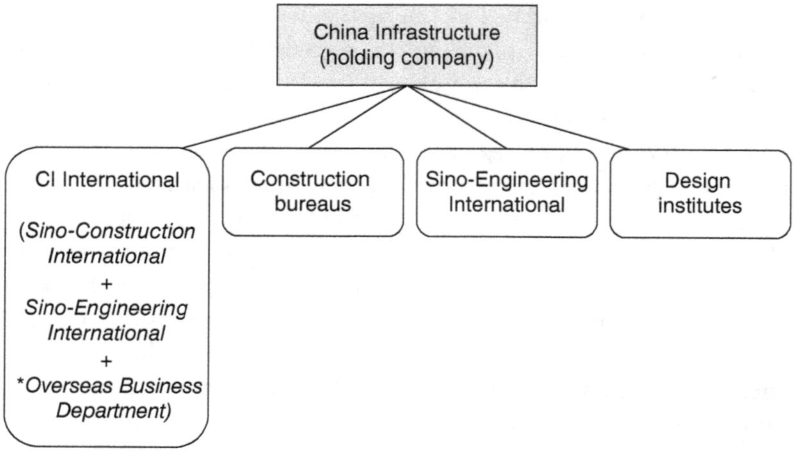

Figure 4.2 China Infrastructure (CI): organizational structure after creation of CI International
Source: Author.

(see Figure 4.2).[19] CI International became the sole entity authorized to manage all of CI's business and offices overseas.[20] As the official company announcement stated: "This is a major event in the history of CI's international business development. It marks entry into a new period of CI's international business operations and management model and it marks the opening of a new chapter in CI's international business."[21]

In theory, the creation of CI International should have increased the company's competitiveness by consolidating resources for international business and deepening vertical industry integration. Within the firm, however, numerous employees viewed the change negatively because it meant more senior managers pooled together in the new

[19] The Overseas Business Department was an internal department with the highest authority to coordinate international business affairs, including managing projects, implementing operational planning and targets, guiding subsidiaries' international projects, facilitating project bidding and contract negotiations, and formulating rules for international project management. After the establishment of CI in the early 2010s and prior to the creation of CI International in 2016, the Overseas Business Department was part of the holding company.

[20] Company document, 2016.

[21] Company document, 2016.

company – and more peers at each level competing for career advancement. "Before I might have had some hope of getting promoted to the leadership of the company [Sino-Construction International]. But now there are twice as many bosses after the merger. … I need to find a way out," an employee shared.[22] Employees expressed their dissatisfaction in ways that ranged from critical expression to shirking and in some cases even quitting their jobs.

Chairman Wu's leadership rapidly yielded a more centralized mode of market expansion. Previously, Chairman Chen had empowered the construction bureaus to "go all out," literally and figuratively, to develop international business. In contrast, overseas market expansion under Chairman Wu's leadership became increasingly centralized, as the holding company directed the process from the top down through CI International. When I asked which country markets a particular construction bureau was responsible for, a CI International employee reprimanded me: "We don't talk about the country markets of construction bureaus anymore."[23] As a construction bureau manager described the change in global expansion efforts: "Under Chairman Chen, construction bureaus played the guiding role, [it was their work that] propelled design. Under Chairman Wu, now design plays the guiding role and design propels the construction bureaus."[24] To illustrate this point, a CI International employee described plans to dispatch engineering teams from Beijing to tour foreign countries and recommend infrastructure projects to their governments, instead of foreign governments identifying projects for potential cooperation based on their own national development plans.[25] An internal summary of the company's work touted its drafting of a development plan for a province in Pakistan and noted that similar efforts were ongoing for a number of other countries.[26]

Chairman Wu's leadership also resulted in a shift in the balance of influence among intra-firm entities. The holding company, Sino-Engineering, and the design institutes won greater authority,

22 Conversation with CI International employee (former Sino-Construction International employee), 2016.
23 Conversation with CI International employee (former Sino-Construction International and construction bureau employee), 2016.
24 Interview with construction bureau employee, 2016.
25 Conversation with CI International employee (former Sino-Construction International employee), 2016.
26 Company document, 2016.

while the construction bureaus and the former Sino-Construction International emerged as losers. As a construction bureau manager expressed: "Now without space to develop, we have no motivation. ... We are not allowed to develop independently. It is a hierarchical system. Whatever it [the holding company] says that you are, then that's who you are."[27] Chairman Wu's strategy of "planning and design come first, technology leads" inverted the prioritization that Chairman Chen had previously granted to the construction bureaus and instead implicitly accorded it to Sino-Engineering and the design institutes. This enabled them to obtain more resources and projects relative to other intra-firm entities. Competition among construction bureaus continued, but it was now subordinate to their struggles for autonomy relative to the holding company.

Sino-Construction International also lost out due to its merger with Sino-Engineering International to create CI International. Instead of the newly formed CI International becoming a larger and more influential counterweight to the holding company, Chairman Wu made clear that it would remain subordinate. As a former Sino-Construction International employee expressed with frustration over lunch in the company cafeteria:

> In the past we had the authority to make project-level decisions, but now we are treated basically as a marketing department, with our past authority for project-level decisions moved to the holding company. On paper it might look like progress, as if the company is improving its formal organization, but in reality, what it is causing is inefficiency.[28]

In contrast, Sino-Engineering and the design institutes felt their positions were improving. A Sino-Engineering employee emphasized that "design takes the lead," contending that design was more important than construction. The two were not equivalent, he stressed, concluding: "Design is design and construction is construction."[29] This separation of roles and the respective hierarchies accorded to them clearly gave Sino-Engineering and the design institutes more influence under Chairman Wu's leadership. Another employee described the new hierarchy among CI's various intra-firm entities even more directly: "The position of the design institutes is the highest – they put forward the

[27] Interview with construction bureau employee, 2016.
[28] Conversation with CI International employee (former Sino-Construction International employee), 2016.
[29] Conversation with Sino-Engineering employee, 2016.

Table 4.2 ***Paired comparison of the tenures of chairmen in CI***

	Chairman Chen	Chairman Wu
Tenure	Early 2010s to mid 2010s	Mid 2010s to early 2020s
Strategy	"Prioritize the international, coordinate with the domestic"	"Planning and design come first, technology leads"
Changes to organizational structure	Increase in the administrative rank of the construction bureaus Authorization for the construction bureaus to conduct "autonomous marketing" overseas	Creation of CI International Withdrawal of authorization for construction bureaus to conduct "autonomous marketing" overseas
Market expansion: degree of decentralization and focus	High Focus on international markets	Low Focus on international markets
Balance of influence among intra-firm entities	Holding company loses influence Construction bureaus gain influence vis-à-vis Sino-Construction International	Holding company gains influence Construction bureaus lose influence Creation of CI International decreases influence of Sino-Construction International Sino-Engineering and the design institutes gain influence

thinking. Next is CI International; it is responsible for implementation. And next are the construction bureaus; they do the actual work."[30]

The accounts given in this chapter provide evidence that the leadership of Chairman Chen and the leadership of Chairman Wu generated

[30] Conversation with CI International employee (former Sino-Engineering employee), 2016.

significant variation over time in CI's reform and overseas expansion. Chairman Chen's strategy of "prioritizing the international, coordinating with the domestic" and changes to organizational structure resulted in decentralized market expansion. The construction bureaus gained influence and emerged as winners at the expense of Sino-Construction International. In contrast, Chairman Wu's strategy of "planning and design come first, technology leads" and his creation of CI International brought about centralized market expansion. The holding company's relative influence increased, as did that of Sino-Engineering and the design institutes. However, the construction bureaus and Sino-Construction International both lost out. Table 4.2 summarizes these findings.

Alternative Explanations

Other explanations might account for the variation in CI's reform outcomes over time. First, one might suggest that intervention by external actors with whom the chairmen had *guanxi* resulted in these differences. In this view, Chairman Chen and Chairman Wu were proxies for outside principals: higher-level officials who could intervene to secure the chairmen's appointments and subsequently influence their decisions and execution. In theory, the ambition of these patrons would be to have the chairmen realize their particular interests and agendas or, in the case of Chairman Wu, to deliberately change course from his predecessor.

However, the circumstances of both chairmen's appointments suggest that this was not the case. Chairman Chen became chairman of CI when it was created in the early 2010s by merging Sino-Construction and Sino-Engineering. This made bureaucratic sense because Chairman Chen was already the head of Sino-Construction and that company was the larger of the two in terms of assets, revenue, profits, and employees. Chairman Wu took over in 2015 because Chairman Chen reached the mandatory retirement age and because Chairman Wu had served as second in command at CI since its founding. Both appointments thus reflect existing bureaucratic norms and rules, not outside intervention. Moreover, there is no evidence available to indicate that either of the two chairmen had *guanxi* with higher-level officials or acted as proxies for external actors. Both men rose to executive leadership positions after working for their entire careers in the state sector; unlike some other central SOE leaders, they were not appointed to their posts from outside positions in central or local government (Lin, 2013a; Lin, 2017).

One might also suggest that major changes in SASAC or State Council policy shaped CI's reform trajectory. For example, SASAC may have issued a directive ordering that central SOEs consolidate authority over business abroad, coinciding with the recentralization of CI's international market expansion. However, policies since the early 2010s suggest a continued trend of greater operational autonomy for central SOEs relative to their administrative superiors, with few exceptions (Politburo, 2015; SASAC, 2017).[31] Beginning in 2014, SASAC launched pilots for state capital management that increased the autonomy of selected SOEs for commercial decision-making. In 2017, the State Council issued new guidelines to shift SASAC's overall function away from state-owned asset management toward state-owned capital management and supervision. These guidelines also confirmed specific areas in which central SOEs possess decision-making authority – including the right of their heads to determine strategies for their companies' development (State Council, 2017).

Employees from different intra-firm entities all noted that CI International's creation reflected an initiative by the leader, not external interference. As one stated: "The merger to create CI International was the idea and initiative of the leadership. Not SASAC. This is a small thing that SASAC does not have time to manage. Leadership came up with a plan and then SASAC approved it. Chairman Wu is under a lot of pressure for this model to be successful."[32] Another explained privately in an online QQ conversation: "The government usually does not instruct the state-owned companies to do this or that in detail. However, it will generally require that the companies follow the national strategy."[33]

31 These exceptions include the anti-corruption campaign that Xi Jinping initiated after coming to power in 2012, which involved the CCDI dispatching investigators to central SOEs to conduct on-site investigations; strengthened requirements, introduced in 2016, for oversight of domestic and overseas state-owned assets; and ongoing efforts to get central SOEs to reduce their commercial activities in noncore business areas like real estate. However, no direct link is apparent between these policies and the observed variation in CI's reform; moreover, some of these policies were initiated well into Wu's tenure as chairman began in the mid-2010s, after significant reform variation relative to Chen's tenure as chairman was already evident.

32 Conversation with CI International employee (former Sino-Engineering employee), 2016.

33 Conversation with CI International employee (former Sino-Construction International employee) QQ conversation, 2016.

Another possible explanation is that changes in market competition explain the observed variation. Major shifts in the markets in which CI operates might have prompted its leaders to adapt the company's strategy and structure. However, there does not seem to have been any significant change in the domestic market after CI's establishment in the early 2010s. The number of central SOEs in the construction industry remained unchanged (SASAC, 2012, 2013, 2014). Nor did the overall level of domestic competition change significantly. The percentage of SOEs among the publicly listed firms in the construction industry between 2012 and 2016 was relatively stable, ranging between 18 percent and 33 percent during this period.[34] The global construction market also did not exhibit any major fluctuations. Between 2012 and 2015, the top 250 international contractors ranked by *Engineering News-Record* reported total contracting revenue from projects outside their home countries ranging from a low of USD 501.14 billion to a high of USD 543.97 billion.[35] This market too was relatively stable year-on-year, with the average annual change in total contracting revenue varying between 4 percent and 6 percent during this period.[36] Finally, although Chairman Chen and Chairman Wu discussed international markets in general terms in their speeches and in company documents, such as the imperative of increasing international competitiveness, I did not find any instances in which they cited specific changes in international markets to justify their decisions concerning organizational strategy or structure.

Ruling out these alternative explanations increases confidence in a leadership explanation, but several caveats remain. First, SASAC and State Council policies may affect central SOEs in different ways depending on the industries in which they operate and their historical relationships with the central government. Furthermore, international market conditions might have varying effects on construction

[34] I calculated levels of market competition based on the proportion of publicly listed companies on both the Shenzhen and Shanghai stock markets in a given industry for which the ultimate parent company is a SOE, using data from the WIND Financial Terminal Database and its industry classification for the construction sector.

[35] The top 250 contractors are ranked on the basis of total contracting revenue outside of their home countries. "Top 250 International Contractors," *Engineering News-Record*, 2017, www.enr.com/toplists/2016-Top-250-International-Contractors1.

[36] Author's calculations using *Engineering News-Record* data, www.enr.com.

companies depending on growth trends in the specific country markets where a company operates. Differential effects could also arise depending on the conditions of secondary industries, such as mining and petroleum, with which the infrastructure a company builds might be related (such as power plants). Further sector-specific and company-specific comparative research is therefore needed to better assess the effects of central policies and economic factors on reform outcomes.

Conclusion

A paired comparison of the consecutive tenures of CI chairmen and process tracing using qualitative and quantitative data provide evidence that Chinese central SOE leaders can generate reform variation by making and executing decisions about organizational strategy and structure. Even in countries such as China where political authority is highly centralized, SOE leaders possess significant autonomy to determine whether, how, and when to respond to central goals, although within the constraints that existing institutions, policies, and economic factors impose. If China's reform process entails "feeling for the stones to cross the river" (摸着石头过河), as a popular metaphor describes it, then the central authorities certainly direct the leaders of public-sector organizations such as SOEs toward certain stones. However, these leaders still make decisions about how to get there, whether to navigate to other stones along the way, or whether to swim in an entirely different direction.

The case of CI shows that the heads of Chinese SOEs enjoy greater autonomy than typically conceived – and that their leadership is consequential. In China, the cadre management system's macro-controls, the broad nature of government policies, and administrative subcontracting all create space for leadership in public-sector organizations. The Chinese term "operational space" (操作空间) – the delineated domain within which one possesses freedom of choice and action – aptly describes this room for maneuver. Such operational space enabled Chairman Chen and Chairman Wu each to respond to the same central goals in divergent ways. The two chairmen's decisions about CI's strategy and structure, and their respective attempts to implement them, ultimately altered the company's reform outcomes. In Chapter 5, I extend the analysis beyond CI to assess the effects of leadership on reform in four additional central SOEs.

5 *China's National Champions*
Leadership and Reform on a Global Stage

This chapter further assesses and refines a leadership explanation through paired comparisons of the consecutive tenures of chairmen in four other Chinese central SOEs. It provides additional evidence that central SOE leaders can generate variation in reform outcomes by making and endeavoring to execute decisions about organizational strategy and structure. Reform variation manifests in the degree to which central SOEs' market expansion is decentralized as well as in the changes in the balance of influence among intra-firm entities. Cross-firm analysis additionally suggests that the effects of leadership on reform are a matter of degree and are conditioned by existing institutions, policies, and economic factors.

Central SOEs vary in terms of the strategic importance of the industries they operate in and their firm type. The Chinese government has formally designated sectors over which the state is to maintain "absolute control" (绝对控制力) and those over which the state is to maintain "relatively strong control" (较强控制力).[1] Leaders of firms in sectors marked for absolute state control might have limited autonomy to make and execute decisions about enterprise strategy or structure, whereas the heads of national champions in industries tapped for lesser state influence might enjoy comparatively greater scope for choice and action.

As discussed in Chapter 1, China's central SOEs are divided into two firm types: core firms and noncore firms. Leaders of core firms have vice-ministerial rank equivalence, and they are appointed by the

[1] For example, in 2006 the State Council specified those industries over which the state will keep "absolute control" (defense, electricity, petroleum, telecommunications, coal, aviation, and shipping) and those sectors over which it will maintain "relatively strong control" (machinery, electronics, information technology, automobiles, steel, nonferrous metals, chemicals, and construction). 《我国明确七大行业将由国有经济保持绝对控制力》 [China Specifies Seven Major Industries in Which the State-Owned Economy Will Maintain Absolute Control], 上海证券报 [Shanghai Securities News], December 19, 2006, http://news.cctv.com/financial/20061219/100221.shtml.

Table 5.1 *Comparative case selection of central SOEs*

	Absolute state control	Strong state control
Core firm	1. State Grid (Power – Electricity)	3. Sinochem (Chemicals)
Noncore firm	2. China General Nuclear Power Group (Power – Nuclear)	4. China Railway Engineering Corporation (Construction)

COD in consultation with higher Party authorities. Leaders of noncore firms have department-level rank equivalence and they are primarily appointed by SASAC. The leaders of core firms who are subject to COD personnel authority might have less autonomy to exercise leadership, whereas the top executives of noncore firms might enjoy greater discretionary room for maneuver.

The four leader pairs and central SOEs examined in this chapter span the full range of industry strategic importance and firm type. The case selection captures maximum variation along these two key dimensions (see Table 5.1). The specific companies analyzed are (1) State Grid; (2) China General Nuclear Power Group (CGN); (3) Sinochem; and (4) China Railway Engineering Corporation (CREC). They represent a variety of industries, from electricity to nuclear power to chemicals and to railway construction. For each national champion, I compare the consecutive tenures of chairmen to evaluate the effects of leadership on the same aspects of reform as in Chapter 4. I again conduct process tracing on qualitative and quantitative data collected through company reports, news articles, and thirteen interviews with current and former employees across all four firms.

State Grid

The Chinese government created the electricity giant State Grid in 2002 by carving up the State Power Corporation of China, the former national electricity monopoly, into multiple central SOEs along functional lines.[2] State Grid, the largest of the two national grid companies established

[2] These included five central SOEs responsible for electricity generation and two central SOEs charged with electricity transmission.

through this restructuring, ranked as the third biggest company in the world by revenue in the 2023 *Fortune Global 500* list. It provides electricity transmission and retail to 1.1 billion people in China, covering nearly 90 percent of the country (Xu, 2017: 1). The company is also a pioneer in developing and applying clean energy technologies. In 2021, State Grid announced plans to expand clean energy generation – including wind, solar, hydropower, and nuclear power – with the goal of meeting 20 percent of China's primary energy consumption needs without fossil fuels by 2025 and 25 percent by 2030.[3]

State Grid has also been increasingly active in international markets. By 2021, the company owned, held shares in, and/or operated overseas electricity assets in Brazil, Italy, Portugal, Austria, Greece, Australia, Georgia, Oman, China, and the Philippines.[4] State Grid has also constructed or upgraded electricity assets in more than thirty countries in Asia, Africa, and Latin America.[5] In addition, the company has exported equipment – iron towers, wiring, transformers, circuit breakers, and safety equipment – to more than seventy countries worldwide.[6] As of 2019, State Grid had set up ten overseas offices to promote acquisitions, investment, contracting, equipment exports, technical consulting, and communications with foreign governments and regulators.[7] It has also inked cooperation accords with partners in the United States and Germany as well as with international nongovernmental organizations to develop new technologies for smart grids, new energy, power big data, and electric vehicles.[8]

[3] Yujie Xue, "State Grid Rolls Out Carbon Neutrality Action Plan to Accelerate China's Clean Energy Drive," *South China Morning Post*, March 1, 2021, www.scmp.com/tech/policy/article/3123650/state-grid-rolls-out-carbon-neutrality-action-plan-accelerate-chinas.

[4] 《'电'亮世界，'网'联四州；'一带一路'上的国家电网》 ["Electricity" Lights Up the World, "Network" Connects the Continents; State Grid in the Belt and Road Initiative], 2021, www.yidaiyilu.gov.cn/ydylgjdw.htm.

[5] Company document provided by interviewee, 2019.

[6] Company document provided by interviewee, 2019.

[7] Company document provided by interviewee, 2019.

[8] Andrew Burger, "US, China Research Institutes Sign Historic Clean Power Grid Accord," *Renewable Energy World*, September 17, 2015, www.renewableenergyworld.com/baseload/us-china-research-institutes-sign-historic-clean-power-grid-accord/#gref; Tom Kenning, "State Grid China Teams Up with German Tech Association on Smart Energy," *PVTech*, August 21, 2018; Tom Kenning, "China's State Grid and IRENA Collaborate on Renewables Grid Integration," *PVTech*, June 9, 2017.

Multiple factors motivate State Grid's continued global expansion. The first is rising demand in international electricity markets.[9] Developed countries aim to adjust their energy structures and increase the scale and capacity of existing power grids, while developing states seek to upgrade aging and inefficient transmission networks. Expansion abroad might also help meet soaring demand for power in China, where electricity consumption is projected to more than double between 2015 and 2050.[10] In theory, a UHV-based smart grid could harness electricity produced domestically from clean energy while linking China with foreign energy sources.[11] By exporting domestically developed technologies in areas such as UHV, smart grids, and new energy, State Grid can also amplify its influence and ability to shape international technical standards in organizations such as the International Electrotechnical Commission. How did State Grid emerge from the restructuring of a lumbering national electricity monopoly at the turn of the twenty-first century to become a global industry leader today? The company's rise is inseparable from the leadership of Liu Zhenya, popularly known as China's "king of power."

Liu Zhenya (2004–2016)

Liu Zhenya was born in 1952 in Shandong. He began his career in the electricity sector at the age of nineteen, working in a local power plant during the Cultural Revolution (1966–76). After earning a degree in power systems and automation from the Shandong Institute of Technology, he spent the next twenty years serving in various roles in provincial power plants and the Shandong branch of the State Power Corporation of China (the national electricity monopoly). Even while

[9] Total world electricity consumption grew at an average rate of 3.3 percent between 1974 and 2017. Each unit of TWh is equivalent to one trillion watts of electrical energy consumed over the period of one hour. International Energy Agency, "Electricity Information: Overview," 2019, www.iea.org/reports/electricity-information-overview/electricity-production.

[10] Michael Meidan, "Glimpses of China's Energy Future," Oxford Institute for Energy Studies, September 2019, www.oxfordenergy.org/publications/glimpses-of-chinas-energy-future/.

[11] Center for Energy, Environmental, and Economic Systems Analysis, Argonne National Laboratory, "Power Play: China's Ultra-High Voltage Technology and Global Standards," Paulson Papers on Standards, April 2015, www.paulsoninstitute.org/wp-content/uploads/2017/01/PPS_UHV_English_R.pdf.

working at the provincial level, Liu attracted attention due to his ambition and drive. With 20 percent of Shandong lacking electricity and a shortage of government funds, Liu led a subsidiary of Shandong Electric Power Company on a fundraising campaign to close the gap, raising RMB 2 billion (USD 240 million) in 1996 alone.[12] He vowed to make Shandong Electric Power Company into a modern utility that could rival foreign counterparts in both size and efficiency. Transferred to Beijing, Liu served briefly as a vice-general manager at the State Power Corporation of China immediately before its dissolution and thereafter he entered State Grid. In 2004, the COD appointed Liu as general manager and Party secretary of State Grid. In 2013, Liu became chairman when State Grid established a board of directors at the holding company level, while he also continued to serve as its Party secretary.

Liu proposed a "one special, four large" (一特四大) strategy for State Grid. This combined the promotion of UHV power grids ("one special") with coal-fired power, hydropower, nuclear power, and renewable energy ("four large").[13] Liu passionately advocated that State Grid's continued monopoly over electricity transmission was essential to meet China's future energy needs.[14] His strategic vision for UHV power grids and State Grid's industry monopoly was mutually reinforcing, because deconstructing a once operational UHV grid into regional grids would be extremely costly and technically difficult. Tasked with achieving the central government's goal of developing globally competitive central

[12] Yang Wei [杨漾] and Zhang Ning [张宁], 《刘振亚时代落幕：57周岁老国网人舒印彪接任国家电网董事长》 [Curtain Closes on the Liu Zhenya Era: 57-Year-Old State Grid Veteran Yin Shubiao Takes Over As State Grid Chairman], 澎湃新闻 [*The Paper*], May 16, 2016, www.thepaper.cn/newsDetail_forward_1465469.

[13] Ultra-high-voltage (UHV) power grids refer to power transmission lines that operate at greater than 800,000 volts (800 kV). They are a controversial technology. Proponents argue that they are cheaper and more efficient than traditional grids, whereas opponents stress the high costs and the risks of systemwide failures. 《刘振亚和他的国家电网12年：说一不二，铁面铁腕》 [12 Years of Liu Zhenya and His State Grid: Standing by His Word, Iron Face and Iron Wrist], 上海证券报 [Shanghai Securities News], May 9, 2016, https://finance.sina.cn/2016-05-09/detail-ifxryhhh1771281.d.html?sid=180966; Liu Lili [刘丽丽]: 《刘振亚身后下了一盘什么棋》 [What Is the Chess Move behind Liu Zhenya?], *Sina Finance*, May 8, 2016, http://finance.sina.com.cn/zl/energy/2016-05-08/zl-ifxryhhi8499433.shtml.

[14] Wang Xiuqiang [王秀强], 《刘振亚出书：争议输配分离改革》 [Liu Zhenya Publishes Book: Transmission Disputes Separate from Reform], 《21世纪经济报道》 [21st Century Business Herald], April 12, 2012.

SOEs, Liu made internationalization a core part of his strategic vision.[15] In later years, he even lobbied for the creation of an ambitious "global energy internet" (全球能源互联网), connecting far-flung clean energy sources with high electricity-consuming urban areas.[16]

Liu altered State Grid's organizational structure in several ways. He quickly ramped up the company's investment in UHV research and development and established a UHV Office, a UHV Power Grid Engineering Leading Group, and a UHV Grid Engineering Advisory Group (Xu, 2017: 32).[17] Liu also modified State Grid's organizational structure by creating a core group of specialized subsidiaries, each of which was responsible for a specific function in domestic and international markets.[18] At home, he reassigned the responsibilities of the regional power grid companies to these subsidiaries. Beginning in 2011, State Grid also transferred operational assets from the regional power grid companies down to the provincial network companies.[19]

15 He detailed these ambitions in "State Grid's International Strategy" and "State Grid's Plan for International Energy Cooperation," which call for expanding the company's international operations and cross-border energy cooperation. State Grid, 《国家电网公司国际化战略》 [State Grid Internationalization Strategy]; State Grid, 《国家电网公司国际能源合作规划》 [State Grid International Energy Cooperation Plan].

16 Liu Zhenya [刘振亚]: 《全球能源互联网》 [Global Energy Internet] (北京：中国电力出版社, 2015).

17 《国家电网公司特高压工程大事记》 [State Grid Corporation UHV Engineering Major Events], 人民网经济频道 [People's Network Economic Channel], November 27, 2006.

18 Liu assigned responsibility for construction contracting to China Power Equipment Incorporated (中电装备), responsibility for financing to Yingda Group (英大集团), responsibility for issuing debt to finance projects to State Grid Overseas Investment Limited (国网海外投资), and responsibility for conducting feasibility studies to the State Grid Economic Research Institute (国网经研院). Guo Kai [郭开], 《神秘公司：中电装备身世》 [Mystery Company: China Power Equipment Incorporated Comes to Life], 《经济观察报》 [*Economic Observer*], July 23, 2011; Wang Xiaoyun [王晓云], 《历时九年 细数国家电网的海外布局战绩》 [Nine Years History: Counting the Overseas Layout Record of State Grid], 能源杂志 [*Energy Magazine*], May 8, 2017, https://m.bjx.com.cn/mnews/20170508/824255.shtml; 《央企金融权力榜：国家电网控股金融机构数量居首》 [The Financial Power Ranking of SOEs, State Grid Tops List in Number of Financial Holdings], *Sina Finance*, 国家电网的金融资产整合之路, July 14, 2017, https://finance.china.com/industrial/11173306/20170714/30967362.html.

19 Liu Lili [刘丽丽], 《刘振亚身后下了一盘什么棋》 [What Is the Chess Move behind Liu Zhenya?], *Sina Finance*, May 8, 2016, http://finance.sina.com.cn/zl/energy/2016-05-08/zl-ifxryhhi8499433.shtml.

To manage the company's overseas investments, Liu created a new subsidiary firm, State Grid International Development Company (SGIDC) in 2008, and in 2012 he placed it directly under the holding company's authority.[20] Liu charged SGIDC with overseeing State Grid's overseas investments, while specialized subsidiaries coordinated contracting, feasibility studies, and financing.[21]

Over time, Liu's leadership resulted in highly centralized market expansion both at home and abroad. His UHV-focused strategy, for which the holding company controlled technological development and approvals, confronted and ultimately overcame domestic opposition.[22] But the shift to UHV technology was by no means inevitable – when Liu first pitched UHV power grids to the Chinese leadership, there were no such power grids in full operation anywhere in the world (Xu, 2017: 30). The downgrading of State Grid's regional power companies and SGIDC's subordination to the holding company further centralized authority for domestic and international market expansion. During Liu's tenure as chairman, State Grid made overseas acquisitions in five countries: Australia, Brazil, Italy, the Philippines, and Portugal.[23] As one media report put it, the top company leaders' control over international market expansion and SGIDC became so centralized that "many even within State Grid know nothing about it."[24]

20 《组织机构》 [Organizational Structure], State Grid website, November 30, 2023, www.sgcc.com.cn/html/sgcc/col2022121211/column_2022121211_1.shtml.

21 《组织机构》 [Organizational Structure], State Grid website, November 30, 2023, www.sgcc.com.cn/html/sgcc/col2022121211/column_2022121211_1.shtml; Zhang Zhe [张哲], 《全球40个找矿计划背后：国家电网的全产业企图》 [Behind Forty Global Prospecting Plans, State Grid's Effort to Expand], 经济观察网 [*Economic Observer*], March 12, 2010, www.eeo.com.cn/2010/0312/165105.shtml; 《走出去智库：案例分析 国家电网海外并购成功策略》 [China Going Global Think Tank: Case Study Analysis State Grid's Successful International M&A Strategy], 凤凰国际智库 [Phoenix International Think-Tank], December 13, 2015, http://inews.ifeng.com/yidian/46649128/news.shtml?ch=ref_zbs_ydzx_news.

22 For a detailed discussion of Liu's "policy entrepreneurship" and lobbying on behalf of UHV while also facing domestic opposition within China, see Xu (2017, 2018).

23 《历时九年 细数国家电网的海外布局战绩》 [Nine Years of History State Grid Counts Its Overseas Buildout], *Sina Finance*, May 8, 2017, https://finance.sina.cn/usstock/mggd/2017-05-08/detail-ifyeycfp9374381.d.html?from=wap.

24 《国家电网再出海：欲17亿美元收购巴西输电公司》 [State Grid Goes Overseas Again: 1.7 Billion Acquisition of Brazilian Transmission Company], *Sina Finance*, May 20, 2010, http://finance.sina.com.cn/chanjing/gsnews/20100520/02457968890.shtml?from=wap.

Liu's decisions about organizational strategy and structure also remade the balance of influence among intra-firm entities in State Grid. Regional power companies, which previously had enjoyed high levels of autonomy and influence, were the biggest losers. After transferring control over assets and operations to the newly created functional subsidiaries, the regional power companies gradually retreated to a regulatory role overseeing interprovincial electricity transmission and infrastructure construction. State Grid's overseas subsidiaries also lost out because they ceded authority to the new specialized subsidiaries. They had to sign cooperation contracts with SGIDC for their international business; China Power Equipment Incorporated became the company's sole platform for construction contracting; and State Grid Overseas Investment Limited took over the issuing of debt to finance projects. The holding company, in turn, tightly controlled these specialized subsidiaries through a combination of direct ownership stakes, personnel ties, and approval authority.[25]

Shu Yinbiao (2016–2018)

In 2016, Liu Zhenya retired and the COD tapped State Grid General Manager Shu Yinbiao to become the company's new chairman and Party secretary.[26] Shu was born in 1958 in Hebei. After earning bachelor's and master's degrees in engineering, he spent a decade working in the Ministry of Power. In 1989, the Ministry of Education selected Shu, as well as other outstanding mid-career officials, to participate in a year-long technical study program in Britain. After returning to China, Shu worked briefly in the State Power Corporation of China before its restructuring created State Grid. He served first in operational and engineering roles before entering management in 2004 as assistant to the company's general manager. While rising in State Grid's managerial ranks, Shu earned a PhD degree in engineering in 2007. He became the company's general manager in 2013, his last stop before becoming chairman.

[25] Take, for example, State Grid International Development Company. Its founding chairman and general manager were both appointed from executive positions in the holding company – the chief economist and the director of the International Cooperation Department, respectively.

[26] Liu retired at the age of sixty-five, significantly past the official retirement age of sixty for officials of vice-ministerial rank.

Shu largely maintained Liu's UHV-focused "one special, four large" strategy for State Grid's development and his vision of building a global energy internet.[27] To complement the company's diversification into clean energy, he proposed a new strategy of "re-electrification" (再电气化) aimed at increasing overall electricity consumption by replacing coal and petroleum with electricity generated using renewable energy sources.[28] The main difference between the two chairmen's strategies concerned State Grid's position in China's electricity industry. Whereas Liu had fought fiercely to maintain and expand the company's monopoly position under both the Hu Jintao and Xi Jinping administrations, Shu took a more cooperative stance toward industry reforms, in particular domestic electricity market liberalization.

Shu made some modifications to State Grid's organizational structure, most of which seemed to accord with central-level policies. The most significant of these changes was State Grid's participation in the establishment of central-level and provincial-level electricity trading centers. In theory, the purpose of these trading centers was to help liberalize electricity prices and increase competition between State Grid and other major industry players – including Datang Group, Huadian, and the Three Gorges Corporation – by facilitating transactions among electricity generators, distributors, and major industrial users.[29] Within State Grid, Shu streamlined the company's organizational structure.[30]

[27] Wang Xuhui [王旭辉],《国网将建世界一流能源互联网企业》[State Grid Will Build a World-Class Energy Internet Company], 中国能源报 [*China Energy News*], January 28, 2019, http://paper.people.com.cn/zgnyb/html/2019-01/28/content_1906870.htm;《舒印彪：国家电网公司2018要这么干!》[Shu Yinbiao: State Grid Wants to Do This in 2018!], 大云网 [*SGC.10*], January 23, 2018, www.sgcio.com/interview/dingcengsheji/46587.html.

[28] 《舒印彪详解国家电网"再电气化"战略》[Shu Yinbiao Explains State Grid's "Re-electrification" Strategy], *China 5e*, http://m.chinaaet.com/article/3000078514, March 18, 2018;《舒印彪解读新时代国家电网新战略》[Shu Yinbiao Interprets State Grid's New Strategy in the New Era], *China 5e*, March 6, 2018, www.china5e.com/news/news-1022447-1.htm.

[29] However, State Grid owned most of these trading centers. Wang Wenyan [王文嫣],《电改博弈:13省份方案中不一样的利益格局》[The Game of Electric Sector Reform: Tracing Varying Interest Networks in Thirteen Provinces], 人民日报 [*People's Daily*], September 14, 2016, http://finance.people.com.cn/n1/2016/0914/c1004-28715016.html.

[30] He reduced the total number of subsidiaries by 437 and cut the management tiers down to three and the layers of legal entities down to two in the main power grid business. Ran Yongping [冉永平],《今年预计为用户减少电费支出七百亿元国家电网 体制改革倒逼内部治理》[State Grid Reduces Customer

Both of these moves aligned with the National Energy Administration's roadmap for reform of the electricity sector as well as with Premier Li's "lean and healthy body" policy for SOEs.

State Grid's market expansion under Shu's leadership remained highly centralized. The holding company continued to direct market activity both at home and overseas. State Grid guidelines released in 2017 detailed numerous areas in which the holding company exercised approval authority, including the right to directly organize and implement major projects.[31] Overseas subsidiaries did not regain autonomy to identify or conduct overseas business; instead, they had to continue to work closely with and through SGIDC.

Under Shu, the balance of influence among intra-firm entities stayed relatively stable. Regional power companies remained weak and consigned to a regulatory role. The functional subsidiaries that Liu had created continued to exert predominant influence over both the regional power companies and the overseas subsidiaries. Of the functional subsidiaries, SGIDC gained influence and resources as State Grid's overseas assets expanded.[32] At the same time, however, these specialized subsidiaries stayed subordinate to the holding company through multiple mechanisms, including ownership shares, personnel appointments, and authority over approvals.

Several inferences about the effects of leadership on the reform of Chinese central SOEs can be made by comparing the two tenures of these chairmen. First, consistent with a leadership explanation, in this case when there was no significant change in leaders' choices about organizational strategy and structure and their execution, there was no significant variation in reform. As a State Grid employee stated simply when asked to compare the two leaders: "There were no major changes in overall thinking or strategy from Chairman Liu to Chairman Shu."[33] Shu kept Liu's modifications to State Grid's

Bills by RMB 700 Billion This Year: Reform Overturns Internal Governance Structure], 人民日报 [*People's Daily*], September 13, 2017.

31 State Grid, 《国家电网公司国际合作工作管理规定》, May 26, 2017.

32 Between 2016 and 2017 alone, State Grid's total overseas assets jumped from USD 40 billion to USD 60 billion. Jiang Lin [姜琳], 《境外投资全部盈利 给世界添点儿"亮"—国家电网加快"一带一路"建设》 [Overseas Investment Profits "Add a Little Light" to the World – State Grid Quickens Speed of "Belt and Road Initiative"], *Xinhua News*, February 2, 2018, http://m.xinhuanet.com/2018-02/01/c_1122356027.htm.

33 Interview with central SOE (State Grid) employee, Beijing, June 2019.

organizational structure intact and carried forward his UHV and global energy internet strategies. After Liu won initial support for UHV power grids and demonstrated their operational and commercial viability, Shu focused on exporting UHV by constructing UHV power grids abroad.[34] As the first State Grid executive to serve as a vice-president of the International Electrotechnical Commission, Shu also helped integrate UHV into international standard-setting in the power industry. Leadership continuity contributed to continuity in reform outcomes at the company level: highly centralized market expansion and a relatively stable balance of influence among intra-firm entities.

Paired comparison of the tenures of these two chairmen also suggests that institutional factors may constrain leaders to varying degrees. Whereas Liu engaged in aggressive political lobbying and molded State Grid from a fledgling grid company into a massive multinational corporation during his twelve-year tenure spanning both the Hu and Xi administrations, Shu showed less entrepreneurialism. Instead, he largely continued to implement his former boss's agenda. Institutional constraints may have decreased Shu's incentives to remake State Grid. Because Shu became chairman in 2016 at the age of fifty-eight, China's mandatory retirement age limited him to a likely tenure of two to five years at most; indeed, he retired in 2018 upon reaching the age of sixty.

China General Nuclear Power Group

China General Nuclear Power Group (CGN) was founded in 1994 as China Guangdong Nuclear Power Corporation.[35] The company played a key role in planning for China's first nuclear power plant in Daya Bay, Guangdong. It was incorporated the year after Daya Bay began operations in 1993. Initially, CGN managed the Daya Bay plant and focused on business in Guangdong. In 2007, the Hu administration decided to double the amount of nuclear energy in China's total installed power capacity from 2 percent to 4 percent by 2020, thereby

[34] State Grid has built UHV transmission lines in Brazil. 《国家电网首个海外独立中标特高压输电项目在巴西开工》[State Grid's First Independently Won UHV Transmission Project Begins Construction], *Xinhua News*, September 29, 2017, http://m.xinhuanet.com/2017-09/29/c_1121744677.htm.

[35] The company changed its name to China General Nuclear Power Group in 2013 so as to indicate that its operations extended beyond Guangdong; however, it still goes by the acronym CGN.

giving CGN a major growth opportunity.[36] Japan's 2011 earthquake and the Fukushima nuclear reactor accident temporarily dampened policy enthusiasm for the development of nuclear power in China, but ultimately it did not arrest CGN's expansion at home or abroad.

Today, CGN is China's biggest nuclear power operator, with more than 50 percent of the domestic nuclear power generation market. It is also the world's largest nuclear power construction company, with operations extending down China's eastern coast and around the globe (Liu, Wang, and Hu, 2021: 119).[37] Economic growth, pursuit of energy security, and a desire to diversify fuel sources have created new markets for CGN in Russia, Kazakhstan, and beyond. As of 2021, CGN had helped to bring nuclear power online in seventeen countries and regions worldwide.[38] However, CGN's successful expansion still faces concerns abroad about nuclear power safety and the national security implications of involvement by foreign firms in critical infrastructure. Qian Zhimin, who led CGN during China's domestic nuclear boom, oversaw its initial transformation from a provincial company to a major multinational.

Qian Zhimin (2005–2010)

Born in 1960 in Jiangsu, Qian Zhimin joined CGN at the age of twenty-five after earning bachelor's and master's degrees in nuclear power engineering. He began his career in planning and operational work at the Daya Bay plant in Guangdong. Even as a junior employee, he had the opportunity to interact with high-level company and national leaders. "When Qian worked in Guangdong, he was in charge of receiving guests," a CGN employee recalled. "He would personally pick up [former Premier] Li Peng and his wife from the airport."[39] These interactions garnered Qian attention and opportunities early

36 《国家核电中长期发展规划(2005–2020年)》 [National Medium- and Long-Term Development Plan for Nuclear Power (2005–2020)], 国家能源局 [National Energy Administration], November 2, 2007, www.nea.gov.cn/2007-11/02/c_131053228.htm.

37 "CGN: A Leader in Clean Energy," CGN website, August 26, 2016, http://en.cgnpc.com.cn/encgn/c100033/2016-08/26/content_8b6b5dafe8194aa19e9bed760172f65b.shtml.

38 《中广核举办2021年度媒体见面会暨高质量发展成果通报会》 [CGN Holds 2021 Media Meeting and High-Quality Development Results Briefing], 能源界 [Energy World], January 21, 2021, www.nengyuanjie.net/article/45375.html.

39 Interview with central SOE employee (CGN), Beijing, June 2018.

in his career. After a stint in executive leadership as general manager of CGN between 2002 and 2005, he was promoted to chairman and Party secretary in 2005. At only forty-five years of age, Qian was the youngest person ever appointed to head a Chinese nuclear company.[40]

Qian proposed a strategy of making CGN a "clean power company, with nuclear power as its core industry."[41] Despite the Hu administration's green light for nuclear power development, Qian believed it was vital for CGN to expand its technical capabilities and business beyond nuclear power into other types of energy. Under his leadership, CGN launched its first wind energy project in Jilin in 2006, hydropower projects in Sichuan in 2007 and in Guangxi in 2008, and its first solar energy project in Gansu in 2009. With the support of the Hu administration's energy security and "going out" policies, Qian also endeavored to cut costs and risks in CGN's industry chain by acquiring mining assets at home and overseas.[42] At the same time, CGN continued to expand its foothold in the domestic nuclear power market by building new plants along China's east coast, from Fujian in the south to Liaoning in the north.

Qian modified CGN's organizational structure to align with his strategy for the company's development. As CGN expanded across China and overseas, and into types of energy beyond nuclear power, Qian amalgamated related assets into subsidiary companies and research institutes directly under the control of the holding company. In CGN's core business area of nuclear power, Qian established new subsidiaries focusing on nuclear technology development.[43] In cooperation with the Chinese electricity company Huaneng and the Chinese Academy of Sciences, he also created a research institute to commercialize and promote applications of CGN's nuclear

40 《钱智民将调任能源局》[Qian Zhimin Will be Transferred to the National Energy Administration], 21世纪网 [*21st Century Business Herald*], March 23, 2010, https://business.sohu.com/20100323/n271020059.shtml.

41 In Chinese, this strategy is "核电为主的清洁能源集团"; 中国广东核电集团, 《清洁能 新发展》 [CGN: New Developments in Clean Energy], CGN website, September 18, 2009, www.cgnpc.com.cn/.

42 An example is CGN's acquisition of the Husab Uranium Mine in Namibia: CGN owns 90 percent of the mine and the state-owned Epangelo Mining Company owns the remaining 10 percent.

43 These included the Shenzhen CGN Nuclear Engineering Design Company, established in 2005, and the Beijing Guangli Nuclear System Engineering Company, also established in 2005. "Mining Operations Begin at Husab," *World Nuclear News*, May 9, 2014; 《北京广利核系统工程有限公司》[China Techenergy Company Description], 《公司概况》 [Company Overview], www.ctecdcs.com/ctecdc2/c102066/list_tt.shtml.

technology.[44] He subsequently transferred CGN's wind power assets to this research institute and merged all of the company's hydropower assets into its existing CGN Energy Company subsidiary.

Qian's decisions about strategy and structure, and their largely successful implementation, yielded highly centralized market expansion. The holding company led planning for all aspects of market activity, from business diversification to identification of new projects at home and abroad, to negotiations and decision-making regarding potential investments, and to project financing and technical and regulatory approvals. For the most part, subsidiaries played only a limited role in market expansion. For instance, CGN Uranium Resources Company helped to research potential uranium mine investments in Australia and the Middle East; however, the holding company led the assessment, negotiations, and project development.[45]

Under Qian's leadership, the holding company dominated commercial decision-making and resource allocation. The subsidiaries had little influence in these areas; instead, their role was confined to project execution, supervision, and research and development work. Whereas subsidiaries in other central SOEs gained influence and resources during the course of expanding into international markets, under Qian the holding company was always the dominant player. In addition, Qian's changes to the organizational structure, whereby he clustered assets and personnel into numerous specialized subsidiaries, prevented the emergence of an intra-firm entity that could serve as a counterweight to the influence of the holding company.

He Yu (2010–2020)

In 2010, General Manager He Yu was promoted to become the new chairman and Party secretary of CGN.[46] Born in 1957, He Yu held

44 中广核CGN核能, 中广核研究院有限公司：关于我们》[China General Nuclear Power: China General Nuclear Power Research Institute: About Us], China General Nuclear Power Research Institute website, 2015, www.cnpri.com.cn/cnpri/c102025/list_tt.shtml; 《一路风雨一路歌，这个企业今天11岁了!》[One Road of Hardship, One Road of Song, This Company Is Turning 11 Today!], 搜狐 [Sohu], November 8, 2017, www.sohu.com/a/203263440_654060.

45 CGN employee, personal correspondence, July 2018.

46 Qian Zhimin was appointed director of the National Energy Administration, the government body responsible at the time for regulating the nuclear power and other energy sectors. In March 2018, the Chinese government

bachelor's and master's degrees in engineering and a PhD in business management. He joined CGN in 1986, first working at the Daya Bay plant in a series of technical and managerial roles before becoming its director. While at the Daya Bay plant, He went to France to participate in a Chinese government-funded training program for leading nuclear power professionals.[47] Upon returning to China, he was promoted to serve as the general manager of CGN between 2005 and 2010.

Chairman He refined his predecessor's strategy of diversifying and internationalizing CGN's business. Facing the post-Fukushima nuclear slowdown in China, He acted more aggressively to promote the development of nonnuclear energy sources, especially wind and solar power.[48] Although He continued to stress the importance of internationalizing CGN's business, he focused on exporting Chinese nuclear technology to international markets and developing overseas projects spanning the entire industry chain.[49] He also led CGN in executing a series of major overseas mergers and acquisitions as well as investments that involved

announced plans to replace the National Energy Administration with a new energy ministry. 《国务院机构改革方案公布：能源局仍由发改委管理》[The State Council's Institutional Reform Plan Is Announced: The National Energy Administration Is Still Managed by the National Development and Reform Commission], *Sina Finance*, March 13, 2018, https://finance.sina.cn/2018-03-13/detail-ifysfits2159673.d.html?cre=tianyi&mod=wpage&loc=12&r=32&doct=0&rfunc=0&tj=none&tr=32&cref=cj.

[47] Those individuals selected to attend training programs in France earned the moniker "gold person" (黄金人) because of the high level of resources that the Chinese government invested in them and also because of their high value to the industry after they returned. 《中国广核集团有限公司党组书记、董事长 贺禹》[China General Nuclear Power's Party Secretary and Chairman He Wei], *Xinhua News*, July 5, 2017.

[48] 《中广核集团：向国际一流清洁能源集团迈进》[China General Nuclear Power: Narrowing the Gap with Top International New Energy Firms], 中国核能行业协会 [China Nuclear Energy Association], February 16, 2011. www.china-nea.cn/site/content/8954.html.

[49] For example, CGN reached an agreement with the state-owned Électricité de France (EDF) in 2016 to partner on several nuclear power projects in the UK that would incorporate the Chinese-designed third-generation nuclear power reactor, known as the HPR 1000 or Hualong One. In addition, CGN was slated to contribute 30 percent of the capital to construct the Hinkley Point C project outside of London, take a minority share in a second project in Sizewell, and hold a majority share in a future third project in Bradwell, which would use the HPR 1000 or Hualong One technology. Aibing Guo, "U.K.'s Aging Nuclear Fleet Offers Target for China Ambitions," Bloomberg, July 9, 2018, https://news.bloomberglaw.com/coronavirus/uks-aging-nuclear-fleet-offers-target-for-china-ambitions?context=article-related.

power assets in the UK, France, Belgium, Ireland, Sweden, and the Netherlands.[50] In addition, he modified his predecessor's strategy by stressing the concept of "marketization" (市场化). This signaled a new willingness to reorient commercial activity toward overseas markets and company actors on the front lines abroad.[51]

Chairman He altered CGN's organizational structure in a number of ways. First, he immediately regrouped departments and subsidiaries into four "pieces" (板块), corresponding to the company's main business areas: nuclear power, nuclear fuel, new energy, and finance and investment. Each of these pieces encompassed both domestic and international market activities. He soon updated this grouping to what he termed "4+X," adding nuclear technology as a fifth piece and a new business area. Toward this end, He founded CGN Nuclear Technology Application Corporation in 2011, a new subsidiary charged with developing non-power applications of nuclear technology, such as medical uses. To accelerate CGN's "going out," He set up new overseas branches and locally incorporated companies in South Africa, France, and the UK.

Chairman He's decisions about CGN's organizational strategy and structure resulted in more decentralized market expansion. Under his leadership, CGN's subsidiaries were encouraged to look for potential business opportunities, especially follow-up projects in geographic areas where they were already operating. Its subsidiaries also began to play a greater role in identifying, operating, and managing projects abroad, including those spanning the entire industry chain.[52]

50 Zheng Xin, "CGN Buys into Swedish Power Project," *China Daily*, July 19, 2018, https://global.chinadaily.com.cn/a/201807/19/WS5b4fe451a310796df4df756a.html.

51 《中广核集团：向国际一流清洁能源集团迈进》 [China General Nuclear Power: Narrowing the Gap with Top International New Energy Firms], 中国核能行业协会 [China Nuclear Energy Association], February, 16, 2011, www.china-nea.cn/site/content/8954.html; 《贺禹荣获中国企业管理最高奖》 [He Yu Receives China's Top Management Award], 中国广核集团 [China General Nuclear Power Group], June 6, 2018, www.toutiao.com/article/6563925107251610116/?wid=1698274483414.

52 For example, in Kazakhstan CGN reached agreements in uranium mining, nuclear fuel pellets, and nuclear fuel fabrication. It also established a joint venture with Kazakhstan's state-owned Kazatomprom to build a fuel fabrication plant. Zheng Xin, "Relationship with Kazakhstan Pays Off," *China Daily*, August 1, 2017, http://europe.chinadaily.com.cn/business/2017-08/01/content_30312997.htm.

However, the subsidiaries did not gain new powers of approval to authorize or finance new projects. The holding company retained centralized authority over these functions.

Chairman He's leadership prompted a small yet noteworthy shift in influence among intra-firm entities. The subsidiaries gained limited influence vis-à-vis the holding company. Both CGN Energy Company, a subsidiary that became the main commercial platform for CGN's new energy business, and the company's overseas subsidiaries gained greater autonomy to identify, operate, and manage projects during He's tenure as chairman. Overall, however, the holding company still retained a strong grip over CGN's subsidiaries.

A paired comparison of the tenures as chairmen of Qian and He provides evidence that SOE leaders can generate reform variation by making and executing decisions about organizational strategy and structure – even in sectors designated for absolute state control. For example, government policies did not dictate Qian's strategy of aggressively diversifying CGN's business and technology during the 2000s. The Hu administration supported the narrower objective of rapid domestic growth in nuclear power. As He continued Qian's strategy of diversifying CGN's business, his emphasis on marketization and accelerated internationalization resulted in more decentralized market expansion and greater, although still limited, influence for subsidiaries relative to the holding company.

Government policies and economic factors, including developments specific to the nuclear industry, were important considerations for He and Qian. The domestic slowdown in nuclear energy development after the 2011 Fukushima disaster surely influenced He's decision to internationalize CGN's business, and government policies incentivized and supported his efforts to "go out" and export Chinese nuclear technology.[53] Long-standing restrictions barring CGN from some domestic industrial activities, such as uranium enrichment due to its military applications, also likely motivated He's pursuit of overseas projects that would enable CGN to upgrade its technology and expertise along the entire nuclear industry chain.

[53] 中国核工业建设集团公司党组 [Party Group of China Nuclear Industry Construction Corporation],《打造核电"走出去"的国家名片》[Creating a Business Card for Nuclear Business Abroad], 中国共产党新闻网 [Chinese Communist Party News Network], January 6, 2017, http://dangjian.people.com.cn/n1/2017/0106/c117092-29003466.html.

The firm's leaders decided the steps and timing to make and execute changes to CGN's organizational strategy and structure. For example, Qian adopted and attempted to implement a strategy of aggressive diversification beyond nuclear power even when government policies and economic factors did not make this politically or commercially imperative. Furthermore, He's strategic emphasis on marketization and internationalization gave the company's overseas subsidiaries a green light to more autonomously identify, operate, and manage projects, ultimately yielding more decentralized market expansion. In contrast, CGN's expansion into new sectors and into overseas markets under Qian were both highly centralized.

Sinochem

Sinochem first began operations in Tianjin in 1950 as China Import Company, the first state-owned foreign trading company of the newly established People's Republic.[54] Mao and the CCP relied on Sinochem to procure vital commodities – such as rubber, petroleum, and fertilizer – to support national industrialization efforts in the 1950s and 1960s. The company soon expanded its international trade activity, partnering with Hong Kong–based China Resources and opening its first overseas representative office in East Berlin in 1952.[55] Sinochem initially traded primarily with other socialist states, including the Soviet Union and East Germany, but later increased its trade with regional neighbors such as Japan and Singapore.[56] By 1994, Sinochem was operating overseas branches in more than twenty countries.[57]

In the twenty-first century, Sinochem has become one of the world's largest chemicals and petroleum companies. It is also the

[54] The company was renamed China Import and Export Company, Ltd. in 1951, China National Chemicals Import and Export Company, Ltd. in 1961, China National Chemicals Import and Export Corporation in 1965, and finally Sinochem Group in 2003.

[55] Sinochem, 《中化集团60周年画册》 [Sinochem Group 60th Anniversary Album], 2010, www.huacew.com/showdm.asp?Articleid=6804.

[56] 《我国公司同日本签订两项贸易合同》 [Chinese Company Signs Two Trade Contracts with Japan], 浙江日报 [*Zhejiang Daily*], November 21, 1963. 《宁波出口两万多吨轻柴油》 [Ningbo Exports More Than 20,000 Tons of Light Diesel Oil], 《浙江日报》 [*Zhejiang Daily*], September 30, 1984.

[57] Sinochem, 《中化集团60周年画册》 [Sinochem Group 60th Anniversary Album], 2010, www.huacew.com/showdm.asp?Articleid=6804.

largest developer and producer of fertilizers and pesticides in China.[58] Sinochem imports and sells foreign fertilizers, such as Roundup, both domestically and overseas in markets including New Zealand and Australia. It is also a leading supplier of animal feed and seeds for major crops, such as rice, corn, wheat, vegetables, and soybeans.[59] In the petroleum sector, Sinochem manages oil fields at home and it also has stakes in oil assets abroad, from Brazil to Ecuador to Colombia and to the United States.[60] The company operates along the industry chain in the exploration, extraction, trading, refinement, and production and sale of petroleum products.[61] Today, it has production bases, research and development facilities, and a marketing network in more than 150 countries and regions around the world.[62] Such commercial success was a distant dream for Liu Deshu, however, when he took the helm of the chemicals and oil giant more than two decades earlier.

Liu Deshu (1998–2015)

Born in 1952 in Hebei, Liu Deshu graduated from the Department of Precision Instruments at Tsinghua University. He then spent the first thirty years of his career working in various capacities at China National Machinery Import and Export Corporation. In 1998, Liu earned an executive master's degree in business administration (EMBA) degree from the China Europe International Business School, an uncommon move for Chinese SOE executives at the time. That year, the COD tapped Liu to lead Sinochem out of financial turmoil. The company was grappling with a severe payment crisis after the 1997 Asian financial crisis, compounded by the Chinese government's ending of the company's monopoly over fertilizer and petroleum products trade. Although Liu embraced a low-profile executive image, he also demonstrated a willingness to seek outside expertise. In 1999,

58 Sinochem, "Life Science," www.sinochem.com/17191.html.
59 Sinochem, "Agriculture Business," www.sinochem.com/english/1474.html.
60 Chen Aizhu and Florence Tan, "China's Sinochem to Re-open U.S. Trading Desk as America's Oil Output Surges," *Reuters*, January 25, 2018, www.reuters.com/article/china-oil-usa-sinochem/chinas-sinochem-to-re-open-u-s-trading-desk-as-americas-oil-output-surges-idUSL4N1PJ36W.
61 Sinochem, 《能源业务》 [Energy Business], www.sinochem.com.cn/1216.html.
62 Sinochem, 《公司简介》公司简介 [Company Profile], www.sinochem.com/16222.html.

Sinochem hired McKinsey & Company to improve its management and internal control systems, marking the first time a Chinese central SOE partnered with a foreign consulting company.[63]

In 2001, Liu proposed what he termed the "1-2-3" strategy for Sinochem's development. The strategy centered on cultivating one ability (market competition), conducting two expansions (expansion into domestic and international markets and expansion upward and downward along the industry chain), and developing three core business areas (petroleum, fertilizer, and chemical products).[64] The "two expansions" expressed Liu's ambition to leverage international markets and resources to support Sinochem's domestic position. The strategy also expressed his desire to selectively diversify Sinochem's broad portfolio through what he termed "focused differentiation of core business areas" (聚焦差异化). Of these, Liu ranked petroleum first, indicating the prioritization of petroleum in his vision for Sinochem's development.

Liu altered the company's organizational structure by reallocating assets, personnel, and authority. He grouped Sinochem's sprawling constellation of subsidiaries into multiple "second-tier business centers" organized along business lines.[65] He also established multiple committees at the holding-company level, such as an interdepartmental Investment Decision Review Committee, to assess and approve potential investments.[66] Liu also set up a new Asset Management

63 Sinochem, 《中化集团60周年画册》 [Sinochem Group 60th Anniversary Album], 2010, www.huacew.com/showdm.asp?Articleid=6804.

64 In 2009, Liu updated the strategy as the "12345" strategy, specifically referring to one ability (market competition), two foundations (domestic and international markets), three links (petroleum, fertilizer, and chemical products), four channels, and five sectors. Wang Wei [王炜]: 《持续创新之路（国企典型）》 [The Road to Continuous Innovation (Typical SOEs)], 人民日报 [People's Daily], May 25, 2007; 《中化自救曲折》 [The Twists and Turns in Sinochem's "Self-Help"], Sinochem website, June 20, 2003, www.sinochem.com.cn/s/1375-4638-8424.html.

65 These second-tier business centers (二级业务中心) were in petroleum, fertilizer, domestic business, and hotels and property management. 《中化自救曲折》 [The Twists and Turns in Sinochem's "Self-Help"], Sinochem website, June 20, 2003. www.sinochem.com.cn/s/1375-4638-8424.html.

66 The Chinese name of the Investment Decision Review Committee was 投资决策审议委员会. This committee was comprised of the directors or vice-directors from relevant departments, such as the Strategy Department and the Finance Department (Sinochem employee, personal correspondence, July 2018).

Department, which, by 2003, had shuttered or transferred more than 400 internal entities and nearly halved the company's workforce from its 1994 levels.[67]

Over time, Liu's decisions regarding strategy and organizational structure brought about more centralized market expansion. When he took office, Sinochem was structured as a "comprehensive trading company" (综合商社) in which the subsidiaries enjoyed significant autonomy for market expansion. By organizing the subsidiaries into second-tier business centers, with only limited autonomy for industry-specific commercial development, the holding company increasingly centralized its authority over market expansion.

Liu's leadership remade the balance of influence among intra-firm entities. Sinochem's subsidiaries had previously operated like "princes," with each enjoying relative autonomy in its particular sectoral or geographic market.[68] Under Liu, many subsidiaries lost authority – and, in some cases, even their independent legal status. A handful of subsidiaries did, however, gain influence. Instead of setting up new overseas offices, Sinochem tapped several existing subsidiaries in regional markets to serve as sector-specific headquarters for its international business.[69] Back in Beijing, the Finance Department became more influential, as financial modeling and risk assessments played a growing role in Sinochem's commercial decision-making and development strategy.[70]

[67] 《刘德树:铁血打造中化"GE"》 [*Liu Deshu: Building a Sinochem "GE" with Iron and Blood*], 21世纪经济报道 [*21st Century Economic Report*], August 2005, www.cec1979.org.cn/huodong/mxqyj/liudeshu/06.htm; 《中化自救曲折》 [The Twists and Turns in Sinochem's "Self-Help"], Sinochem website, June 20, 2003, www.sinochem.com.cn/s/1375-4638-8424.html.

[68] 《刘德树:铁血打造中化"GE"》 [*Liu Deshu: Building a Sinochem "GE" with Iron and Blood*], 21世纪经济报道 [*21st Century Economic Report*], August 2005, www.cec1979.org.cn/huodong/mxqyj/liudeshu/06.htm.

[69] For example, Liu designated Sinochem Trading Singapore Company to serve as its overseas headquarters for its chemicals business. Huang Yue [黄越], 《中化海外企业石化业务发展战略》 [*A Study of Development Strategy for Sinochem Overseas Petrochemical Enterprises*] (Xiamen: Xiamen University Press, 2008).

[70] 《刘德树:铁血打造中化"GE"》 [*Liu Deshu: Building a Sinochem "GE" with Iron and Blood*], 21世纪经济报道 [*21st Century Economic Report*], August 2005, www.cec1979.org.cn/huodong/mxqyj/liudeshu/06.htm; Wang Feng [王枫], 《刘德树：打造中国的"通用电气"》 [Liu Deshu: Building China's "General Electric"], 人民日报 [*People's Daily*], October 23, 2006.

Ning Gaoning (2016–2022)

After Liu retired in 2016, ending one of the longest executive tenures of any Chinese central SOE leader, Ning Gaoning took over as chairman and Party secretary. Ning was an experienced and well-known Chinese business leader. Born in 1958 in Shandong, he earned a bachelor's degree in economics from Shandong University and an MBA degree from the University of Pittsburgh. If it was rare to earn a business degree in China in the 1990s, as his predecessor Liu did, it was even more unusual to have earned one abroad in the 1980s. After returning to China, Ning joined central SOE China Resources and ultimately became its chairman. In 2004, the COD transferred him to helm another central SOE: China National Cereals, Oils, and Foodstuffs Corporation (COFCO). Ning led COFCO for more than a decade before he was appointed to head Sinochem in 2016. An avid proponent of mergers and acquisitions, Ning had earned the moniker "China's Morgan [Stanley]" for initiating more than thirty mergers and acquisitions at China Resources and approximately fifty more at COFCO.[71] Ning embraced public attention with frequent media appearances and a string of books. For instance, in a volume simply titled *Why?*, Ning penned essays on topics ranging from meeting General Electric chairman Jack Welch to Starbucks' global expansion and to the commercialization of Christmas.[72]

In 2017, Ning proposed a new strategy for Sinochem's development – "in science we trust."[73] Three interrelated "i's" expressed its key tenets: innovation, industrial upgrading, and investment.[74] Through the "in science we trust" strategy, Ning sought to remake Sinochem into an innovative petrochemical and chemical company and an investment company with limited diversification in agriculture, real estate,

[71] 《宁高宁掌舵中粮11载发起50起并购 子品牌业绩平平》 [Ning Gaoning Takes the Helm of COFCO 11 and Launches 50 Mergers and Acquisitions: Sub-brand Performance Is Flat], 投资者报 [*Investors News*], January 4, 2016, www.ce.cn/cysc/sp/info/201601/04/t20160104_8023222.shtml.

[72] Ning Gaoning [宁高宁], 《为什么》 [*Why?*] (Beijing: Zhongguo zhongxin chubanshe, 2008).

[73] The Chinese phrase for the strategy is "科学至上." Sinochem's official English translation is "in science we trust." Sinochem, 《中化集团2018–2020年发展战略指引》 [Sinochem 2018–2020 Development Strategy Guide].

[74] 《宁高宁：从明天起，中化会发生什么？》 [Ning Gaoning: From Today Forward, What Will Happen at Sinochem?], *Phoenix New Media*, April 4, 2018.

and finance.[75] He identified emerging industries such as new materials and new energy as targets for future innovation.[76] Specifically, Ning envisioned that Sinochem would become an "innovation platform" (创新平台) and "platform company" (平台公司) focusing on improving technology and making capital investments rather than acquiring and operating fixed assets, especially in petroleum.[77]

Ning remolded Sinochem's organizational structure. First, he reorganized the company's business centers into strategic development units corresponding with the core business areas: energy, chemicals, agriculture, finance, and real estate. He directed the holding company to act as an investment company, with the strategic development units conducting the actual business.[78] Toward this end, in eighty-six areas he delegated decision-making power to the strategic development units.[79] Similarly, he authorized the strategic development units to independently implement the company's innovation strategy.[80] Ning's new strategy of "in science we trust" mandated the creation of positions of chief scientist and chief technology officer at all levels, from the holding company down to the strategic development units, with the aim of strengthening the science–industry nexus and boosting the company's number of scientific patents.[81] He also increased funding

[75] 黄鑫 [Hua Xin]: 《中化集团: 做实做优主产业 增强国际竞争力》[Sinochem: Doing Well in the Core Business Enhances International Competitiveness], 《经济日报》 [*Economic Daily*], September 23, 2017, http://cpc.people.com.cn/n1/2017/0923/c412690-29554386.html.

[76] 《我们的能源梦》[Our Energy Dream], Sinochem website, n.d., www.sinochem.com/m/s/10757-29123-117178.html.

[77] 《这家低调的央企总部，要有大变化!》[This Low-Key Central SOE Headquarters Will Undergo Major Changes!], Sinochem WeChat official account, April 19, 2017.

[78] 《中化减少总部一半部门 酝酿五大事业部上市》 [Sinochem Reduces Half of Its Headquarters Departments and Plans to IPO Five Major Divisions], December 7, 2016. www.sohu.com/a/120921309_284327.

[79] 《这家低调的央企总部，要有大变化!》[This Low-Key Central SOE Headquarters Will Undergo Major Changes!], Sinochem WeChat official account, April 19, 2017.

[80] Ning emphasized: "In practice, the headquarters does not directly carry out the operational business; therefore it is the business units that are the point of implementation for scientific and technological innovation; we must rely on their general managers and their teams." Ning Gaoning [宁高宁], 《科学至上》 [Science First], Sinochem website, March 2018, www.sinochem.com/s/8959-24289-118028.html.

[81] Ning Gaoning [宁高宁] 《科学至上》 [Science First], Sinochem website, March 2018, www.sinochem.com/s/8959-24289-118028.html.

across the board to support research and development.[82] Finally, Ning continued to streamline the company's organizational structure by abolishing more than fifty departments at the holding-company level and merging or selling a number of subsidiary firms.[83]

Ning's leadership led to a more decentralized mode of market expansion for Sinochem. Strategic development units and subsidiaries assumed a greater role in commercial decision-making, including the identification of potential acquisition targets.[84] However, the holding company and even Ning personally still led the large-scale mergers and acquisitions. Ning initially lobbied heavily in support of the 2017 blockbuster USD 43 billion acquisition of the Swiss biotech firm Syngenta by ChemChina, another central SOE whose merger into Sinochem was approved by Chinese regulators.[85] These acquisitions reflected Sinochem's efforts to expand along the industry chain in agriculture as well as to diversify its business into the new sectors targeted by Ning.[86]

Ning's decisions about strategy and structure catalyzed a shift in the balance of influence among intra-firm entities. The holding company ceded influence to subsidiaries while continuing to exercise control through mechanisms such as investment, assessment, and oversight. Strategic development units emerged as winners by gaining decision-making authority and control over resources and front-line market

82 Ning also approved 69 percent and 33 percent increases in spending on technological innovation for Sinochem International Corporation, the flagship subsidiary of the company's chemicals business. 《中化国际2017年科技创新投入激增69%》 [Sinochem International's Investment in Science and Technology Innovation Surges 69 Percent in 2017], Finance World website, June 5, 2018, https://read01.com/zh-mo/E8K2zA7.amp.

83 For example, Ning sold Sinochem subsidiary Zhejiang International Group (英特集团) to the Zhejiang provincial government and merged Sinochem Blue Sky (中化蓝天) with Sinochem International (中化国际). Kang Yin [康殷], 《中化集团整合剥离药企 英特集团改嫁浙江国资》 [Sinochem Integrates and Divests its Pharmaceutical Companies, While INTEC Group Changes Its Relationship with Zhejiang State-Owned Assets], Securities Times website, January 11, 2017, http://finance.sina.com.cn/roll/2017-01-11/doc-ifxzkfuk3579033.shtml.

84 Ning Gaoning [宁高宁], 《科学至上》 [Science First], Sinochem website, March 2018, www.sinochem.com/s/8959-24289-118028.html.

85 Colin Qian and Tom Daly, "China Approves Long-Planned Merger of Sinochem and ChemChina," *Reuters*, March 31, 2021.

86 《并购之王宁高宁：中化与中国化工合并谈判最重要推手》 [Ning Gaoning, The King of M&As: The Most Important Promoter of Sinochem's Merger with China's Chemical Industry], *Sina Finance*, October 17, 2016, https://finance.sina.cn/chanjing/gl/2016-10-17/detail-ifxwvpar8245939.d.html?

activity. Research and development institutes within Sinochem benefited because "in science we trust" granted them new resources for technological upgrading in core business areas, research and development in new and emerging sectors, and permission to establish and operate new subsidiaries. Research and development institutes, and technical personnel more generally, also gained influence on the basis of their specialized scientific expertise. They enjoyed a privileged position to assess the technological merits and commercial potential of merger and acquisition targets involving advanced or new technologies.

A paired comparison of the tenures of these two chairmen of Sinochem further corroborates that there has been no fixed trend of increased centralization in the market expansion of central SOEs. One might argue that initial decentralization occurs naturally because at the outset the holding company is inexperienced and lacks the capacity to manage international business. Others might suggest it reflects a learning process for Chinese firms "going out," whereby different entities within the firm experiment and the holding company subsequently implements a standardized approach based on the method of the most successful performer.[87] Still others might contend that increased centralization over time has little to do with leadership and instead results from the Xi administration's tightening oversight of SOE business, especially overseas (SASAC, 2017). However, as analysis of the consecutive chairmen of both Sinochem and CGN suggests, leaders' decisions about strategy and structure can also yield more decentralized market expansion. Furthermore, this was the case even during periods of tighter political control, such as during the Xi era.

China Railway Engineering Corporation

China Railway Engineering Corporation (CREC) originated in 1950 as the General Bureau of Construction and the General Bureau of Design

from=wap; Wang Yajie [王雅洁], 《中化集团揭秘全新战略定位 宁高宁将带领企业干这些大事儿!》 [Sinochem Unveils a New Strategic Positioning: Ning Gaoning Will Lead the Company to Do These Big Things!], 经济观察网 [*Economic Observer*], November 16, 2017, http://m.eeo.com.cn/2017/1116/316931.shtml.

[87] Such an approach would be analogous to Sebastian Heilmann's concept of "experimentation under hierarchy," in which the central government fosters localized experimentation and then uses the successful cases as the basis for national policymaking (Heilmann, 2008a, 2008b).

under the Ministry of Railways. Its roots extend further back to the Railway Corps of the People's Liberation Army during the Chinese Civil War (1945–49) (Chan, 2022). Over the following decades, railroads built and run by the Ministry of Railways played a crucial role in China's national industrialization, mass mobilization, and military logistics. During the Mao era, "[T]he railroads represented the speed, economic efficiency, punctuality, discipline, technological advances, professionalism, dedication, and heroism necessary to promote the ideals of the party and the government at large" (Köll, 2019: 247). During the reform-era restructuring under Deng Xiaoping, the government carved out assets from the Ministry of Railways in 1989 and incorporated them to create CREC.[88] The State Council later placed CREC under central government administration, first under the Central Large-Scale Enterprise Work Commission in 2000 and then under SASAC after it began operations in 2003.

Today, CREC is a leading developer of transportation infrastructure both in China and abroad. Within China, the company has constructed more than two-thirds of the national railway network, three-fifths of the urban railways, and one-eighth of the highways.[89] Internationally, CREC ranks as the second largest global infrastructure contractor in the world.[90] As of the end of 2019, the company had operations or projects under construction in more than ninety countries and regions.[91] These projects included railways in Russia, Indonesia, Laos, Singapore, and Ethiopia, as well as numerous highways, bridges, airports, ports, and municipal works around the world.[92] Leaders of CREC, such as Shi Dahua, have been tasked with managing the company's growing business in both domestic and international markets.

88 《公司简介》 [Company Profile], China Group Railway Limited official website, www.crecg.com/chinazt/1116/1120/1124/index.html.

89 《公司简介》 [Company Profile], China Group Railway Limited official website, www.crecg.com/chinazt/1116/1120/1124/index.html.

90 This is according to the *Engineering News-Record* 2023 rankings of the top 250 global contractors. *Engineering News-Record* ranks companies according to construction revenue generated outside of the home country. The 2023 rankings are based on 2022 revenue, www.enr.com/toplists/2023-Top-250-Global-Contractors-1.

91 《公司简介》 [Company Profile], China Group Railway Limited official website, www.crecg.com/chinazt/1116/1120/1124/index.html.

92 CREC, "Overview of Overseas Business," November 26, 2018, www.crecg.com/english/2745/2808/17498/index.html.

Shi Dahua (2006–2010)

Born in 1951 in Hubei, Shi Dahua joined the People's Liberation Army when he was only seventeen years old. After serving in the military for more than a decade, he joined the Ministry of Railways and earned a college degree in engineering management. After graduation, he held positions on the Party committee of the China Railway Construction Corporation in 1995 and then the Party committee of CREC in 1997. He later became the chairman and Party secretary of CREC in 2006.

Shi's strategy for CREC stressed limited diversification of the company's business into related areas (有限相关多元化), both domestically and overseas. Specifically, he aimed to gradually expand CREC's core strength in constructing basic infrastructure, such as railways, highways, and municipal projects – which in 2007 constituted 89 percent of the company's operating revenue – to include business in real estate, trade, and logistics.[93] Although the domestic market in China remained CREC's top priority, Shi advocated a strategic shift toward "two markets" – domestic and international. He encouraged the company's engineering design institutes and construction bureaus to work together to develop its international business.

Shi modified CREC's organizational structure by refining and marketizing the company's assets. During his leadership, CREC acquired twenty-two railway construction SOEs, increasing total firm assets by 25 percent.[94] He also led CREC to create the subsidiary China Railway Real Estate Group to diversify beyond basic infrastructure.[95] In addition, he led CREC in transferring, restructuring, or selling off nearly 100 subsidiary entities unrelated to its core business areas.[96]

93 Ou Yangbo [欧阳波], 《中国中铁：大单大工程打造基建"航母"》 [China Railway: Big Single Project to Build Infrastructure "Aircraft Carrier"], 中国证券报 [*China Securities Journal*], June 27, 2008, www.cs.com.cn/jnj/jngs/ssgsjj2018/08/201810/P020181025448357612070.pdf.

94 Cao Xu [曹煦], 《专访中国中铁董事长李长进：中铁40年成就得益于政策环境+内生动力》 [Interview with Li Changjin, Chairman of China Railway Group: China Railway's Forty Years of Achievements Benefit from the Policy Environment + Self-Power], 中国经济周刊 [*China Economic Weekly*], July 23, 2018, www.ceweekly.cn/2018/0723/229993.shtml.

95 《中国中铁股份有限公司2007年年度报告》 [*China Railway Corporation Limited 2007 Annual Report*], www.sse.com.cn/disclosure/listedinfo/announcement/c/2008-05-10/601390_2007_n.pdf.

96 《中国铁路工程总公司进入世界双500强》 [China Railway Engineering Corporation Enters the World's Top 500 Rankings for Size and Brand

In 2007, CREC transferred a large portion of its assets to China Railway Group Limited, a newly created subsidiary wholly owned by the holding company, and, in the following year, it publicly listed part of China Railway Group Limited's assets in Hong Kong and Shanghai.

Shi's changes to organizational strategy and structure resulted in some decentralization of CREC's international market expansion. As CREC diversified and expanded its business overseas, the holding company still controlled market development. At the same time, the construction bureaus and design institutes gained autonomy over project management and execution. In both domestic and international markets, CREC evolved from being simply a railroad builder to becoming an adviser on railroad design. In addition to railway project construction, the company began to offer technical consulting and engineering survey and design services.

Under Shi's leadership, CREC's construction bureaus and design institutes enjoyed greater albeit still limited influence vis-à-vis the holding company. The design institutes gained influence and resources with the growth of CREC's technical consulting and engineering survey and design businesses. However, the holding company retained primary control over identifying domestic as well as overseas market opportunities. Overall, Shi's leadership resulted in the holding company leading business development, the design institutes collecting information and executing project designs, and finally the construction bureaus doing the actual building work.

Li Changjin (2010–2019)

Li Changjin took over as chairman and Party secretary of CREC in 2010, when SASAC appointed Shi to serve on its board of supervisors. Born in 1958 in Guangxi, Li was a railway man from his earliest days, earning bachelor's and master's degrees in railway and transportation engineering. Following a brief stint in one of the Ministry of Railways' survey and design institutes, he joined CREC's Second Construction Bureau, where he worked in technical and managerial roles for more than a decade. In 2002, CREC promoted him to the holding company, where he held a series of executive positions before becoming chairman. Those

Influence], 中国青年报 [*China Youth Daily*], August 3, 2006, http://zqb.cyol.com/content/2006-08/03/content_1466856.htm.

who worked with Li described him as a risk-taker and someone who was willing to innovate to advance CREC's development. "Chairman Li is very good at grasping and using opportunities," observed one employee. Quoting Deng's well-known aphorism – "It doesn't matter whether the cat is black or white, as long as it catches mice" – he continued: "For Chairman Li, any project that makes money is acceptable."[97]

Li proposed a development strategy for CREC of "grasping the railway market, accelerating expansion into non-railway markets, and actively entering into emerging markets."[98] He maintained Chairman Shi's strategy of business diversification, but he deepened and reoriented it toward international markets. Even as CREC rode the peaks of China's stimulus-fueled railway construction boom and high-speed rail became a priority sector, Li argued that the company's highly concentrated industrial structure made it overly vulnerable to shifts in government spending.[99] He accelerated CREC's expansion into new business areas, including finance, hydropower, airport construction, and dredging. In line with policies supporting high-tech manufacturing, especially during the Xi administration, Li prioritized railway technology and machinery, in particular tunnel boring machines and track switches used for high-speed rail.[100]

Li altered CREC's organizational structure by redistributing assets and authority within the state-owned enterprise group. He led the establishment of the subsidiary China Railway International Group Limited in 2013 to serve as the company's main platform for international business. At the same time, he merged numerous other subsidiaries to consolidate resources and decrease competition among CREC's member firms. Li described his goal of developing a two-level

97 Interview with central SOE employee (CREC), Beijing, June 2018.

98 The Chinese description of this strategy is "突出抓好铁路市场，加快拓展非铁路市场，积极进入新兴市场"; Jiang Lei [姜雷], 《中国中铁告急》[China Railways Is in Crisis], 经济观察报 [Economic Observer], July 29, 2011, https://finance.sina.cn/sa/2011-07-29/detail-ikftpnnx9072636.d.html?from=wap.

99 Railways accounted for more than 50 percent of the business of the entire company and more than 80 percent of the business of some construction bureaus in 2011. Jiang Lei [姜雷], 《中国中铁告急》[China Railways Is in Crisis], 《经济观察报》 [*Economic Observer*], July 29, 2011, https://finance.sina.cn/sa/2011-07-29/detail-ikftpnnx9072636.d.html?from=wap.

100 《李长进作为央企唯一代表参加品牌国际论坛企业家对话》 [Li Changjin, As the Sole Representative of the Central Enterprises, Participated in the Brand International Forum's Entrepreneurial Dialogue], 中国中铁股份有限公司 [China Railway Group Ltd.]. May 21, 2018, www.crecg.com/zgztsjz/10050114/10050996/34102/index.html

organizational structure in which the headquarters and the holding company led operations while the subsidiaries, including the construction bureaus, were organized beneath it by region.[101] Li also reassigned responsibility for directly managing CREC's twenty largest key projects to company leaders at the holding-company level.[102]

Over time, Li's leadership yielded more centralized market expansion for CREC. The holding company reclaimed authority for market development that the construction bureaus, design institutes, and subsidiaries had previously exercised. The "flattening out" of the company's organizational structure, as a CREC construction bureau employee described it, shortened the chains of command between the holding company and the subsidiaries.[103] The relative influence of the construction bureaus and overseas subsidiaries was also diminished by the wave of internal consolidation and restructuring that Li initiated during his tenure as leader.

Li's adjustments to CREC's organizational strategy and structure shifted the balance of influence among the players within the firm. The holding company was the biggest winner. Instead of permitting the marketing departments to partner with the construction bureaus and subsidiaries to lead market development, Li wanted investment to drive CREC's business. As a result, the holding company and its Investment and Development Department gained influence. The Investment and Development Department's resources and product offerings – now including trusts, investment funds, and insurance – expanded in tandem with the Department's internal authority to assess and determine the commercial potential of projects.

A paired comparison of Shi's and Li's tenures as chairmen of CREC highlights how a leader might formally maintain his predecessor's strategy while refining specific components and the timing of implementation, thereby generating limited variation in reform outcomes.

101 曹煦 [Cao Xu]: 《专访中国中铁董事长李长进：中铁40年成就得益于政策环境+内生动力》 [Exclusive Interview with Li Changjin, Chairman of China Railway Group: China Railway Group's 40 Years of Achievements Benefit from the Policy Environment + Self-Propulsion], 经济网 [*CE Weekly*], July 23, 2018, www.ceweekly.cn/2018/0723/229993.shtml.

102 For example, Li established a new "232 leadership marketing institution" (领导营销"232"制度) in which company leaders were required to visit two clients, three or more design institutes, and follow up personally on two or more projects. CREC, 《2013年集团公司年终工作总结》 [2013 Holding Company Year-End Work Summary].

103 Personal communication with CREC employee, July 2018.

Table 5.2 ***Paired comparison of the tenures of chairmen in selected central SOEs***

Company	Leader	Centralization of market expansion	Balance of influence among intra-firm entities
Core firms			
State Grid	Liu Zhenya	High	Holding company dominates; regional power companies and overseas subsidiaries lose influence to functional subsidiaries and State Grid International Development Company
	Shu Yinbiao	High	Holding company dominates; regional power companies and overseas subsidiaries remain subordinate to functional subsidiaries and State Grid International Development Company
China Guangdong Nuclear (CGN)	Qian Zhimin	High	Holding company dominates; subsidiaries have limited influence
	He Yu	Moderate	Holding company directs; subsidiaries have greater but still limited influence
Noncore firms			
Sinochem	Liu Deshu	High	Holding company dominates; second-tier business centers and research and development institutes lose influence
	Ning Gaoning	Moderate	Holding company directs; strategic development units and research and development institutes gain influence
China Railway Engineering Corporation	Shi Dahua	Moderate	Holding company directs; construction bureaus, design institutes, and subsidiaries have some but limited influence
	Li Changjin	High	Holding company dominates; construction bureaus, design institutes, and subsidiaries have less influence
China Infrastructure (CI)	Chairman Chen	Low	Holding company cedes influence; construction bureaus gain influence; design institutes and Sino-Construction International lose influence
	Chairman Wu	High	Holding company dominates; construction bureaus and CI International lose influence; design institutes gain influence

Consider, for instance, Li's continuation of Shi's emphasis on business diversification. Whereas Shi focused primarily on "limited" and "related" diversification into sectors such as real estate and trade and logistics, Li targeted areas such as high-tech manufacturing and investment that would move CREC up the industry chain and pivot the company from managing assets to capital. The two men also diverged in terms of the speed and orientation of their desired diversification efforts. Shi pursued gradual, domestic-focused diversification, whereas Li advocated rapid, international-oriented diversification. Table 5.2 summarizes the key findings from the four paired comparisons of the tenures of the central SOE chairmen presented in this chapter.

Conclusion

This chapter presents paired comparisons of the tenures of the chairmen of four Chinese central SOEs that were selected to capture variation in industry strategic importance and firm type. I used process tracing of qualitative and quantitative data to assess leadership's effects on two aspects of reform: the degree to which a company's market expansion is decentralized and the balance of influence among intra-firm entities. This analysis yields additional evidence that leaders' decisions about organizational strategy and structure can generate variation in reform outcomes. Since the cases span sectors with different levels of strategic importance and examine both core and noncore firms, these findings increase confidence that leadership affects reform outcomes across China's portfolio of central SOEs. Although the cases analyzed are selected to maximize variation in industry strategic importance and firm type, no clear correlations are evident between these factors and the observed reform outcomes summarized in Table 5.2.

Several general inferences about leadership and its effects on reform in Chinese SOEs can be made from these cases. First, leaders frequently make decisions about organizational strategy and structure that diverge from those of their predecessors. This suggests that leadership succession may indeed function as a mechanism for innovation in socialist bureaucratic contexts (Bunce, 1981). Second, these cases imply that although the effects of leadership on reform are significant, they are often limited in terms of degree. For example, changes in the centralization of market expansion typically involve movements from low to moderate to high (or vice versa); shifts from one extreme to another are less common. Third, these cases also confirm that enterprise reform trajectories are often nonlinear. Market expansion might become more centralized after a period of decentralization, while the balance of influence among intra-firm entities may shift back and forth. Finally, consistent with a leadership explanation, in cases where there was no significant change among consecutive leaders in terms of their decisions about organizational strategy and structure as well as their execution, there was no significant variation in reform outcomes over time.

Further empirical research is needed to assess the validity of these inferences and the extent to which this chapter's findings might apply to a broader group of Chinese SOEs. Such research could systematically investigate the tenures of more chairmen across firms of different types over time. Such a study would help to gauge whether sectors marked for absolute state control might have a higher "threshold" for the level of decentralization in market expansion that SOE leaders can bring about. Examining multiple consecutive leaders over a longer time frame in a larger number of firms would also facilitate identification of potential firm, industry, and time-specific factors that might systematically condition the exercise of leadership and its effects. A more immediate question concerns how leaders implement their choices about organizational strategy and structure, particularly if they face internal opposition. How are these decisions actually carried out and how do they shape reform outcomes? Chapter 6 investigates the tactics that Chinese SOE leaders use to execute their leadership agendas and the variety of ways in which their subordinates respond.

6 Leader–Subordinate Dynamics in Chinese SOEs

When SOE leaders make decisions about organizational strategy and structure, they need their subordinates to execute them. Although most employees support or at a minimum comply with implementing the leader's agenda, others may resist particular choices or any changes to the status quo. Accumulation of pushback can impede the leaders' execution ability and negatively affect enterprise operations and performance, even if the effects of individual employee resistance are limited. As Chinese SOE leaders navigate political priorities and market pressures externally, how do they work to carry out their agendas internally – and how do their subordinates respond? To what extent do leaders' tactics and efficacy differ between the leaders of SOEs and the leaders of private firms in China?

Analysis of CI and other Chinese central SOEs reveals a common set of SOE leader tactics and subordinate responses. Leader tactics include leveraging position authority, conducting personnel ploys, emphasizing material and status gains, invoking external threats, underscoring the directives and policies of superiors, and appealing to personal duty and morality. Subordinates may respond rhetorically by praising the leaders' decisions, raising alternative views, or engaging in critical expression. They can also counter by delaying or subverting implementation, or even by shirking or quitting. Both the leaders' tactics and the subordinates' responses vary in their risk and efficacy.

This chapter develops an integrated framework of leader–subordinate dynamics in Chinese SOEs. Grounded in multiple bases of power – reward, coercion, and legitimation – it shows how leader tactics interact with subordinate responses and evolve over time (French and Raven, 1959).[1] For example, SOE leaders' appeals to personal duty and morality may limit their subordinates' ability to advance

[1] On other bases of power, see French and Raven (1959); Raven (1965); and Yukl and Falbe (1991).

alternative views or to engage in critical expression because the former draw upon legitimate power. Subordinates may also be more likely to support a leader's agenda until the threats the leader invokes have passed. The following sections outline leader tactics and subordinate responses to present an integrated framework of leader–subordinate dynamics in Chinese SOEs.

Leader Tactics

Position Authority

Leaders can leverage the authority of their position by invoking their superior rank to secure subordinate support. This tactic induces compliance by referencing formal hierarchies and social norms requiring that subordinates obey superiors. Leveraging position authority enables a leader to use the existing power structure in their organization to influence subordinates (Elias, 2008). This tactic works best in workplaces where subordinates believe they have minimal control over their work environment (Elias, 2009: 373). In Chinese SOEs, norms about vertical order are strong and employees have traditionally exhibited high acceptance of organizational hierarchy and centralized decision-making (Walder, 1986).[2] As Redding (2013: 61) describes such a context:

> The individual has a built-in sense of the legitimacy of the superior-subordinate relationship. ... This is not to say that compliance is mute and unthinking, as there are endless possibilities for subtle resistance and for disguising the unwillingness to conform, but the general tone of vertical relationships is that there is not an issue of principle at stake about rights and duties.

Over time, repeated leveraging of position authority reinforces existing hierarchies and norms for subordinate compliance.

Leaders of SOEs leverage their position authority both formally and informally. They can establish it formally by citing their titles and responsibilities. For instance, leaders may reference their official

[2] However, some variation exists. For example, a study of participative leadership in Chinese SOEs finds that employees with shorter organizational tenures exhibit a greater desire for self-control and intrinsically motivating tasks than employees with longer work histories (Huang et al., 2006).

designation as the organization's legal representative (法人) or as the responsible party in responsibility contracts with administrative superiors. They may also informally invoke position authority in visible, top-down ways, such as inspecting their subordinates' work, calling subordinates in to their office, assuming the customary seat of the leader in meetings, and designating areas of an organization's physical space for their exclusive use. In CI, for example, the chairman routinely met with subordinates in his office, which was located on a floor exclusively for use by top management. There was also a separate VIP room in the company's cafeteria for the chairman and other top managers. Both formally and informally, conveying superior rank in such ways can help SOE leaders secure support from their subordinates.

Personnel Ploys

Personnel ploys occur when leaders appoint their allies to key leadership posts. These formal moves reshape the informal networks of patronage relationships, whereby allies exchange their allegiance to the leader for tangible and intangible individual benefits (Farh et al., 1998; Hillman, 2014; Paik and Baum, 2014). Personnel ploys bolster the leaders' influence because they build a network of allies through which the leaders can affect decision-making, shape resource allocation, coordinate behavior, and obtain information.[3] Leaders can also use personnel ploys to sideline critics and potential rivals. Through personnel ploys, a SOE leader can remake *guanxi* networks, thus improving their interpersonal relationships and ability to exercise authority inside the firm.

In CI, personnel ploys entailed the chairman posting his allies – often former colleagues from the same intra-firm units – to top positions in key departments in the holding company and the subsidiaries. Take, for example, Chairman Wu's moves after succeeding Chairman Chen. Chairman Wu appointed an ally with whom he had worked closely earlier in his career to head the regional department with the largest overseas business revenues in CI International – even though that individual had scant experience in the region compared with

[3] On how the development of patronage networks affects the exercise of power and its institutionalization within the state, see Boone (1992).

the other candidates. In CI International's reconstituted Investment Department, Chairman Wu created a new requirement that 50 percent of its employees come from Sino-Engineering – which he had previously led – even though Sino-Engineering accounted for less than 40 percent of CI's total assets, revenue, profits, and personnel at the time of the merger creating CI.[4] Similar examples can be found in other central SOEs. For example, when Liu Zhenya was chairman and Party secretary of State Grid and he established SGIDC as a flagship subsidiary to coordinate international business, he appointed two of his former right-hand men in State Grid's holding company to serve as the new chairman and general manager of SGIDC.[5]

However, there are limits to leaders' ability to carry out personnel ploys. Leaders may incite a backlash if their subordinates perceive that such appointments violate norms for professional advancement or that the appointees are unqualified. Mediation or even discipline by SASAC are possible if appointments of allies are excessive or cause discord. Leaders may also struggle to displace employees whom their predecessors previously appointed. This helps to explain, for instance, why the number of vice presidents in CI International ballooned to twenty-seven after it was created.[6] In SOEs and other public-sector organizations in China, it is extremely difficult to demote or fire employees, especially those in senior positions. As a CI employee wryly observed: "Have you ever seen someone at our company get fired? No one in our company will be laid off unless it is national policy."[7] Instead of firing employees, SOE leadership will typically transfer or demote employees, wait until they retire, or attempt to get them to quit on their own by curtailing their authority or promotion opportunities. As another CI employee explained: "People don't really get fired. If the leaders think your ability is inadequate, they will give you a simple job. Or if the leaders really want to fire you, they

[4] Moreover, Sino-Engineering accounted for a much smaller portion of the company's overall international business. In 2015, Sino-Engineering International signed twelve new contracts for overseas projects, with a total contract value of approximately USD 5 billion, far less than Sino-Construction International's 115 new contracts for overseas projects, with a total contract value of approximately USD 11 billion. Company document, 2016.

[5] Liu appointed Du Zhigang, State Grid's chief economist, as chairman and Sun Jinping, the former director of State Grid's International Cooperation Department, as general manager.

[6] Conversation with CI International employee, 2016.

[7] Conversation with CI International employee, 2016.

will talk to you and get you to quit yourself."[8] Internal backlash and limited capacity to terminate employees thus constrain but do not eliminate leaders' ability to conduct personnel ploys.

Material and Status Gains

Leaders also attempt to execute their agendas by emphasizing material and status gains for their organizations and subordinates.[9] In Chinese SOEs, material gains refer primarily to accomplishments related to performance metrics, such as revenue, profitability, and asset growth. Status gains occur when a company moves up in domestic or international rankings such as the *Fortune Global 500*. Another important type of status gain occurs when administrative superiors designate particular organizations or even individual employees as models, or award them prizes for their achievements. Linking one's leadership with organizational status gains can increase subordinates' deference because the subordinates' own status is linked with that of the organization (Pearce, 2011). Material and status gains can also amplify subordinate support by highlighting the progress already achieved during a leader's tenure, thereby suggesting that subordinate allegiance and efforts will earn future rewards.

Both CI chairmen emphasized material and status gains. In addition to touting the company's performance achievements during their respective tenures, each chairman vowed that his decisions regarding organizational strategy and structure would yield future prosperity. For example, Chairman Chen promised that his new strategy for CI's development would produce a "surge effect" (井喷式的效应) as the adjusted production relations would release productive forces.[10] He also noted that SASAC had awarded CI the "Outstanding Enterprise Performance Prize" and annual "A grade" evaluations under his leadership.[11] Similarly, Chairman Wu stressed CI's rapid rise in the *Fortune Global*

8 Conversation with CI International employee (former Sino-Engineering employee), 2016.

9 Status refers to an individual's standing in a particular group or society (Pearce, 2011).

10 Speech by Chairman Chen at the Sino-Construction International 2013 work meeting and the annual meeting of employee representatives, February 2013.

11 Speech by Chairman Chen at CI's 2014 work meeting, February 2014. In addition to the "Outstanding Enterprise Performance Prize" (业绩优秀企业奖),

500 rankings during his leadership. The company jumped sixty ranks the year that Chairman Wu took the helm, and again fifty more ranks the following year. In the opening sentence of a speech to employees, he emphasized these status gains as evidence of its "remarkable production and operation results" and CI's "steadily rising global influence" under his command.[12]

Growing employee estrangement in SOEs today may weaken the persuasive effects of organizational status gains. Such alienation from work occurs when subordinates experience work as totally separate from the rest of their lives (Sarros et al., 2002: 286). During the Mao era, work alienation was relatively low; SOEs provided workers with lifetime employment and welfare, social solidarity, and a stable, recognized status (Lü and Perry, 1997). Organizational attachments were neither transactional nor based on individual material incentives. Instead, they were a kind of "moral contract" characterized by workers' loyalty to their superiors and to the work unit. As Child and Warner (2003: 34) describe: "In traditional SOEs, the culture has been one of top-down leadership and authority, collectivism and mutual dependence, with an emphasis on conformity and attachment to the organization based on moral rather than material incentives."

In contrast, many SOE employees now have a more conditional, commercialized, and transactional relationship with their employers and the ruling CCP. As a CI employee explained: "Now Sino-Construction International is not a work unit. It is only a company. I contribute my time and work and I receive a salary – this is the deal."[13] Individual material benefits – salaries, bonuses, and fringe benefits – are of greater concern to many employees than overall gains in organizational status.[14] When I asked a CI employee privately what

other special prizes that SASAC awards to central SOEs are the "Technology and Innovation Enterprise Prize" (科技创新企业奖), the "Managerial Advances Enterprise Prize" (管理进步企业奖), and the "Outstanding Energy Savings and Emissions Reductions Enterprise Prize" (节能减排优秀企业奖) (SASAC, 2009).

12 Speech by Chairman Wu reviewing the company's work in 2016, January 2017.

13 Conversation with Sino-Construction International employee, 2015.

14 Sino-Construction International employees continued to receive many fringe benefits in addition to their salaries, including company-issued work uniforms, shoes, and ties (for men), dry cleaning credits, cell phone credits, bookstore gift cards, movie theater gift cards, union-issued credits to purchase vegetables, and

motivated his efforts to achieve the company's annual targets, he answered: "Both my individual interest and our departmental pride. But mostly my individual interest."[15] For today's SOE employees, there is a growing disjuncture between their feeling of belonging to a group working toward a common end and the commodification of individual capacities for private gain (Sabel and Stark, 1982: 444). Since SOEs no longer directly control the allocation of housing, healthcare, education, and ration coupons for basic staples, employees are less dependent on their employers. They thus have greater space to resist implementing their leaders' agendas.

External Threats

Leaders also invoke external threats to mobilize subordinate support. This benefits leaders because it promotes internal unity and raises the costs of opposition and foot-dragging.[16] As Mulder and Stemerding (1963: 317) find: "Small groups and larger organizations, even nations, 'close the ranks' in threatening situations and accept strong, dominant leadership, concentrated to a high degree in the hands of one man. Leaders who hope to gain more power than they already have make use of this 'fact' by calling the attention of their followers to large, imminent threats." External threats may be economic, political, or social in nature and either domestic or international in orientation. For example, CI chairmen frequently emphasized rising competition, declining demand, and economic slowdown in domestic and overseas markets as serious threats demanding concerted action. Some employees agreed that external threats made it imperative that they work to implement their leaders' agendas – even if this meant reduced professional opportunities for some and the dislocating effects of change for all. For example, a CI employee described why he supported Chairman Wu's contentious creation of CI International: "If our company does not undertake these changes and become better positioned in overseas

a gift box of meats for the Chinese New Year holiday. The company's cafeteria also provided three subsidized meals a day – breakfast, lunch, and dinner – ranging in cost from approximately USD 1.00 to USD 3.50 as of 2016.

15 Conversation with Sino-Construction International employee, 2014.

16 National leaders similarly invoke real or perceived international threats to mobilize domestic resources and support for particular political or economic agendas (Christensen, 1996; Zhu, 2002).

markets, then other [Chinese] companies will do so and our company will lose this historical opportunity."[17]

However, leaders' ability to invoke external threats depends on how subordinates perceive their relevance and immediacy. For example, a SOE leader's emphasis on rising competition in international markets may seem like a distant worry to employees in a human resources department. In contrast, this threat would be of pressing concern to marketing department employees whose bonuses and job security are tied directly to the achievement of business targets. Invoking external threats may also be less effective to mobilize junior employees because any failure to respond on their part is ultimately their superiors' responsibility. For this tactic to work, leaders must tailor threats so that their subordinates perceive them to be urgent and relevant.

Superiors' Directives and Policies

Leaders of SOEs may also underscore directives from administrative superiors and existing policies to advance their agendas. Extending the logic of orders from a superior in a military context, leaders stress the upward chain of command to induce subordinate compliance. This also functions to reduce leaders' individual accountability and mitigate any perception that they are pursuing individual interests (Van Verseveld, 2016). This tactic is effective because the superiors' authority typically exceeds that of any potential opposing entities within an organization, thereby increasing the costs of resistance. Moreover, since subordinates often lack information about their leaders' communications with administrative superiors, this information asymmetry creates an opportunity for the leaders to selectively frame directives and policies in ways that support their own agendas (Smith, 1997).

Leaders may use their superiors' directives and existing policies in two ways. First, they may cite superiors' mandates in broad terms to bolster their authority and quell potential resistance. For example, Chairman Chen emphasized that the merger in the early 2010s to create CI was a decision made by SASAC and the State Council. He urged subordinates to:

[17] Conversation with CI International employee (former holding-company employee), 2016.

Guarantee completion of the task assigned to the organization and resolutely implement the overall requirements of SASAC's Party committee for participant companies during the reorganization period: "no chaos in thinking, no disruption in production, no dispersal of the team, no loss of state assets, and protection of corporate and social stability."[18]

Second, leaders may argue that their decisions regarding organizational strategy or structure are advisable because they will advance existing policies. In this way, they can promote their own agendas by "wrapping" them with policy images and rhetoric (Raines and Prakash, 2005). Chairman Wu, for example, contended that his strategy for CI of "planning and design comes first, technology leads" and the associated practice of directly drafting development plans for foreign governments was advancing the BRI – even though there was no obvious direct link between the two. For example, CI's 2016 Work Plan claimed that the company would "on the basis of deeply researching and closely following 'One Belt One Road' [BRI] implement international industrial capacity cooperation and other national strategies ... [and] continue to actively participate in other countries' development planning and research."[19] This practice is neither a mere repetition of the official line nor an attempt to change the substance of existing policies. Instead, it shows how public-sector leaders in China can simultaneously be subject to state authority while also strategically appropriating state authority to minimize opposition and mobilize support within their organizations.[20]

However, emphasizing the directives and existing policies of administrative superiors still cannot eliminate implementation challenges. For example, while CI employees recognized that SASAC mandated the merger that created CI in the early 2010s, this did not remove what they perceived to be its negative effects on their daily lives and future careers. One employee, for example, expressed her frustration at having had to work in four different departments during a two-year span and experiencing stalled professional advancement after the merger.

18 Speech by Chairman Chen at Sino-Construction International's 2011 meeting on operations and management work, April 2011.

19 Company document, 2016.

20 Weldes (1996) similarly highlights the crucial role of elite manipulation by showing how elite-generated associative chains combine to produce contextually specific and contingent representations of the world.

"In theory, we are supposed to move up one level every year," she explained, "but I have been at the company for five years and my level has not changed."[21]

Appeals to Personal Duty and Morality

Leaders may also appeal to personal duty and morality to garner subordinate support and to execute their agendas.[22] Leaders may stress personal duty or provide moral encouragement in formal speeches and in informal "heart-to-heart" conversations with groups or individuals (Granrose et al., 2000: 488). Moral appeals enhance subordinates' sense of self-worth and personal commitment by connecting their self-concept and individual behavior with the realization of important shared values (Meier and O'Toole, 2006; Shamir, House, and Arthur, 1993). Moral appeals resonate most strongly when these values align closely with subordinates' self-image, for example as professionals, organization members, or citizens (Yukl and Gardner, 2019). Such "values work" articulates what is right or wrong, good or bad, in the operation and design of an organization (Raynard et al., 2020). Appealing to personal duty and morality may be especially effective if a leader's proposed actions contradict their subordinates' material or ideological interests. By shaping perceptions of appropriateness, leaders can generate subordinate support as well as positive evaluations of credibility and moral legitimacy (Raynard et al., 2020; Suchman, 1995).

In CI, leaders' appeals to personal duty and morality included but also exceeded standard Party slogans about individual integrity. For example, following the creation of CI, Chairman Chen urged employees to prioritize the new company's interests, irrespective of any organizational changes. He told them:

> People have self-awareness, and with self-awareness it is possible to be rational and equitable when judging gains and losses, to avoid being impetuous and irrationally feeling underappreciated, and to rationally and

[21] Conversation with Sino-Construction International employee, 2014.

[22] In contrast to Weber's claim that the rationalization and routinization of behavior in organizations constrain and ultimately negate such "meaning-making" by charismatic leaders, others argue that the leader's importance as a source of organizational values in fact facilitates coordination and efficiency in modern organizations (Polodny, Khurana, and Hill-Popper, 2004; Weber, 1998 [1946]).

pragmatically face change. I believe that most comrades have this type of basic quality – and also they should have this type of quality.[23]

In a similar vein, Chairman Wu called upon employees to cultivate a mindset of personal striving – an "attitude of always being on the way" (永远在路上的心态) – and to create an environment of positive public discourse for the company's reform and development.[24]

Yet the changing relationship between Chinese SOEs and their employees means that personal considerations and material interests also affect employee thinking and behavior. Balancing company and individual interests can create acute dilemmas. In CI, for example, not all personnel were willing to spend years or even decades of their lives being transferred at their employer's will or working in faraway locales. In CI, one employee resigned within weeks of being assigned to a project in central Africa because he was not willing to spend the next several years apart from his spouse and soon-to-be-born child.[25] It is also becoming increasingly common for SOE employees and officials who work "within the system" (体制内) to choose to leave it entirely.

Risk and Efficacy of Leader Tactics

Leader tactics vary in terms of their risk and efficacy. Personnel ploys involve the greatest risk but are also potentially the most effective. Placing an ally in an influential position immediately extends the leader's control, but it risks subordinate backlash if the appointee is unqualified or lacks the internal networks to secure compliance. Other tactics, such as stressing external threats and underscoring superiors' directives and policies, are less risky for leaders but also potentially less effective. Subordinates are less likely to perceive these tactics as manipulation or to blame their leaders for failures, because they recognize that these factors are largely beyond a leader's control. However, leaders risk subordinate skepticism or fatigue if external threats lack credibility or if they overemphasize superiors' directives and policies. Leader appeals to personal duty and morality can be effective and

23 Speech by Chairman Chen at Sino-Construction International meeting for all headquarters employees, December 2011.
24 Speech by Chairman Wu at CI's 2017 work meeting, January 2017.
25 Sino-Construction International employee, 2014.

relatively low-risk; however, their efficacy ultimately depends on how much subordinates identify with and feel obligated to the organization.

Firm-specific factors, such as industry type and degree of internationalization, also affect tactic efficacy. For example, although SOE leaders in all sectors commonly promote their agendas using emotive language of personal duty and morality, those in strategic industries may be better positioned than their counterparts in commercial sectors to make such appeals. Conversely, heads of SOEs in nonstrategic industries that are subject to less state control – and enjoy less state support – can more credibly and effectively stress external threats, such as rising competition or market slowdowns. The same is true for SOE leaders whose firms have more international business and are therefore more vulnerable to foreign competition and market fluctuations.

Subordinate Responses

Support

Supporting a leader's agenda is the most common response by subordinates in Chinese SOEs and other public-sector organizations. Subordinates interpret their leaders' decisions about organizational strategy and structure from the vantage point of their own positions and interests. If they perceive implementation will have a minimal or gradual impact, they are likely to support such decisions and continue with "business as usual." For example, a SOE employee responsible for facilities management may not have strong preferences about a leader's decision regarding whether to prioritize domestic or international market expansion. Conversely, if employees perceive that their leaders' agenda might strongly and/or immediately benefit them, they will intensify their support. Since resistance is always riskier, subordinates are more likely to respond with support unless or until they are personally affected.

Employees of SOEs support their leaders in varied ways. Rhetorically, subordinates express support by either publicly or privately praising the leader and their choices about organizational strategy and structure. In practical terms, subordinates show support through their implementation efforts. Walder (1983: 65) describes two types of supporters in Chinese SOEs: "activists" (积极分子) and "backbones" (骨干分子). Activists are typically younger, more ambitious employees who display support for the leader by praising them and acting to implement their agenda. Backbones are older, more experienced employees who serve a leader and their agenda, albeit less vocally and with less individual ambition (Walder, 1983: 66–67). Both types of supporters can be found in Chinese SOEs today.

Resistance

Workers across China engage in various forms of resistance. Strikes, mass protests, and even suicides elicit either repression or responsiveness from employers and the government (Elfstrom, 2019, 2021; Frazier, 2010). However, workers may also exercise agency in numerous ways short of direct confrontation. They might use classic "weapons of the weak," such as foot-dragging, noncompliance, feigned ignorance, or slander (Scott, 2008 [1987]). Through grumbling, cursing, making jokes, sharing rumors, and other forms of critical face-to-face or online expression, employees can carve out oppositional space with like-minded colleagues to build solidarity and to resist a leader's agenda (Johnston and Mueller, 2001; Li, 2012). When individuals feel a sense of group identity, even if the group is informal, they are more likely to resist (Cartwright, 1965). Practices such as proposing alternatives when leaders seek feedback or reading the newspaper at one's desk instead of working to signify dissatisfaction can reshape existing rules and norms, especially when many individuals engage in them (Bayat, 2013). Examining SOE employees' responses to leaders' tactics reveals multiple types of potential resistance through either rhetoric or action.

Expression of Alternative Views

Subordinates interpret their leaders' decisions about organizational strategy and structure from the perspective of their own positions and interests. As a former CI employee described this process: "I begin by thinking about the leader's strategy, the logic it represents, and how this framework is related to the content of my work."[26] Such interpretation is itself an act of agency because it involves subordinates thinking about how they can interpret their leaders' agendas

[26] Conversation with former CI International employee, 2018.

to advance their own interests. At the same time, however, employees expressed that a leader's decisions about organizational strategy and structure create clear parameters for discussion and action. As the same individual stated: "It would be stupid to blindly oppose the leader. It is like in the military – is there any room for open disagreement there?"[27] Subordinate interpretations of the leader's agenda are especially important when a new leader assumes office. As a CI employee explained: "In China when a new leader arrives, he might have totally different ideas. ... It is important to see what the leader wants to do."[28]

Subordinates can choose whether to express alternative views about a leader's decisions or their implementation. This means of upward influence relies on rational persuasion: the use of logical arguments and facts to persuade the leader that the proposed alternative is feasible and consistent with shared objectives (Yukl and Tracey, 1992). As Prasad and Prasad (2000: 389) explain, expressing alternative views can itself be a form of resistance: "Specific actions and events occurring in organizations may hold oppositional connotations for certain local actors. When these actors vocalize these oppositional meanings (in a wide spectrum of private and public domains), they discursively constitute routine resistance." In SOEs, subordinates can express alternative views orally during one-on-one conversations with leaders, group discussions with senior staff, or meetings with other employees. They can also do this in writing via private correspondence or formal reporting. Leeway for subordinates to express alternatives is greater when multiple possible choices are on the table, because this creates more room for input and adjustment. By framing different approaches as part of a collective brainstorming process aimed at advancing shared objectives, subordinates can subtly reorient, if not redirect, their leaders' agendas.

Delay or Subversion

Subordinates may also delay or subvert the implementation of a leader's agenda. This response is more likely if subordinates perceive that a leader's decisions will harm their interests or disrupt a status quo from

[27] Conversation with former CI International employee, 2018.
[28] Conversation with Sino-Construction International employee, 2015.

which they benefit. As Guth and MacMillan (1986: 319–20) describe: "Middle managers who feel that their goals are compromised can not only redirect the strategy, delay implementation or reduce the quality of implementation, but they could also even totally sabotage the strategy." Subordinates may justify postponing implementation by arguing that timing or conditions are not yet right. This frames inaction positively by characterizing the leader's strategic or organizational choices as "too advanced" for the current situation. Or subordinates may subvert implementation by broadly adhering to the leader's agenda while simultaneously tailoring its specifics to their departmental or individual interests. As an employee at CGN explained: "Sometimes the leader's strategy is quite general, so when one gets to the middle of the implementation stage, things can shift. For example, when we have meetings at the departmental level, the strategy can be changed a bit."[29]

Subordinates may also exploit internal differences of opinion as political cover for delays or subversion. As the same CGN employee described: "In our company there was an overseas project that the chairman thought one thing about and the general manager thought another. So one way to resist was to play those internal differences off of one another by picking the person whose view you agree with most and then citing their view to support your own position."[30] Citing others' viewpoints is especially effective when individuals whose views differ from those of the leader enjoy strong backing within the organization. Rhetorical approaches are more common in the Chinese context than "end-running," whereby a resistor appeals directly and usually covertly to higher bosses to circumvent a leader's direction (Carr and Brower, 2000: 114). This is because insubordination carries high costs in China and few communication channels exist for subordinates to reach a leader's superiors.

Shirking

Shirking, specifically dissent-shirking, is another way that subordinates may react to their leaders' decisions about organizational strategy and structure.[31] Dissent-shirking entails abstaining from work due to disagreement with a particular decision. It differs from leisure-shirking,

[29] Interview with CGN employee, Beijing, June 2018.
[30] Interview with CGN employee, Beijing, June 2018.
[31] The Chinese term for shirking in SOEs is "not acting" (不作为).

which involves not working due to a lack of motivation or desire (Brehm and Gates, 1999: 30). Shirking encompasses various behaviors including foot-dragging, deliberate inefficiency, evasion or dereliction of assigned duties, false compliance, and absenteeism. A common theme among these is the withholding of physical effort, cooperation, and/or psychological commitment from the organization (Carr and Brower, 2000). Shirked labor may be consumed as leisure or deployed through part-time work in the private sector (Ghosh and Whalley, 2008).

Chinese SOE employees express disapproval by dissent-shirking. Resisting in this way is less risky than individual confrontation or collective action. For example, after CI's internal restructuring to create CI International, I observed a junior employee spending at least one hour mid-afternoon each workday reading a paper copy of *The Beijing News*, fully fanned out on his desk, a behavior I had not witnessed previously. Several months later, he quit CI and took a job at another central SOE in the same industry. He expressed his dissatisfaction with Chairman Wu's decisions about organizational structure by deliberately withholding his labor and engaging in nonproductive activities.

Critical Expression

Subordinates also respond through critical expression. Few avenues exist for SOE employees to challenge leaders directly; those who attempt to do so will likely be reassigned or dismissed. Gossiping or complaining among trusted peers is an important way to exchange information, express dissatisfaction, reduce individual pressure and anxiety, and create solidarity. As a form of resistance, critical expression may involve a pointed retelling of events or observations about people and conditions that highlight perceived affronts or injustices (Sotirin and Gottfried, 1999: 58). Even innocuous jokes or nostalgic talk about "the good old days" are safe ways for subordinates to voice disenchantment with their leaders' decisions (Hafen, 2004: 232–33).

In CI, subordinates frequently engaged in face-to-face critical expression. Critical expression occurred most often during in-person exchanges over lunch in the company cafeteria. Although department employees typically ate together, informal mixing with coworkers from other departments and with higher-ranking colleagues was also routine. The midday break also offered non-napping employees additional opportunities to gossip and complain, especially while chatting during walks inside the office building, taking breaks to smoke cigarettes in the stairwells or outside, or strolling in the surrounding residential areas.

Subordinates may also express critical views virtually. At CI, employees used the Chinese instant messaging program QQ to communicate and coordinate work activities. The ping of an incoming message could be heard frequently throughout the workday as employees chatted on QQ accounts with light-hearted status messages in Chinese and English like "Young For You!" and "Let your dreams fly!"[32] When employees used QQ to complain, they most commonly used it as a private medium to vent with colleagues in one-on-one chats. Virtual criticism of their leaders' decisions about organizational strategy and structure occasionally, albeit rarely, spilled over into work team-wide or department-wide group QQ chats. For example, in a department-wide group QQ chat in January 2015, a Sino-Construction International employee wrote sardonically:

> The leadership of CI and how CI is managed are things that are pretty far away from us and we do not really understand what happens there. If you are good at speaking, you can go to the discussion meeting [about plans for forthcoming restructuring] and make a speech, and then you may be promoted to the holding company.

The department head responded in the same group QQ chat: "Establishing regional bureaus [an internal consolidation that preceded creation of CI International] means having yet another mother-in-law, and work efficiency will be lower."[33] Online conversations such as this one provide subordinates in Chinese SOEs with another important means for critical expression.

Quitting

Quitting is the final way in which subordinates can respond to their leaders' tactics. Professional exodus is a strong form of resistance for those who refuse to implement or abide by a leader's decisions. Resignation from Chinese SOEs, as elsewhere, is typically a private, personal matter between employee and employer. Indeed, many exit

[32] Sino-Construction International employee QQ account individual status messages, 2014.
[33] Sino-Construction International, department QQ conversation, 2015.

quietly without openly expressing criticism or dissatisfaction. However, some treat quitting as a statement of defiance and voice their reasons for resignation in the hope it will "send a message" to the leaders or motivate colleagues to follow suit (Lutgen-Sandvik, 2006: 415). When employee turnover is significant, subordinates can cite their colleagues' resignations as proof of valid grievances.

Employee resignations in SOEs remain rare, but they are becoming more common. The popular term "iron rice bowl" (铁饭碗) expresses the Mao-era promise of lifetime work and welfare. Today, however, waves of employee attrition routinely follow major restructuring events.[34] In some cases, a leader's decisions may immediately affect subordinates' material interests and daily work, thereby prompting them to resign. In other cases, subordinates may choose to leave because they perceive fewer avenues for professional advancement. This may occur, for example, when a leader's personnel ploys place a new boss in a department or when subordinates are unconvinced by a leader's appeals to personal duty and morality. Although resignations remain rare, it is becoming increasingly common for Chinese officials and SOE employees to quit and enter the private sector (Li, 2019).[35]

Risk and Efficacy of Subordinate Responses

Subordinate responses differ in terms of both risk and effectiveness. Delaying or subverting implementation is most effective, but it is also the riskiest. Expressing alternative views is less risky because it does not involve action, but it may still be perilous because an individual's opposition to a leader's agenda can be singled out. Such risks are lower if subordinates frame alternative views as providing help to the leader, or if the leader themself solicits alternative views. Expressing alternative views can be effective for subordinates if a leader adopts their ideas. Shirking and complaining are also less risky – especially if shirking is unrelated to a leader's agenda and if complaining is done

[34] Examples of major restructuring events include a merger of two firms, internal consolidation of multiple departments in an existing enterprise, or major reallocations of assets, capital, and personnel within a state-owned enterprise group.

[35] Jobs "within the system" (体制内) also include positions in other public-sector organizations such as government bodies, Party organs, research institutes, and universities.

privately. Both can be moderately effective if shirking affects implementation or if complaining builds oppositional solidarity. Quitting poses relatively few risks for subordinates, but its larger effects are limited. Supporting and implementing a leader's agenda is clearly the least risky of possible subordinate responses.

Employee resistance within SOEs has real-world effects despite its limited scope. Aggregate employee behavior may affect organization-level outcomes, even if the consequences of individual action are circumscribed. Resistance through delay or subversion, shirking, or attrition may directly impede the implementation of a leader's agenda. It can also generate dysfunction and costs that harm company operations and performance. For example, after Chairman Wu's creation of CI International, employees pushed back against his personnel ploys. Describing the situation after the restructuring as "a chaotic situation" (混乱的局面), an employee stated:

> The earlier assessment criteria were very clear. There were three areas of assessment: work experience, overseas experience, and professional qualifications. A division-level (处级) position required at least three years of overseas experience. ... Now people are being appointed to leadership positions from outside the departments, but they do not meet the requirements. This makes people in the departments feel that they cannot find expression for their abilities and it often causes people to quit their jobs.[36]

In this case, employee complaints, shirking, and resignations resulted in a loss of morale, workplace tension, inefficient communication, miscommunication, and staffing changes – all contributing to longer project time frames and increased costs.

An Integrated Framework of Leader–Subordinate Dynamics

Chinese SOE leaders' tactics are grounded in multiple bases of power: legitimate power, reward power, and coercion power. Legitimate power is activated when leaders reference formal hierarchies and social norms requiring subordinates to comply with their superiors (French and Raven, 1959). Both subordinates and leaders act according to "role prescriptions" based on their positions in the existing power structure (Raven, 1965: 375). Legitimation is achieved when

[36] Conversation with CI International employee (former Sino-Construction International employee), 2016.

subordinates accept and internalize the leader's right to require them to implement and comply with decisions (Raven, 2008). This is an implicit mutual understanding rather than an explicit formal contract (Yukl and Gardner, 2019). Legitimate power helps leaders obtain the assistance, cooperation, and information necessary to implement their agendas (Yukl and Falbe, 1991). Tactics such as leveraging position authority, emphasizing administrative superiors' directives and policies, and appealing to personal duty and morality involve legitimation because they stress a leader's rights and their subordinates' obligations.

Reward power exists when leaders pledge or provide positive incentives, either tangible or intangible, to induce subordinate compliance. Leaders can often review and modify reward decisions made at lower levels (Yukl and Gardner, 2019). When an individual's degree of organized dependence on their employer is relatively high, as in the case of Chinese SOEs, leaders can control the allocation of a wide variety of rewards (Walder, 1983). Tangible rewards might include bonuses, promotion opportunities, salary increases, opportunities to change one's household registration (户口) to a more desirable locality, or obtaining better office space.[37] Intangible rewards can include public praise, personal approval from superiors, model employee designations, or perceived fulfillment of one's patriotic duties. Tactics such as personnel ploys and emphasis on material and status gains are grounded in reward power. Leaders' appeals to personal duty and morality also involve reward power because they confer the intangible benefit of "doing the right thing."

Coercion power manifests when a leader threatens their subordinates with negative, undesirable consequences if they do not comply. Threats may be either specific or ambiguous (Yukl and Gardner, 2019). The strength of coercion power varies with the magnitude of the threatened punishment and subordinates' perceived probability of avoiding punishment by conforming (French and Raven, 1959). For intimidation to be effective, a leader must show subordinates that they have coercive ability and are willing to assume the costs of using it (Raven, 1992). Leaders of SOEs can coerce subordinates in varied ways, including public criticism, reduced work responsibilities,

[37] China's household registration system, known as *hukou*, is a hereditary, mostly nontransferable identity document that classifies individuals as local citizens in a specific city or county. Access to government services such as education and pensions is restricted to an individual's place of registration (Vortherms, 2019).

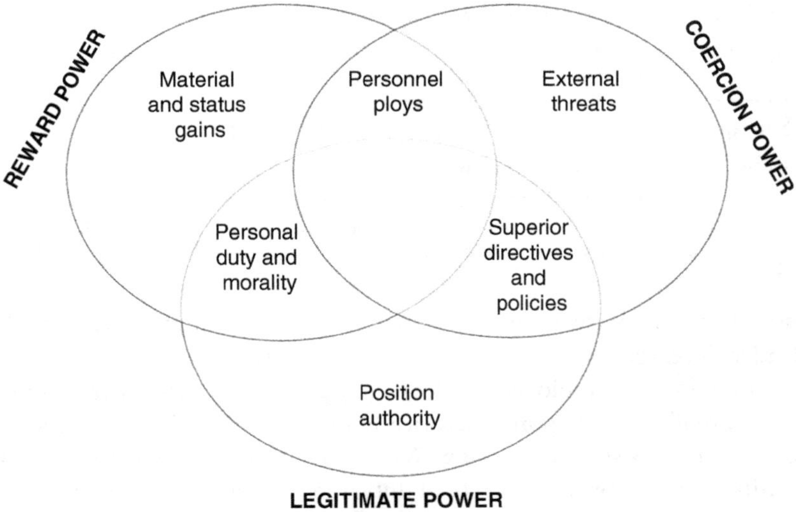

Figure 6.1 Chinese SOE leader tactics and power bases
Source: Author.

allocation of less desirable projects, compensation cuts, professional title changes, sidelining for promotion, transfers, demotions, investigations, or even dismissals (Prakash, 2000: 29). Tactics such as invoking external threats or emphasizing superiors' directives and policies force subordinate compliance with a leader's preferred agenda. Figure 6.1 summarizes how Chinese SOE leader tactics are grounded in legitimate, reward, and coercion power.

As subordinates respond to the leader's tactics, they may eclectically combine rhetoric with action and support with resistance. For example, a subordinate may publicly praise a leader's decisions about organizational strategy and structure, while concomitantly delaying or subverting implementation. Conversely, a subordinate may engage in critical expression while simultaneously acting to implement a leader's agenda. Subordinates may also shift between different response types and orientations. For instance, a SOE employee might initially support a leader's agenda with rhetoric and action, then later move to resist it with words and deeds, or vice versa. Table 6.1 summarizes subordinate responses by type and orientation.

Although introduced separately for clarity, in practice leader tactics interact with subordinate responses. Put simply, which tactics a leader

Table 6.1 *Subordinate responses, by type and orientation*

	Rhetoric	Action
Support	• Praise	• Implement
Resist	• Alternative views • Critical expression	• Shirk • Delay/subvert • Quit

uses affects how their subordinates respond. For example, when SOE leaders leverage position authority or cite their superiors' directives and existing policies, employees are less likely to resist overtly. Instead, they are more likely to respond rhetorically by expressing alternative views or with actions such as shirking. When leaders emphasize material and status gains or appeal to personal duty and morality, they might deliberately include organizational and individual targets to disincentivize resistance. In such cases, subordinates will likely eschew visible, quantifiable forms of resistance, such as shirking and implementation delay or subversion, and instead respond rhetorically or even quit.

Conversely, subordinate responses – and a leader's expectations about them – may also affect the leader's tactics. If subordinates directly counter a leader's agenda by criticizing it or by delaying or subverting implementation, the leader is more likely to react with tactics grounded in coercive and legitimate power. For example, a leader can raise the costs of resistance by emphasizing superiors' directives and policies, thereby linking their agenda with the authority of higher-ranked third parties. A leader may also exercise coercion power by replacing resistors or by installing allies with personnel ploys. In contrast, a leader is more likely to react to rhetorical resistance by subordinates with tactics grounded in rewards and legitimate power, such as emphasizing gains and appealing to personal duty and morality.

Leader tactics and subordinate responses are both interactive and iterative. The success or failure of any particular tactic may prompt the leader to reassess and adjust their tactics in the future. As Raven (2008: 9) explains: "The target may now be amenable to influence strategies that would not have worked the first time around or be more resistant to strategies that earlier might have been effective." Consider, for example, a leader's invocation of external threats. If either a threat or its implied negative consequences fail to materialize, this tactic will become less effective. A coercive tactic, regardless of its effectiveness, could incite subordinate hostility and consequently limit a leader's options in the future. Similarly, subordinates may adapt their responses to a leader's tactics. Perhaps the most obvious example is a SOE employee's decision to resign after other attempted responses fail. Interaction and iteration generate feedback effects through which leader–subordinate dynamics gradually evolve.

Comparing SOEs and Private Firms

The differences between SOEs and private firms give rise to disparate leader tactics with varying degrees of effectiveness. For instance, SOE leaders are more likely than private company executives to attempt to mobilize subordinate support by underscoring the directives and policies of superiors. This is logical because SOEs are embedded more deeply in the Chinese bureaucratic hierarchy than private firms. This tactic is also more effective in SOEs because employees understand that they are "within the system" and therefore more accountable to the state. For the same reason, SOE leaders' appeals to subordinates' personal duty and morality resonate more strongly than such appeals by their private-sector counterparts. Even though SOE employees today have a more conditional, commercialized, and transactional relationship with their employers, they nevertheless recognize that working for a SOE supports important nonmaterial objectives, such as national development under CCP leadership. As a CI employee described: "Even if being employed at a state-owned enterprise provided only a low salary, could not help to solve the *hukou* [household registration] issue, and was unstable, there would still be people willing to work there because of their belief in the Chinese Communist Party."[38] Private-sector employees in China may also demonstrate similar "corporate commitment," evident in a strong sense of loyalty and obligation to their companies and especially to the top executive (Useem, 2022).

Conversely, SOE leaders are less well-positioned to use other types of tactics compared to private-firm executives. For instance, SOE leaders are more limited in their ability to use material and status

[38] Conversation with CI International employee (former Sino-Engineering employee), 2016.

gains to incentivize their subordinates. Although SOE executives may emphasize improvements in company performance and rankings, their highly regimented wage systems prevent significant increases in individual compensation. Personnel ploys face constraints and scrutiny as well. This is because SOE leaders have less discretion over personnel appointments than do private-firm executives, especially for senior management positions. Xi's anti-corruption campaign and the recent policies of lifetime accountability for SOE leaders further augment scrutiny of their behavior. This has made SOE leaders cautious about using personnel ploys too frequently or appointing unqualified loyalists.

Guanxi plays a greater role in leader–subordinate dynamics in SOEs than it does in private firms. Regardless of a company's ownership type, *guanxi* may positively foster trust and loyalty between leaders and subordinates. At the same time, however, it may lead to subordinates perceiving inequities or prioritizing impression management (Han and Altman, 2009). *Guanxi* prevails in SOEs because SOE reward systems in general are comparatively more subjective (Walder, 1983). Although formal institutions of corporate governance, employee evaluation, and performance-based compensation all now exist in state firms, their functions are considerably different from those in private firms (Rosen, Leutert, and Guo, 2018). State ownership and a stronger collective identity among SOE employees disincentivize the development of market-centered, rule-based systems of individual exchange (Chen, 2020). As SOE leader tactics such as personnel ploys suggest, leader–subordinate dynamics in SOEs remain heavily relationship-based and personalistic despite decades of reform (Peng, 2003).

In private firms, *guanxi* is also prevalent but it is less influential in leader–subordinate dynamics. *Guanxi* may complement formal institutions in the private sector by coordinating economic and social exchanges (Horak and Restel, 2016). Externally, private companies rely on *guanxi* even more than SOEs to protect themselves when legal protections for private business are weak (Xin and Pearce, 1996). These coordinative and protective functions were particularly prominent during the early reform period (Guthrie, 1998). Inside private firms, however, leader–subordinate interactions exhibit a stronger market logic, characterized by the capitalization of human activities based on prices generated via competition. Reward allocations in the private sector thus center more on individual, market-oriented performance metrics applied universally to all employees regardless of *guanxi* (Pearce, Branyiczki, and Bigley, 2000). Such a "market pricing model" therefore reduces the importance of *guanxi* in leader–subordinate dynamics in the private sector (Chen, 2018).

Despite their differences, leader tactics in SOEs and private firms may become more similar in the future. Greater state intervention in the private sector under Xi is making it more difficult for some executives to prioritize profit-making and to incentivize subordinates using market-based reward systems. Some private business leaders are former SOE managers and they may borrow leader tactics from SOEs, either deliberately or unconsciously (Zhang, 2015). Conversely, Chinese SOE leaders face the increasingly acute paradox of fulfilling strategic functions for the state while simultaneously improving performance amid economic downturn at home and intensifying competition abroad. As organized dependence on SOEs wanes among the next generation of state-sector employees, pressure may grow for company leaders to increase the use of leader tactics involving rewards for subordinates. Executives themselves, however, will likely remain firmly embedded in the CCP's internal labor market and incentive structure.

Conclusion

This chapter has introduced an integrated framework of leader–subordinate dynamics in Chinese SOEs, linking leader tactics and subordinate responses. Grounded in legitimate, reward, and coercive bases of power, leader tactics include leveraging position authority, conducting personnel ploys, emphasizing material and status gains, invoking external threats, underscoring directives by superiors and existing policies, and appealing to personal duty and morality. Although subordinates usually support the leader's agenda, they may also resist it by raising alternative views, delay or subversion, shirking, critical expression, or even quitting. Multifaceted subordinate responses may combine rhetoric with action or blend support with resistance.

Leader tactics and subordinate responses are both interactive and iterative. Which tactics a leader uses affects how their subordinates respond. For instance, when a leader emphasizes administrative superiors' directives and existing policies, this limits their subordinates' space for direct opposition. Instead, subordinates will be more likely to respond rhetorically or to resist indirectly. If particular tactics fail to advance the leader's agenda, they will reassess and adjust them in the future. To overcome subordinate resistance, a leader might shift from tactics grounded in legitimate and reward power, such as invoking position authority or emphasizing gains, to more coercive measures, such as invoking external threats or emphasizing superiors' directives and policies. In this way, leader–subordinate dynamics can evolve over time.

Leaders of SOEs are better positioned to use some tactics than are private-firm executives. Appealing to personal duty and morality, for example, is more effective in SOEs. However, SOE leaders are less able to incentivize subordinates using material and status gains. Additionally, personnel ploys in state firms face growing scrutiny because of Xi's anti-corruption campaign and policies of lifetime accountability for SOE leaders. *Guanxi* matters more for SOE leader–subordinate dynamics, which remain strongly relationship-based and personalistic even today. In contrast, leader–subordinate interactions in private firms exhibit a stronger market logic, with reward allocations based more on individual, market-oriented performance metrics.

Overall, SOE leaders appear to be generally successful in implementing their agendas – albeit sometimes with a time lag and considerable costs. They have multiple tactics at their disposal to influence subordinates and secure their compliance. However, the execution process requires significant time and resources, especially if subordinates resist. If pushback is widespread and accumulates, it will impose real-world costs on SOE operations and performance, thereby exacerbating existing productivity and profitability challenges. As leaders' agendas evolve over time, they must continually mobilize internal support to carry them out, setting in motion repeated cycles of leader–subordinate interactions and execution efforts.

The SOE leader tactics and subordinate responses analyzed here are not exhaustive; further study is needed to identify other behaviors and the conditions under which they may occur. For example, SOE leaders may also alter budgets, create new internal communication mechanisms, or publicly shame employees as they endeavor to implement their respective agendas. Subordinates may respond in additional ways as well, such as falsifying information in internal reports or organizing strikes. More systematic analysis of leader tactics and subordinate responses might examine additional SOEs and other public-sector organizations in China to identify additional behaviors beyond those discussed here. For small-n studies, deeper investigations into intra-organizational politics, grounded in divergent organizational cultures, histories, and geographies, would further illuminate patterns of internal cooperation and conflict.

7 *Rethinking the Domestic Politics of Reform as SOE Leadership Goes Global*

"Feeling for the stones to cross the river" is a well-known metaphor for China's reform process. Those who view the state as the architect of reform might interpret this metaphor as describing an adaptive yet controlled process, one in which central authorities direct lower-level actors toward particular stones to reach the other side. However, it is the leaders of the public-sector organizations engaged in reform – at all levels – who choose when to proceed, which stones to grasp, or whether to swim somewhere else entirely. If the swimmers reach the opposite shore, they do so at varied places and times. The objective of traversing the river is fixed (state goals and policies), the placement of the stones is preexisting (geography and resource endowments), and there may be currents or other obstacles (institutional and external constraints). Yet the swimmers themselves matter just as much as these other factors in understanding how reform really occurs and what direction it takes.

The importance of leadership in China's public sector is self-evident to those who actually work in it. As a department head at the NDRC, a central-level economic planning agency, described the potential scope of leadership's effects: "A leader's way of thinking can influence an industry, a locality, even a country."[1] Many Chinese officials like him view the heads of public-sector organizations – from central-level government bodies such as the NDRC to ministries to SOEs to local planning commissions – as highly consequential in the bureaucratic settings where they operate. As Lampton (2013: 3) writes:

> Leadership in China is broader in scope than simply the small number of members of the Standing Committee of the Politburo who sit at the apex of the national power hierarchy. One of the most important changes in Chinese

[1] Interview with government official (National Resource and Development Commission), May 2016, Beijing.

society during the reform era has been the gradual enlargement of the scope and diversity of individuals who can reasonably be counted as leaders.

A leadership approach, this book argues, helps to explain the variation in reform outcomes in Chinese SOEs. Even in countries such as China where political authority is highly centralized, state designs do not automatically translate into particular reform responses and results. Leaders of public-sector organizations at all levels must interpret government goals and economic environments, often under conditions of significant uncertainty. They exercise leadership by making decisions about organizational strategy and structure and by attempting – sometimes unsuccessfully and with a significant time lag – to mobilize subordinates to carry them out. As Burns (1978: 298) puts it: "To the extent that bureaucracy is in practice the simple application of authority from the top down, it is not leadership. To the extent that it exemplifies conflict, power, values, and change in accordance with leader–follower needs, it embodies leadership." The operations of public-sector organizations in China, or anywhere else for that matter, rarely involve absolute control from above.

But the state does serve multiple important functions. State actors determine reform goals, design pilot programs, and designate models. They can also disseminate successful approaches by organizing meetings, arranging visits and exchanges among leaders, and featuring cases during official trainings or circulating them in internal publications. The state can facilitate the movement of people and information among organizations, especially those at different administrative levels or in disparate geographic locations, and it mediates these flows and the competition among actors. It is not an impartial referee that defines the criteria of success and then steps back and waits until the winners appear. Certain organizations and their leaders may gain disproportionate political and material support because of their personal connections or if their approaches accord with the policy agendas of particular political elites (Cai and Treisman, 2006). However, all heads of public-sector organizations possess some degree of bounded autonomy to exercise leadership, regardless of the nature of their individual ties to the state.

Despite its importance, leadership in China's public sector remains under-examined. Powerful national figures and more accessible local officials still draw the bulk of scholarly attention, while leaders of public-sector organizations remain largely hidden in closed and complex bureaucratic worlds. The ability of researchers to enter these organizations and observe those who work inside them, even for short periods of time, is crucial to differentiate between actors' behavior on the "front-stage" versus the "back-stage" of the Chinese state (Ding, 2022; Goffman, 1959). Opening up the black box of Chinese central SOEs reveals that much of the process and politics of reform plays out inside public-sector organizations. How does studying leadership and leader–subordinate dynamics contribute to a rethinking of the domestic politics of reform?

The Intra-organizational Politics of Reform

Studies of reform in post-socialist settings around the world emphasize its distributional consequences and power shifts involving elites, marginalized actors, and cross-class coalitions. Since the near-term material costs of reform may generate fierce resistance, economic liberalization may initially appear to require compensating, suppressing, or politically incorporating the "losers" (Frye and Mansfield, 2003; Milner and Kubota, 2005). Yet the "winners" too are capable of opposing or stalling reform if they benefit from the distortions in a partially reformed economy (Hellman, 1998; Przeworski, 1991). Conversely, when coalitions emerge between governments and domestic economic interest groups, the implementation of market-oriented reforms becomes more likely (Skålnes, 2016). Other domestic determinants of reform outcomes include crises, dependence on foreign capital, competitive signaling and global status aspirations of reform proponents, and particular liberalizing policies pursued (Appel and Orenstein, 2018; Brooks and Kurtz, 2007; Lin and Katada, 2022; Vachudová, 2005).

Another influential perspective on the politics of reform stresses the institutional dynamics of bargaining and competition at the subnational level. In this view, fragmented authority at and below the central level motivates officials to negotiate over resources and forge deals to execute major projects (Lieberthal and Lampton, 1992). Decentralized competition among local officials for economic resources (and associated opportunities to gain rents) generates buy-in for central reforms (Shirk, 1993). "Tournament competition" among local officials to deliver economic growth – and subsequently to advance politically because of it – functions to align bureaucratic interests (Li and Zhou,

2005; Zhou, 2018). Without such incentives, subnational actors may be more likely to favor particularistic policies that undermine national reform efforts (Remmer and Wibbels, 2000).[2]

Although much of the analysis of reform invariably involves public-sector organizations, their leaders and internal politics are rarely studied. An obvious reason is simply a lack of access. It is very difficult to gain direct, repeated entry to public-sector organizations or to gather data about their internal functioning because these are official bodies with operations involving restricted and in some cases even classified information.[3] Although the obstacles to access are greatest in authoritarian states like China, they exist even in democratic countries with greater transparency and established mechanisms for the disclosure of public information. The closed nature of public-sector organizations thus often renders their leaders and what happens inside them invisible to the outside.

By going inside Chinese central SOEs, this book reveals what I term the "intra-organizational politics of reform": the daily dynamics of cooperation and conflict between leaders and their subordinates inside public-sector organizations. As this book has shown, leaders can shape reform outcomes by deciding whether to maintain or modify organizational strategies and structures, and by attempting to influence subordinates to do the same. As Morgan (1993: 156) observes: "An organization's politics is most clearly manifest in the conflicts and power plays that sometimes occupy center stage … More fundamentally, however, politics occurs on an ongoing basis, often in a way that is unobservable to all but those directly involved." What happens inside SOEs and other public-sector organizations constitutes the everyday substance of reform and shapes its ultimate course.

The intra-organizational politics of reform range from cooperative to conflictual. As the integrated framework of leader–subordinate dynamics in Chinese SOEs in Chapter 6 makes clear, leaders can draw

[2] For example, local officials may resist the privatization of local SOEs, budget cuts, or other reform policies that might negatively affect their short-term economic and political interests, despite the potential for long-term collective gain (Remmer and Wibbels, 2000: 422).

[3] Only a handful of scholars have gained access to public-sector organizations in China, and almost all have been market rather than government or CCP organizations. See, for example, Battat (1986), Ding (2022), Hanser (2008), Lee (1998), and Zhang (2014).

from a menu of tactics to execute their agendas. These tactics include leveraging position authority, personnel ploys, emphasizing material and status gains, invoking external threats, underscoring directives and policies of administrative superiors, and appealing to personal duty and morality. Subordinates may react in ways ranging from support to resistance to criticism and to exit. Which tactics a leader ultimately uses will affect how their subordinates respond and vice versa.

This book's study of the intra-organizational politics of reform makes several contributions to a rethinking of the domestic politics of reform in China and beyond. First, it extends efforts to disaggregate the state – and public-sector organizations, in particular – to uncover multiple, diverse actors. Each of these actors has its own distinctive strategies and interests (Tan, 2021). The difficulty or even impossibility of accessing public-sector organizations might make treating them as unitary actors the only practical option. This approach may also be analytically tempting because it facilitates broader generalizations about "SOEs" or "ministries" or "provincial governments." However, such aggregation risks obscuring the internal politics that generate important variation in structure, behavior, and outcomes. Opening up public-sector organizations illuminates a diverse cast of internal actors: leaders and their subordinates, as well as other entities such as SOE subsidiaries or local government departments.

A focus on intra-organizational politics shows that reform winners and losers also exist *inside* public-sector organizations. Scholars conventionally conceptualize reform's winners and losers as aggregate economic or political groups, such as private entrepreneurs or former Communist elites, or as collective actors, such as local officials, workers, or SOEs (Hellman, 1998; Shirk, 1993). Winners and losers might also involve the various agencies inside a government bureaucracy (Tan, 2021). Others identify winners and losers at the firm level, for example finding that companies without lobbying experience benefit least from reform (Szakonyi and Urpelainen, 2014). However, evidence from CI and other Chinese central SOEs suggests that reform winners and losers may also exist within a single firm or within a single public-sector organization. Moreover, the roster of who gains and who loses inside any given firm or public-sector organization can change over time.

Examining the intra-organizational politics of reform also helps to explain why reform trajectories are often nonlinear, even during periods of relative institutional stability. The language of "transition" implicitly posits unilateral movement along a continuum toward fully market-based resource allocation. It is important, however, to consider "that behind such seemingly descriptive terms are teleological constructions in which concepts are driven by hypothesized end-states" (Stark and Bruszt, 1998: 83). The path of reform for even a single SOE may be nonlinear, as CI and its oscillating mode of international market expansion shows. Indeed, as Prakash (2000: 2) writes: "Though factors external to firms create incentives and expectations for managers, intra-firm politics influences how managers perceive and interpret external pressures and act upon them." The study of leadership and intra-organizational politics thus helps to explain why reform trajectories are frequently nonlinear.

Chinese SOE Leadership Goes Global

The context and consequences of leadership in Chinese SOEs are now global in nature. Historically, SOEs have provided the bulk of China's outward direct investment, buoyed by strong policy support and access to export buyers' credits and concessional loans from Chinese policy banks (Brautigam, 2009; Scissors, 2017). A growing number of SOEs have also acquired minority or majority shares in foreign companies. Chinese state firms have racked up nearly 200 mergers and acquisitions annually since 2012, hitting a peak of more than 500 deals in 2017 (Gordon and Milhaupt, 2019: 221). Central SOEs alone held RMB 6 trillion (USD 904 billion) in assets in more than 185 countries worldwide as of 2017.[4]

The expansion of SOEs into international markets has crucial strategic value for China. Boosting SOEs' overseas business helps to address domestic challenges, such as surplus industrial capacity and unemployment. By partnering with or buying into foreign firms and exporting indigenously developed technologies, SOEs support China's broader effort to move up the global value chain in high-tech and strategic sectors. An expanding network of Chinese SOE-operated or SOE-owned

[4] "Overseas Assets Held by China's Centrally Owned Firms Top 6 Trillion Yuan," Reuters, October 18, 2017, www.reuters.com/article/uk-china-congress-soes/overseas-assets-held-by-chinas-centrally-owned-firms-top-6-trillion-yuan-idUKKBN1CN1EN.

infrastructure projects abroad also provides important support for the Chinese military's worldwide operations and for the protection of China's citizens and interests abroad (Kardon and Leutert, 2022). Individual "mega-projects" may also be political linchpins in China's bilateral relations, especially with developing countries (Mohan and Tan-Mullins, 2019).

As China's economy falters in the wake of the COVID-19 pandemic, the strategic value of SOEs to the state is greater than ever. Since 2020, Beijing has directed SOEs to recruit and hire more university graduates so as to mitigate the stability risks of youth unemployment, which hit a record high of 21.3 percent in June 2023 and prompted the government to stop releasing age group–specific unemployment data in August 2023.[5] As a CI employee explained: "For SOEs, it is not about compensating people according to their work contribution. It is about maintaining jobs. SOEs have many different priorities with which they must contend, not only profit maximization." He recalled:

> When I was in Tanzania working on a project, I did not understand why if we wanted to lower costs, then we weren't hiring more local staff instead of flying over Chinese workers who require not only higher salaries but also travel costs from China. I have a positive impression of people from Africa, especially the college students whom I met. I told my boss we could train more local staff. My boss explained that one of our company's priorities is to maintain people's employment.[6]

With the domestic economy struggling and overseas business now a bigger part of Chinese SOEs' portfolios, the ability of SOE leaders to serve the state and society in China depends increasingly on their ability to win and execute profitable projects abroad. As a CI employee explained: "The company is owned by the [Chinese] government. We have to do business in order for the company to survive. SOEs can thus assist local people and places [in China] to

[5] "Youth" are officially defined as those between the ages of sixteen and twenty-four. Guo Jinhui [郭晋晖]: 《支持国企等"体制内"岗位扩容，国务院再推稳就业新举措》 [Support the Expansion of SOE and Other "In-System" Jobs, State Council Again Launches New Measures to Stabilize Employment], 第1财经 [First Finance], April 26, 2023, https://m.yicai.com/news/101742343.html; Thomas Hale, "China Stops Reporting Youth Unemployment as Economic Pressures Mount," *Financial Times*, August 15, 2023.

[6] Conversation with CI International employee [former Sino-Engineering employee], 2016.

develop. We are a company and we operate for the Chinese people and for the government."[7]

Leadership directly affects how, when, and where Chinese SOEs expand abroad. Executives determine which regional or national markets a SOE will target and what types of investments – such as greenfield projects or acquisitions – it will use to enter those markets. Education, experience, and state ties can mold SOE leaders' perceptions of the political risks of a host country and its overall "investability" (Camba, 2022). More broadly, leadership affects a company's prioritization of new technologies and its industry diversification. Recall, for example, how Ning Gaoning steered Sinochem's overseas business away from petroleum and toward capital investments and development of new materials, new energy, and other emerging technologies. Government policies might support global market expansion or promote the export of technologies such as UHV or high-speed rail, but it is SOE leaders who ultimately determine how to implement them. Conversely, some SOE leaders may also co-opt government policies or campaigns to pursue the particular internationalization strategies that they desire (Child and Rodrigues, 2005).

Leaders of SOEs may even direct their firms to go after specific overseas projects. "The degree to which the Chinese state can direct the firms to invest or participate in a project vary. ... However, the decision to participate or to bid for the project is often up to the firm" (Camba, 2022: 2016). There are numerous cases in which Chinese SOE leaders are the driving force behind particular deals, especially major acquisitions or large-scale projects. Take, for example, Ren Jianxin, the former chairman of central SOE ChemChina. Ren's initiative was crucial to the company's courtship and ultimate 2017 acquisition of Syngenta. "For most outside China," reports Reuters in a 2016 profile, "Ren is the biggest dealmaker they may never have heard of."[8]

Local SOE leaders also personally pursue and negotiate projects abroad. For instance, the chairman of the local SOE Shenzhen Energy, Gao Zimin, visited Ghana and negotiated personally with Asogli State

[7] Interview with CI International employee, Beijing, December 2019.

[8] Matthew Miller and Chen Aizhu, "Industrialist Turned Dealmaker, ChemChina's Ren Thinks Big with Syngenta," Reuters, February 3, 2016, www.reuters.com/article/us-syngenta-ag-m-a-chemchina-ren/industrialist-turned-dealmaker-chemchinas-ren-thinks-big-with-syngenta-idUSKCN0VC14Y.

Paramount Chief Togbe Afede XIV in 2006 to clinch the company's first overseas project, the Sunon Asogli Power Plant (Afede, 2013). "We took a big risk commercially and we were willing to do it," a Shenzhen Energy representative recalled.[9] With its first gas turbine operational in 2010 and its second in 2017, the power plant became the largest new independent power producer in Ghana.[10] Shenzhen Energy provided 60 percent of the funding for the project, with the remaining 40 percent provided by the China Africa Development Fund (CADF).[11] The Ghanaian government purchased the power generated through the Electricity Company of Ghana and guaranteed the supply of natural gas to the plant.[12] Executive deal-making, however, remains subject to regulation and input from multiple company and external actors, including SOE boards of directors, Party committees, SASAC, NDRC, and in rare cases even top Chinese leaders.

As Chinese SOE leadership goes global, international actors are increasingly exposed to its effects. Executive decisions about organizational strategy and structure invariably affect the many foreign companies that have entered into joint ventures with Chinese SOEs. Global index maker MSCI's addition of Chinese A-shares to its Emerging Markets Index since 2018 means that international institutional investors in the United States and elsewhere now have direct, long-term exposure to SOE governance and performance.[13] Furthermore, international nongovernmental organizations (INGOs) and intergovernmental organizations (IGOs) have begun to actively partner with Chinese SOEs and their leaders to deliver overseas projects, ranging from infrastructure works to training programs for local officials in third-party countries (Leutert, Plantan, and Strange, 2023; Plantan, Leutert, and Strange, 2024).

9 Interview with Shenzhen Energy country representative, Accra, August 2015.

10 "About Us," Sunon Asogli Power website, https://sunonasogli.com/index.php/about-us-2/.

11 China Development Bank established the China-Africa Development Fund (CADFund) in 2007 with initial capital of USD 1 billion. As of December 2023, its capital amount has grown to USD 10 billion. "Introduction," China-Africa Development Fund website, December 31, 2023, http://en.cadfund.com/Column/25/0.htm.

12 Interview with state-owned bank official (China Development Bank), Accra, Ghana, May 2019.

13 MSCI, "MSCI Emerging Markets Index (USD)," Factsheet, July 29, 2022, www.msci.com/documents/10199/c0db0a48-01f2-4ba9-ad01-226fd5678111.

Decisions by SOE leaders and their execution also affect communities and environments abroad. Chinese SOEs have earned a reputation for their ability to implement overseas projects quickly, reducing bureaucratic red tape but also potentially neglecting social, environmental, and other safeguards (Mwase and Yang, 2012). Variation in the degree to which market expansion is decentralized during the tenures of various SOE leaders, for example, may affect compliance with health, safety, and environmental regulations in SOEs' overseas projects. More decentralized market expansion involves fewer intra-firm mechanisms for top-down oversight and less standardization and dissemination of best practices. Conversely, greater centralization of market expansion can help to strengthen internal coordination and monitoring, but it risks weakening SOEs' ability to take local perspectives and conditions into account.

Chinese SOEs' evolving roles in overseas business will amplify leadership's effects on a global scale. No longer mere construction contractors, companies such as CI are moving up the value chain to operate, own, and invest in infrastructure projects abroad.[14] Take, for instance, China Construction Communications Corporation (CCCC), a central SOE that explicitly advocates a strategy of transforming itself from a contractor focused primarily on construction to become an operator, investor, and owner of overseas infrastructure.[15] The CCCC subsidiary China Harbour Engineering holds an equity share in a public–private partnership (PPP) port project that it is building in Cameroon and it is pursuing similar arrangements elsewhere.[16] Other SOEs are investing their own capital to build, own, and operate infrastructure projects overseas. Local SOE Shenzhen Energy, for example, provided the majority of the capital to fund the construction of the Sunon Asogli Power Plant in Ghana.[17] The result of these developments is

14 Wendy Leutert, "The Global Expansion and Evolution of Chinese State-Owned Enterprises," Fairbank Center for Chinese Studies Blog, Harvard University, July 11, 2019, https://medium.com/fairbank-center/the-overseas-expansion-and-evolution-of-chinese-state-owned-enterprises-3dc04134c5f2.

15 《中国交建：国企改革"模范生"》 [China Construction Communications Corporation: "Model Student" in SOE Reform], 《国资报告》 [State-Owned Assets Report], September 12, 2017.

16 《破冰非洲！中国交建探索"第三方市场合作"模式》 [Breaking the Ice in Africa! China Construction Communications Corporation Explores the "Third Party Market Cooperation" Model], 《华夏幸福》 [*China Fortune*], March 30, 2018.

17 "About Us," Sunon Asogli Power website, http://sunonasogli.com/index.php/about-us-2.

that Chinese SOEs are assuming long-term commercial and strategic stakes in countries around the world. Actors abroad are responding by endeavoring to increase communications and oversight on infrastructure quality, technical standards, labor practices, and environmental impact. The shift of state firms from contractors to operators, investors, and owners of infrastructure abroad, while still in its early stages, makes Chinese SOE leadership increasingly consequential on the global stage.

Leading the Way Forward? The Future of Leadership in China's Public Sector

What does the future hold for leadership in China's public sector during the Xi Jinping era? The NPC in October 2022 officially confirmed that Xi will remain in place as the country's top leader.[18] This makes Xi the first Chinese leader in the twenty-first century to extend his rule for a third five-year term (2022–27). To some observers, Xi has already ushered in a new, "counter-reform era," characterized by greater centralized CCP control over the country's economy, politics, and society (Minzner, 2018). In this view, Xi is engineering a profound shift from state capitalism to Party-state capitalism, from China Inc. to CCP Inc. (Blanchette, 2020; Economy, 2018; Pearson, Rithmire, and Tsai, 2022). In the state-owned economy specifically, Xi has embraced CCP-centered tools of command and control to pursue the Chinese leadership's long-standing vision of globally competitive, state-controlled SOEs (Leutert and Eaton, 2021).

On the surface, Xi's rule appears to drastically limit leadership in SOEs and other public-sector organizations. The logic here is that strengthened Party institutions restrict space for leadership by increasing officials' responsiveness to state directives and by incentivizing conformity and conservatism. As a CI department manager told me privately: "The most critical question is whether the executives of central SOEs will be given the authority to act as businesspeople

[18] This move follows the elimination of term limits in 2018 for Xi's position as CCP general secretary. Ben Blanchard and Christian Shepherd, "China Allows Xi to Remain President Indefinitely, Tightening His Grip on Power," Reuters, March 11, 2018, www.reuters.com/article/us-china-parliament/china-allows-xi-to-remain-president-indefinitely-tightening-his-grip-on-power-idUSKCN1GN07E.

in the best interests of the company rather than as political figures or only thinking of themselves."[19] Xi's anti-corruption campaign and the formalization of a lifetime accountability system for the major decisions by SOE leaders have certainly had a chilling effect. Indeed, as this book's review of enterprise reforms since 1978 shows, the scope for leadership can vary significantly over time and across issue areas. Leaders of SOEs have consistently enjoyed increasing autonomy for commercial decisions – even during the Xi administration – but trends in space for leadership are not necessarily linear.

Yet no matter how the Xi era continues to unfold, leadership in the public sector will remain crucial to the functioning of China's politics and economy. This is because it is leaders at all levels who decide whether, how, and when to respond to central-level goals and policies about economic growth, social stability, and environmental protection. It is these individuals who actually implement Xi's initiatives, such as the BRI and the poverty alleviation campaign. And as Xi continues to remake the Chinese bureaucracy by eliminating and amalgamating government bodies and establishing new ministries and leading small groups, studying leaders of public-sector organizations will be critical to understanding the functioning and evolution of the Party-state apparatus. More fundamentally, studies of leadership in China's public sector during the Xi era challenge the simplifying and inaccurate impulse to ascribe reform variation to the machinations of a handful of top leaders, no matter how powerful they may appear – or to China's "authoritarian state" writ large. Leadership therefore remains a vital subject for those who want to understand China's future.

Further research could address several key questions. First, does leadership in China's public sector have wider diffusion effects? The CCP explicitly implements a cadre rotation system, whereby officials are routinely transferred between different posts and/or localities across the sprawling Chinese bureaucracy. The replication of successful experience (复制成功经验) is cited as a key motivation for this practice. Do public-sector leaders credited with success in a specific policy or geographic area actually make similar decisions about organizational strategy and structure when they are transferred elsewhere? Scholars

[19] Conversation with Sino-Construction International department manager, 2014.

are beginning to investigate the mechanisms behind spatial policy diffusion in China (Bulman, 2024; Zhu, 2018). Analysis of leadership and its effects would be particularly helpful in longitudinal studies of this phenomenon, through both case studies and large-N analyses.

Second, how do time and environment condition leadership's effects? As Donaldson (2009: 422–23) finds regarding leadership in China's provinces: "Once a particular course is set and receives central support, a form of path dependency can encourage the strategy to continue even after the original leaders have departed." What factors make such a "leadership lock-in effect" more likely? Environment also matters. If space for leadership is greater during times of crisis or rapid change when uncertainty is high, its subsequent effects may persist longer. During critical junctures, the range of plausible choices and scope for policy action expand and the consequences of actions are greater (Capoccia and Kelemen, 2007; Soifer, 2012). A leader's remaking of organizational strategy and structure at such times may be more likely to endure into the future. Analyses of consecutive leaders could employ qualitative and quantitative data to assess the correspondence among tenures of leaders, external shocks, and variation in outcomes of interest. Studies with a longer time frame could also investigate processes of learning and adjustment during individual leaders' tenures and over the course of their careers (Lant, Milliken, and Batra, 1992; Pettigrew, 1987).

Third, how do international and industry-specific factors affect leaders' influence? Such factors include strategic partnerships between Chinese enterprises and leading multinationals, shifting conditions in global industry chains and markets, and industry and business associations at home and abroad. Leaders might be able to leverage these factors to access additional resources and take advantage of new opportunities, thereby bolstering their ability to lead. For example, Yeung (2016) analyzes case studies of East Asian national champions to show how "strategic coupling" with global multinationals made some firms so strong that they could remake developmental states back home. Conversely, market conditions or industry ties with other actors may constrain a leader's decision-making and execution ability.

Fourth, what are the determinants of leadership? This question reverses the causal chain to treat leadership as the dependent variable, not an explanatory variable as is done in this book. Such work could assess the effects of individual-level attributes, risk dispositions, experiential and environmental factors, and cognitive frames (Carpenter, Geletkanycz, and Sanders, 2004; Hambrick and Mason, 1984; Horowitz, Stam, and Ellis, 2015; Kowert and Hermann, 1997; Marquis and Tilcsik, 2013). Statistical analyses using original datasets of observational data on leaders' attributes and decisions, content analysis of leaders' speeches, survey experiments, and case studies are all potential methodological approaches for such research. Leaders' tenure, age, education, and previous work experience are easily measurable, and evidence exists that these factors affect decision-making. Other factors, such as leaders' risk propensity and "imprinting" through exposure and indoctrination with Communist ideology, may also be consequential (Marquis and Qiao, 2020). Existing typologies of leadership styles or "political personalities" in China's public sector could be expanded by categorizing leaders according to these attributes (Hasmath, Teets, and Lewis, 2019; Jiang and Luo, 2021; Ramamurti, 1987).

Fifth, and finally, what are the international consequences of leadership in China's public sector? How do particular leaders' decisions and their execution affect the types of overseas business that Chinese firms pursue, governance of projects on the ground, and their effects on local communities, public opinion, and the environment? Are some leaders of Chinese SOEs and other public-sector organizations more likely than others to seek out collaboration with counterparts abroad by forming joint ventures, inking memoranda of understanding (MOUs), or forging relationships with local actors? The increasingly global context and consequences of leadership in Chinese public-sector organizations call for further investigation, both within and beyond China.

Appendix A
Methodology and Research Design

Methodology and Research Design

This study combines paired comparisons with process tracing (Bennett and Checkel, 2015; George and Bennett, 2005). I first selected the units of analysis: the consecutive tenures of chairmen in CI and other Chinese central SOEs. This identification strategy exploits the change of chairmen largely according to fixed bureaucratic rules, for example about mandatory official retirement ages, which are exogenous to organization-level factors. Paired comparisons also generate high internal validity and reduce the possibility that unobserved variables will impact the outcomes of interest (Tarrow, 2010). This is because studying the consecutive tenures of chairmen in the same company increases confidence that these cases are similar along a range of variables that might affect reform at the organization level.

I next employed process tracing to investigate the relationship between leadership and selected indicators of reform at the firm level. I used original qualitative and quantitative data gathered in three ways: fifteen months of participant observation that I conducted at CI between 2014 and 2017; semi-structured interviews with SOE managers and employees; and written sources, including company documents and yearbooks. As I carried out the process tracing, I systematically assessed the possible effects of other factors, such as external interference in company affairs, major policy changes, and market fluctuations. A fieldwork strategy of long-term, iterative immersion over fifteen months of on-site research at CI enabled me to collect both "measurement evidence" (that events in a particular process tracing chain actually occurred) and "identifying evidence" (that rules out confounding variables and processes) (Nielsen, 2016).

The observable implication of a leadership approach is that the decisions of successive chairmen about organizational strategy and structure and their execution will yield variation in a company's reform over time. I examined two specific aspects of reform: changes in the degree to which a company's market expansion is decentralized and the balance of influence among intra-firm actors.[1] Evidence refuting a leadership explanation would be found if a change of chairman does not result in any variation in these aspects of reform, or if any observable changes in reform outcomes are instead systematically related to other factors, such as external interference in company affairs, major policy changes, or market fluctuations.

Case Selection

I chose to study the consecutive tenures of chairmen in CI because the company is representative of central SOEs both in the construction industry and overall, in terms of size, revenue, profitability, and official designation of strategic industry importance. Out of the eight central SOEs in the construction industry in 2013, when I began my field research, CI ranked second in size in terms of total assets; fifth in revenue; fifth in ratio of state capital preserved; and sixth in profits.[2] Its ratio of state capital preserved and profitability was closely equivalent to that of central SOEs as a group: it posted profits of approximately RMB 11 billion, compared to an average of RMB 13 billion among the ninety-seven reporting central SOEs in that year.[3] Its 107 percent ratio of state capital preserved equaled the average for the eighty-five reporting central SOEs.[4] As a construction company, CI operates in a semi-protected industry that is in between strategically important sectors in which the state maintains "absolute control" and more commercially oriented sectors where no explicit protections for state ownership are given.[5] During the study's time frame, CI did not experience any significant changes in size, performance, or official industry designation.

1 There are other possible measures of reform at the company level, such as changes in the specific proportion of a company's assets that are publicly listed or variation in the relative amounts and types of state support that the company receives; however, data for these indicators are not publicly available.
2 I use the official industry categorization of China's government ownership agency, SASAC, to identify this group of firms (SASAC, 2014).
3 Author's calculations using SASAC yearbook data (SASAC, 2014).
4 Author's calculations using SASAC yearbook data (SASAC, 2014).
5 According to the State Council designations in 2006, as cited previously.

Data Collection and Analysis

I gained access to CI by applying for an unpaid internship through a formal process after an employee introduced me to the company. I submitted a cover letter, CV, and two letters of recommendation in December 2013 and subsequently was interviewed by CI's human resources department in January 2014. I worked in the company's office in Beijing during three different time periods over fifteen months between 2014 and 2016: from January to June 2014, from September 2014 to March 2015, and from April to June 2016. I worked two days a week full-time, from 8:30 a.m. to 5:00 p.m.

I collected qualitative and statistical data in three ways: participant observation, semi-structured interviews, and written sources. I participated in a range of activities at CI: market research (such as writing memos on infrastructure projects identified in various countries' national development plans and current political developments); English-to-Chinese and Chinese-to-English translation; development of company marketing materials; and employee training. I kept detailed daily logs recording my observations of company activities and exchanges with employees as well as my own activities, questions, and reflections. I typed these daily logs directly onto my computer using the notepad function. I also took handwritten notes during group meetings and one-on-one interviews and then typed them up afterward. Together, this data collection yielded more than 200 pages of single-spaced notes. Semi-structured interviews with department managers and company leaders began with a set of fixed questions, followed by a series of open-ended queries tailored to the interviewee's background and expertise. Finally, I supplemented this firsthand data with an extensive record of written sources: company notices and documents (such as newsletters and work reports), company yearbooks, and media reports. All sources cited in this book are my own English translations from the original Chinese.

Two factors were critical to the success of my fieldwork at CI. The first factor was a fieldwork strategy of long-term and iterative immersion. Long-term immersion permitted sustained accumulation of trust and understanding. Periodic removal from the research setting facilitated critical reflection and improved my ability to consciously discern between informants' first-order reports and notions of what was happening in the corporate setting and my second-order conceptions as a researcher about what was actually occurring (Van Maanen, 1979). The second factor was my fluency in Mandarin. This was essential to participate in daily activities at CI, to interact with employees, and to collect and incorporate written sources. Through these activities, I gained a deeper and more accurate understanding of how the organization was structured and what were the interests of and relationships among different intra-firm entities.

To my knowledge, this study is the first in political science to employ data gathered through participant observation in a Chinese central SOE. In this approach, "the researcher takes part in the daily activities, rituals, interactions, and events of a group of people as one of the means of learning the explicit and tacit aspects of their life routines and their culture" (DeWalt and DeWalt, 2011). Participant observation has multiple advantages over other data collection methods. First, it can generate reliable data that is simply unavailable elsewhere. Beyond scholarly concerns about incomplete or unreliable data in China – particularly given widespread manipulation of official statistics – researchers have been unable to access many of the Party, state, and other organizations that make and implement reform policies (Wallace, 2016). Data gathered through participant observation therefore provide essential context for analysis by enabling accurate identification of internal decision-making participants and processes. Participant observation is especially well-suited for analyzing the reform process because it illuminates the relevant drivers, mechanisms, and constraints in particular organizational and institutional environments. This is extremely difficult to do through interview-based fieldwork, in which the researcher typically has a single brief interaction with one person that frequently occurs outside of the organizational environment. Finally, participant observation enables improved construct validity, for instance how "reform" should be conceptualized and measured.

Potential Sampling Bias

I identified several sources of potential sampling bias during the fieldwork and took steps whenever possible to address them. First, I naturally interacted most with CI employees who also worked in the department and subsidiary where I was based in Beijing. Fortuitously, this subsidiary's office building became the headquarters for the entire enterprise group just one month after I began my fieldwork; this enabled me to interact regularly with employees of the holding company as well as with other intra-firm entities when they visited the headquarters. In addition, I attended internal training sessions and meetings that brought together employees from across the company, ate meals with employees who worked in other parts of the firm, and traveled outside of Beijing to visit construction bureau offices. In 2016, I also gave three trainings on cross-cultural communication to employees from different subsidiaries; I concluded these sessions with written questionnaires to gather additional information about the experiences and views of employees in various parts of the company.[6] Second, because I was not a paid full-time employee I did not have access to the company's internal computer network, which included an intranet with detailed information about employees and projects. I therefore participated actively in the semi-official online QQ chat groups (QQ is a Chinese social messaging software) for my department. I communicated regularly with employees about their work through this medium as well as in person. Third, I did not collect any information that was marked for internal reference (内部参考) or that I considered proprietary or sensitive, such as statistics on employee salaries or project finances. I did this to respect company regulations and to protect my own position as a foreign scholar affiliated with an American academic institution who was conducting research in a Chinese public-sector organization. In particular, the Xi administration's launch of a nationwide anti-corruption campaign after coming to power in 2012 heightened the potential sensitivity of my presence because it increased scrutiny of the internal operations of central SOEs.

Researcher Positionality

Throughout this study, I critically considered the issue of researcher positionality and how it affected my field research and findings. Researcher positionality refers to the effects of individual attributes (such as race, gender, age, nationality, and social and economic status), personal experiences, and political and professional beliefs about

[6] These questionnaires were informal and anonymous. I could relate responses to particular subsidiaries because I asked participants where in the company they worked; however, I did not ask for any information that would have enabled identification of particular individuals, such as the titles of their positions.

data collection, quality, and analysis in a given research context (Berger, 2015; Hsueh, Jensenius, and Newsome, 2014). During the fieldwork, I introduced myself as a researcher from a foreign university interning with the company in order to study its organization and operations; my interlocuters were also aware of my identity as a white American woman.

My outsider status aided the research process in several ways. First, it enabled me to engage candidly with actors across the company without their thinking that I represented the vested interests of a particular intra-firm entity. In addition, since I was a foreign academic, employees assumed that I was unfamiliar with the company and industry; on numerous occasions this prompted them to share additional information and materials or to invite me to sit in on company meetings.

However, the liability of my status as an outsider and temporary employee was that I had to invest significant time and effort to build trust with the employees and to increase my own knowledge of the company's structure and operations. I did this by participating in the company's daily work as well as in social activities outside the office, such as meals with employees and employee outings. Depending on the extent to which intra-firm actors saw me as part of their organization, they may have withheld certain information about company operations or their own experiences and views. Frequently engaging with employees in groups where exchanges were not only with me individually helped to mitigate this issue but cannot entirely rule out any possible effects.

External Validity and Further Research

The main trade-off of this study's research design is its restricted external validity. Additional empirical analysis is needed to assess whether this study's findings can be extended to additional central SOEs, to SOEs at different levels of government in China, or to SOEs in other countries. Future work could therefore employ a subnational or cross-national comparative approach. For instance, such studies might investigate the effects of leadership on reform in central versus local SOEs, on SOEs at the same level of government but located in different geographic areas or different industries, or on reform outcomes in comparable Chinese and foreign SOEs.

Appendix B Participant Observation and Interviews in CI

This Appendix presents details about the participant observation and interviews at CI that are cited in the book in the order in which the quotations appear. I conducted the participant observation and interviews at CI primarily between 2014 and 2016, with additional follow-up in 2018, 2019, and 2023; all participant observation and interviews were conducted in-person. The "Intra-firm entity" column denotes the specific part of the company in which the individual worked. The "Individual" column identifies each individual's area of functional responsibility within the company as well as their position level. The "Format" column indicates the nature of the exchange, ranging from informal and unstructured to formal and structured. The "Time frame" column specifies the total time period during the fieldwork in which I interacted with each individual. The "Context" column identifies the settings in which our exchanges occurred.

Citation	Intra-firm entity	Department	Individual	Format	Time frame	Context
Chapter 1	CI	Holding company	Chairman	Formal	2014	Annual shareholders meeting at headquarters
Chapter 1	CI International	Regional marketing department	Employee (former Sino-Construction International employee)	Unstructured, informal	2016	Daily work at CI International office
Chapter 1	Construction bureau	Construction bureau (outside Beijing)	Manager	Semi-structured, formal	2016	On-site visit to construction bureau
Chapter 4	Sino-Construction International	Regional marketing department	Employee	Unstructured, informal	2014	Daily work at headquarters
Chapter 4	Sino-Construction International	Corporate communications department	Employee	Unstructured, informal	2014	Daily work at headquarters
Chapter 4	Construction bureau	Construction bureau (outside Beijing)	Manager	Semi-structured, formal	2015	On-site visit to construction bureau
Chapter 4	CI International	Regional marketing department	Employee (former Sino-Construction International employee)	Unstructured, informal	2014	Daily work at headquarters
Chapter 4	CI International	Regional marketing department	Employee (former Sino-Engineering employee)	Unstructured, informal	2016	Daily work at CI International office

(*cont.*)

Citation	Intra-firm entity	Department	Individual	Format	Time frame	Context
Chapter 4	CI International	Regional marketing department	Employee (former Sino-Construction employee)	Unstructured, informal	2016	Daily work at CI International office
Chapter 4	CI International	Regional marketing department	Manager (former Sino-Construction International and construction bureau employee)	Unstructured, informal	2016	Daily work at CI International office
Chapter 4	Construction bureau	Construction bureau (outside of Beijing)	Manager	Semi-structured, formal	2016	On-site visit to construction bureau
Chapter 4	CI International	Regional marketing department	Employee (former Sino-Construction International employee)	Unstructured, informal	2016	Daily work at CI International office
Chapter 4	Construction bureau	Construction bureau (outside Beijing)	Manager	Semi-structured, formal	2016	On-site visit to construction bureau
Chapter 4	CI International	Regional marketing department	Employee (former Sino-Construction International employee)	Unstructured, informal	2016	Daily work at CI International office
Chapter 4	Sino-Engineering	Engineering design department	Design institute	Semi-structured, formal	2016	On-site visit to Sino-Engineering office

Chapter 4	CI International	Regional marketing department	Employee (former Sino-Engineering employee)	Unstructured, informal	2016	Daily work at CI International office
Chapter 4	CI International	Regional marketing department	Employee (former Sino-Construction employee)	Unstructured, informal	2016	Daily work at CI International office
Chapter 6	Sino-Construction International	Regional marketing department	Employee	Unstructured, informal	2016	Daily work at CI International office
Chapter 6	CI International	Legal department	Employee (former Sino-Construction International employee)	Unstructured, informal	2016	Daily work at CI International office
Chapter 6	Sino-Construction International	Regional marketing department	Employee	Unstructured, informal	2015	Daily work at headquarters
Chapter 6	Sino-Construction International	Regional marketing department	Employee	Unstructured, informal	2014	Daily work at headquarters
Chapter 6	CI International	Regional marketing department	Employee (former holding-company employee)	Unstructured, informal	2016	Daily work at CI International office
Chapter 6	Sino-Construction International	Regional marketing department	Employee	Unstructured, informal	2014	Daily work at headquarters
Chapter 6	Sino-Construction International	Regional marketing department	Employee	Unstructured, informal	2014	Daily work at headquarters
Chapter 6	CI International	Regional marketing department	Former employee (former Sino-Construction International employee)	Semi-structured, formal	2018	Meeting at coffee shop in Beijing

(*cont.*)

Citation	Intra-firm entity	Department	Individual	Format	Time frame	Context
Chapter 6	Sino-Construction International	Regional marketing department	Employee	Unstructured, informal	2015	Daily work at headquarters
Chapter 6	CI International	Regional marketing department	Employee (former Sino-Construction International employee)	Unstructured, informal	2016	Daily work at CI International office
Chapter 6	CI International	Regional marketing department	Employee (former Sino-Engineering employee)	Unstructured, informal	2016	Daily work at CI International office
Chapter 7	CI International	Regional marketing department	Employee (former Sino-Engineering employee)	Unstructured, informal	2016	Daily work at CI International office
Chapter 7	CI International	Regional marketing department	Employee (former Sino-Construction International employee)	Semi-structured, formal	2019	On-site visit to CI International office
Chapter 7	Sino-Construction International	Regional marketing department	Manager	Unstructured, informal	2014	Daily work at CI International office

Appendix C
List of Interviewees

Between 2013 and 2019, I conducted more than 100 interviews with individuals in the Chinese government and the CCP, central SOEs, state-owned banks, academia, think tanks, and other sectors. Only a small subset of these interviews are cited in the book, but all informed the research and my understanding. These exchanges took place primarily in China (Beijing, Shanghai, Tianjin, Haikou, and Hong Kong) and also in the United States and Ghana, where I met with SOE representatives on the front lines of international business.

Interviews were typically semi-structured and ranged between 30 minutes and 2 hours in duration. They began with a short set of fixed questions followed by open-ended questions tailored to the interviewee's specific background and expertise. Interviews were carried out in a variety of public and private settings depending on the interviewee's preference, including restaurants and cafés, offices, and homes. All were conducted in person, unless otherwise indicated. The vast majority of interviews were one-on-one; a small number, denoted with asterisks, were group conversations at which other researchers were present. Interviews were conducted in accordance with Institutional Review Board protocols for research involving human subjects.

For each interviewee listed in this appendix, I provide a description of their position, interview location, and date.

Government and CCP

Government official (Ministry of Commerce), Beijing, November 2013.
Government official (Ministry of Commerce), Beijing, December 2013.
Government official (Ministry of Commerce), Beijing, March 2014.
Government official (National Development and Reform Commission), Beijing, May 2014.
Government official (National Development and Reform Commission), Beijing, May 2014.

Retired government official (Beijing city government), Beijing, November 2014.

Retired government official (State Council), Beijing, December 2014.

Retired senior government official (secretary to leader), Beijing, February 2015.

Former government official (State-Owned Assets Supervision and Administration Commission), United States, October 2015.

Former government official (State-Owned Assets Supervision and Administration Commission), United States, November 2015.

Retired government official (National Development and Reform Commission), Beijing, March 2016.

Retired government official (National Development and Reform Commission), Beijing, April 2016.

Retired senior government official (State Council), Beijing, April 2016.

Retired government official (State Council), Beijing, April 2016.

Former government official (State Assets Administration Bureau), Beijing, April 2016.

Retired government official (National Development and Reform Commission), Beijing, May 2016.

Senior government official (National Development and Reform Commission), Beijing, May 2016.*

Retired senior government official (secretary to leader), Beijing, June 2016.

Retired government official (National Development and Reform Commission), Beijing, June 2016.

Retired senior government official (State Council), Beijing, June 2016.

Senior CCP official (Party Literature Research Office), Beijing, July 2016.*

Senior CCP official (International Liaison Department), Beijing, July 2016.*

Senior CCP official (Central Committee for Discipline Inspection), Beijing, July 2016.*

Retired government official (National Development and Reform Commission), Beijing, July 2016.

Government official (Ministry of Transportation), Beijing, June 2018.

SOEs

Central SOE department manager (CI), January 2013.

Retired central SOE department manager (Sinosteel), January 2013.

Central SOE employee (Minmetals), September 2013.

Central SOE employee (Sinochem), September 2013.

Central SOE employee (Metallurgical Corporation of China), Beijing, March 2014.

Central SOE employee (Sinochem), Beijing, March 2014.

Central SOE employee (Metallurgical Corporation of China), Beijing, April 2014.

Central SOE employee (Minmetals), Beijing, April 2014.

Central SOE employee (State Grid), Beijing, May 2014.

Central SOE department manager (Metallurgical Corporation of China), Beijing, May 2014.

Central SOE department manager (Metallurgical Corporation of China), Beijing, May 2014.

Central SOE department manager (CI), Beijing, May 2014.

Central SOE department manager (CI), Beijing, June 2014.

Central SOE department manager (China International Engineering Consulting Corporation), Beijing, November 2014.

Retired central SOE senior manager (CI), Beijing, November 2014.

Central SOE department manager (CI), Beijing, December 2014.

Central SOE senior manager (CI), Beijing, January 2015.

Central SOE senior manager (CI), Beijing, February 2015.

Central SOE department manager (CI construction bureau), Tianjin, February 2015.

Central SOE department manager (CI construction bureau), Tianjin, February 2015.

Central SOE department manager (CI construction bureau), Tianjin, February 2015.

Central SOE department manager (CI construction bureau), Tianjin, February 2015.

Central SOE department manager (CI), Accra, Ghana, August 2015.

Central SOE department manager (CI), Accra, Ghana, August 2015.*

Local SOE employee (Shenzhen Energy), Accra, Ghana, August 2015.

Central SOE employee (Sinochem), Beijing, April 2016.

Retired central SOE department manager (CI), Beijing, May 2016.

Central SOE department manager (China General Nuclear Power Group), Beijing, June 2016.

Central SOE department manager (Metallurgical Corporation of China), Beijing, June 2016.

Central SOE department manager (CI construction bureau), Tianjin, June 2016.

Central SOE department manager (CI construction bureau), Tianjin, June 2016.

Central SOE department manager (CI construction bureau), Tianjin, June 2016.

Central SOE department manager (CI), Beijing, June 2016.

Former central SOE employee (China Aerospace Science and Technology Corporation), Beijing, June 2018.

Retired central SOE senior manager (China Resources Group), Beijing, June 2018.

Retired central SOE department manager (CI), Beijing, June 2018.

Retired central SOE employee (CI), Beijing, June 2018.

Central SOE employee (China Communications Construction Company), Beijing, June 2018.

Central SOE employee (China Railway Engineering Corporation), Beijing, June 2018.

Central SOE employee (Sinochem), Beijing, June 2018.

Central SOE department manager (China General Nuclear Power Group), Beijing, June 2018.

Central SOE department manager (CI), Accra, Ghana, May 2019.

Local SOE employee (Shenzhen Energy), Accra, Ghana, May 2019.

Central SOE department manager (State Grid), Beijing, June 2019.*

Central SOE employee (State Grid), Beijing, June 2019.*

Central SOE employee (State Grid), Beijing, June 2019.*

Central SOE department manager (State Grid), Beijing, June 2019.*

Central SOE employee (State Grid), Beijing, June 2019.*

Central SOE employee (CI), Beijing, December 2019.

Central SOE employee (CI), Beijing, December 2019.

Central SOE department manager (CI), Beijing, December 2019.

Central SOE employee (CI), Beijing, December 2019.

Retired central SOE employee (CI), Beijing, December 2019.

Central SOE employee (CI), Beijing, December 2023.

Central SOE employee (CI), Beijing, December 2023.

State-Owned Banks

Retired state-owned bank senior executive (China Merchant Bank), Hong Kong, January 2016.

State-owned bank official (China Development Bank), Beijing, May 2016.

State-owned bank official (China Development Bank), Accra, Ghana, May 2019.

Academia and Think Tanks

Think-tank researcher (Chinese Academy of Social Sciences), Beijing, October 2013.

Think-tank researcher (China Center for International Economic Exchanges), Beijing, October 2013.

Academic (Zhejiang Normal University), Beijing, October 2013.

Academic (Peking University), Beijing, December 2013.
Academic (Renmin University), Beijing, December 2013.
Academic (University of International Business and Economics), Beijing, November 2014.
Academic, Beijing (Peking University), December 2014.
Academic, Beijing (Tsinghua University), December 2014.
Think-tank researcher (Unirule), Beijing, January 2015.
Academic (Peking University), Beijing, March 2015.
Think-tank researcher (China Academy of Social Sciences), Beijing, August 2015.
Academic (Renmin University), Beijing, March 2016.
Retired think-tank researcher (Chinese Academy of Social Sciences), Beijing, April 2016.
Retired think-tank researcher (Chinese Academy of Social Sciences), Beijing, April 2016.
Academic (Hong Kong University), Beijing, May 2016.
Academic (Central Institute of Socialism), Beijing, May 2016.
Think-tank researcher (Chinese Academy of Social Sciences), Beijing, May 2016.
Academic (Tsinghua University), Beijing, May 2016.
Think-tank researcher (China Institute for Reform and Development), Hainan, June 2016.
Think-tank researcher (China Institute for Reform and Development), Hainan, June 2016.
Think-tank researcher (China Institute for Reform and Development), Hainan, June 2016.
Think-tank researcher (National Economic Research Institute), Beijing, June 2016.
Academic (China Executive Leadership Academy in Pudong), Shanghai, July 2016.*
Academic (Chinese University of Hong Kong), Hong Kong, July 2016.

Law

Lawyer (international law firm), Beijing (by telephone), May 2019.

References

Aberbach, Joel D., Robert D. Putnam, and Bert A. Rockman (1981). *Bureaucrats and Politicians in Western Democracies*. Cambridge, MA: Harvard University Press.

Afede XIV, Togbe (2013). *Making the Difference: Ten Years of Progress, 2003–2013*. Ho, Volta Region, Ghana: Asogli State Council, in collaboration with Carrie Brown.

Andrews, Kenneth R. (1971). *The Concept of Corporate Strategy*. Homewood, IL: Dow Jones-Irwin.

Ang, Yuen Yuen (2023). "Ambiguity and Clarity in China's Adaptive Policy Communication." *The China Quarterly*, no. 257: 20–37. https://doi.org/10.1017/policypage

Ang, Yuen Yuen (2016). *How China Escaped the Poverty Trap*. Ithaca, NY: Cornell University Press.

Appel, Hilary, and Mitchell A. Orenstein (2018). *From Triumph to Crisis: Neoliberal Economic Reform in Postcommunist Countries*. Cambridge, UK: Cambridge University Press.

Aycan, Zeynep (2006). "Paternalism: Towards Conceptual Refinement and Operationalization." Pp. 445–66, in Uichol Kim, Kuo-Shu Yang, and Kwang-Kuo Hwang, eds., *Indigenous and Cultural Psychology: Understanding People in Context*. New York: Springer.

Bai, Chong-en, and Yijiang Wang (1998). "Bureaucratic Control and the Soft Budget Constraint." *Journal of Comparative Economics* 26, no. 1: 41–61.

Bai, Shuaijiao, Henrique Duarte, and Dong Guo (2016). "Drivers of Organizational Reorientations in Planned Economies: The Case Study of a Chinese Third-Front Company." *Journal of Organizational Change Management* 29, no. 4: 551–79.

Bajona, Claustre, and Tianshu Chu (2004). *China's WTO Accession and Its Effect on State-Owned Enterprises*. Economics Study Area Working Paper, no. 70. Honolulu: East-West Center.

Battat, Joseph Y. (1986). *Management in Post-Mao China: An Insider's View*. Ann Arbor: UMI Research Press.

Bayat, Asef (2013). *Life as Politics: How Ordinary People Change the Middle East*, 2nd edn. Palo Alto, CA: Stanford University Press.

Beck, Kasper I. (2022). "Reforming the Chinese State Sector: Mixed Ownership Reforms and State-Business Relations." *Journal of Contemporary China* 32, no. 140: 264–79.

Bedi, Akanksha (2020). "A Meta-Analytic Review of Paternalistic Leadership." *Applied Psychology* 69, no. 3: 960–1008.

Bennett, Andrew, and Jeffrey T. Checkel, eds. (2015). *Process Tracing: From Metaphor to Analytic Tool*. Cambridge, UK: Cambridge University Press.

Berger, Roni (2015). "Now I See It, Now I Don't: Researcher's Position and Reflexivity in Qualitative Research." *Qualitative Research* 15, no. 2: 219–34.

Blanchette, Jude (2020). "From 'China Inc.' to 'CCP Inc.': A New Paradigm for Chinese State Capitalism." *China Leadership Monitor*, no. 66: 1–13. www.prcleader.org/post/from-china-inc-to-ccp-inc-a-new-paradigm-for-chinese-state-capitalism

Blecher, Marc, and Vivienne Shue (2001). "Into Leather: State-Led Development and the Private Sector in Xinji." *The China Quarterly*, no. 166: 368–93.

Boisot, Max H. (1987). "Industrial Feudalism and Enterprise Reform: Could the Chinese Use Some More Bureaucracy?" Pp. 217–37, in Malcolm Warner, ed., *Management Reforms in China*. London: Frances Pinter.

Boisot, Max H., and John Child (1988). "The Iron Law of Fiefs: Bureaucratic Failure and the Problem of Governance in the Chinese Economic Reforms." *Administrative Science Quarterly* 33, no. 4: 507–27.

Boone, Catherine (1992). *Merchant Capital and the Roots of State Power in Senegal: 1930–1985*. Cambridge, UK: Cambridge University Press.

Brautigam, Deborah (2009). *The Dragon's Gift: The Real Story of China in Africa*. Oxford: Oxford University Press.

Brehm, John O., and Scott Gates (1999). *Working, Shirking, and Sabotage: Bureaucratic Response to a Democratic Public*. Ann Arbor: University of Michigan Press.

Breznitz, Dan, and Michael Murphree (2011). *Run of the Red Queen: Government, Innovation, Globalization, and Economic Growth in China*. New Haven, CT: Yale University Press.

Brødsgaard, Kjeld E., ed. (2016). *Chinese Politics as Fragmented Authoritarianism: Earthquakes, Energy and Environment*. London: Routledge.

Brødsgaard, Kjeld E. (2012). "Politics and Business Group Formation in China: The Party in Control?" *The China Quarterly*, no. 211: 624–48.

Brødsgaard, Kjeld E., and Kasper I. Beck (2021). "Big Business and Cadre Management in China." *The Copenhagen Journal of Asian Studies* 39, no. 2: 53–76.

Brooks, Sarah M., and Marcus J. Kurtz (2007). "Capital, Trade, and the Political Economies of Reform." *American Journal of Political Science* 51, no. 4: 703–20.

Brunetti, Aymo, and Beatrice Weder (2003). "A Free Press Is Bad News for Corruption." *Journal of Public Economics* 87, no. 7: 1801–24.

Buckley, Peter J., Jeremy Clegg, and Hui Tan (2005). "Reform and Restructuring in a Chinese State Owned Enterprise: Sinotrans in the 1990s." *Management International Review* 45, no. 2: 147–72.

Bulman, David J. (2024). "Control, Career Development, and Diffusion: The Evolving and Contradictory Roles of Cadre Rotation in China." Unpublished Working Paper.

Bulman, David J. (2016). *Incentivized Development in China: Leaders, Governance, and Growth in China's Counties.* Cambridge, UK: Cambridge University Press.

Bunce, Valerie (1981). *Do New Leaders Make a Difference? Executive Succession and Public Policy under Capitalism and Socialism.* Princeton, NJ: Princeton University Press.

Burns, James M. (1978). *Leadership.* New York: Harper & Row.

Burns, John P., ed. (1989). *The Chinese Communist Party's Nomenklatura System: A Documentary Study of Party Control of Leadership Selection, 1979–1984.* Armonk, NY: M. E. Sharpe.

Byrd, William A. (1987). "The Market Mechanism and Economic Reforms in Chinese Industry." Ph.D. dissertation, Harvard University.

Cai, Hongbin, and Daniel Treisman (2006). "Did Government Decentralization Cause China's Economic Miracle?" *World Politics* 58, no. 4: 505–35.

Camba, Alvin (2022). "How Chinese Firms Approach Investment Risk: Strong Leaders, Cancellation, and Pushback." *Review of International Political Economy* 29, no. 6: 2010–35.

Capoccia, Giovanni, and R. Daniel Kelemen (2007). "The Study of Critical Junctures: Theory, Narrative, and Counterfactuals in Historical Institutionalism." *World Politics* 59, no. 3: 341–69.

Carothers, Christopher (2022). *Corruption Control in Authoritarian Regimes: Lessons from East Asia.* Cambridge, UK: Cambridge University Press.

Carpenter, Mason A., Marta A. Geletkanycz, and Wm. Gerard Sanders (2004). "Upper Echelons Research Revisited: Antecedents, Elements, and Consequences of Top Management Team Composition." *Journal of Management* 30, no. 6: 749–78.

Carr, Jered B., and Ralph S. Brower (2000). "Principled Opportunism: Evidence from the Organizational Middle." *Public Administration Quarterly* 24, no. 1: 109–38.

Cartwright, Dorwin (1965). "Influence, Leadership, Control." Pp. 1–47, in James G. March, ed., *Handbook of Organizations.* Chicago: Rand McNally.

Central Committee of the CCP (1999).《中共中央关于国有企业改革和发展若干重大问题的 决定》[Decision of the Central Committee of the CCP on Several Major Issues Concerning the Reform and Development of SOEs]. September 22. www.reformdata.org/1999/0922/4632.shtml

Chan, Kyle (2022). "Inside China's State-Owned Enterprises: Managed Competition through a Multi-Level Structure." *Chinese Journal of Sociology* 8, no. 4: 453–73.

Chandler, Alfred D. (1962). *Strategy and Structure: Chapters in the History of the American Industrial Enterprise*. Cambridge, MA: MIT Press.

Chen, Derong (1994). *Chinese Firms between Hierarchy and Market: The Contract Management Responsibility System in China*. New York: St. Martin's.

Chen, Feng (2000). "Subsistence Crises, Managerial Corruption and Labour Protests in China." *The China Journal*, no. 44: 41–63.

Chen, Hui [陈晖] (2008). 《新中国第一个生产资料广告》 [New China's First Advertisement for the Means of Production]. 《四川党的建设: 城市版》 [Sichuan Party Building: City Version]. August.

Chen, Qingtai [陈清泰] (1995). 《抓住当前深化企业改革的有利时机, 进一步推动企业集团 试点工作》 [Seize the Current Opportunity to Deepen Enterprise Reform, Further Promote Enterprise Group Pilot Work]. Pp. 8–20, in《我国企业集团试点的政策与实践》[*Policies and Practice of China's Enterprise Group Pilots*]. Beijing: Zhongguo jingji chubanshe.

Chen, Xi (2020). "The State-Owned Enterprise as an Identity: The Influence of Institutional Logics on *Guanxi* Behavior." *Management and Organization Review* 16, no. 3: 543–68.

Chen, Xi (2018). "Revisiting the Relationship between Justice and Extra-Role Behavior: The Role of State Ownership." *Management and Organization Review* 14, no. 3: 607–39.

Chen, Xiao-Ping, and Chao C. Chen (2004). "On the Intricacies of the Chinese *Guanxi*: A Process Model of *Guanxi* Development." *Asia Pacific Journal of Management* 21, no. 3: 305–24.

Chen, Yun [陈云] (1980).《经济形势与经验教训》[The Economic Situation and the Lessons Learned]. Speech at the Central Work Conference. December 16.

Child, John (1994). *Management in China during the Age of Reform*. Cambridge, UK: Cambridge University Press.

Child, John, and Yuan Lu (1990). "Industrial Decision-Making under China's Reform, 1985–1988." *Organization Studies* 11, no. 3: 321–51.

Child, John, and Suzana B. Rodrigues (2005). "The Internationalization of Chinese Firms: A Case for Theoretical Extension?" *Management and Organization Review* 1, no. 3: 381–410.

Child, John, and Malcolm Warner (2003). "Culture and Management in China." Pp. 24–47, in Malcolm Warner, ed., *Culture and Management in Asia*. London: Routledge Curzon.

Christensen, Thomas J. (1996). *Useful Adversaries: Grand Strategy, Domestic Mobilization, and Sino-American Conflict, 1947–1958*. Princeton, NJ: Princeton University Press.

Chung, Jae H. (2005). "Preferential Policies, Municipal Leadership, and Development Strategies: A Comparative Analysis of Qingdao and Dalian." Pp. 105–40, in Jae H. Chung, ed., *Cities in Post-Mao China: Recipes for Economic Development in the Reform Era*. London: Routledge.

Chung, Jae H. (1999). "A Sub-provincial Recipe of Coastal Development in China: The Case of Qingdao." *The China Quarterly*, no. 160: 919–52.

Coplin, Abigail E. (2019). "Domesticating Biotechnological Innovation: Science, Market and the State in Post-Socialist China." Ph.D. dissertation, Columbia University.

DeWalt, Kathleen M., and Billie R. DeWalt (2011). *Participant Observation: A Guide for Fieldworkers*, 2nd edn. Lanham, MD: Rowman AltaMira.

Ding, Iza (2022). *The Performative State: Public Scrutiny and Environmental Governance in China*. Ithaca, NY: Cornell University Press.

Donaldson, John A. (2009). "Why Do Similar Areas Adopt Different Developmental Strategies? A Study of Two Puzzling Chinese Provinces." *Journal of Contemporary China* 18, no. 60: 421–44.

Downs, Anthony (1967). *Inside Bureaucracy*. Boston: Little, Brown.

Duckett, Jane (1998). *The Entrepreneurial State in China: Real Estate and Commerce Departments in Reform Era Tianjin*. London: Routledge.

Eaton, Sarah (2016). *The Advance of the State in Contemporary China: State-Market Relations in the Reform Era*. Cambridge, UK: Cambridge University Press.

Eckstein, Harry (1975). "Case Study and Theory in Political Science." Pp. 79–137, in Fred J. Greenstein, and Nelson W. Polsby, eds., *Handbook of Political Science*, vol. 7. Reading, MA: Addison-Wesley.

Economy, Elizabeth (2018). *The Third Revolution: Xi Jinping and the New Chinese State*. Oxford: Oxford University Press.

Elfstrom, Manfred (2021). *Workers and Change in China: Resistance, Repression, Responsiveness*. Cambridge, UK: Cambridge University Press.

Elfstrom, Manfred (2019). "Two Steps Forward, One Step Back: Chinese State Reactions to Labour Unrest." *The China Quarterly*, no. 240: 855–79.

Elias, Steven M. (2009). "Restrictive Versus Promotive Control and Employee Work Outcomes: The Moderating Role of Locus of Control." *Journal of Management* 35, no. 2: 369–92.

Elias, Steven M. (2008). "Fifty Years of Influence in the Workplace: The Evolution of the French and Raven Power Taxonomy." *Journal of Management History* 14, no. 3: 267–83.

Elizabeth, Wendy Leutert, and Austin Strange (2024). "Pivoting to Overseas Development: INGOs' Changing Engagement with China." Working Paper.

Elster, Jon (1993). "Constitution-Making in Eastern Europe: Rebuilding the Boat in the Open Sea." *Public Administration* 71, no. 1–2: 169–217.

Fan, Shitao [范世涛], and Xue Xiaohe [薛小和] (2022). 《薛暮桥年谱: 1904–1952》 [*Xue Muqiao Chronicle: 1904–1952*]. Beijing: Zhongxin chuban jituan.

Farh, Jiing-Lih, and Bor-Shiuan Cheng (2000). "A Cultural Analysis of Paternalistic Leadership in Chinese Organizations." Pp. 84–127, in J. T. Li, Anne S. Tsui, and Elizabeth Weldon eds., *Management and Organizations in the Chinese Context: An Overview*. London: Palgrave Macmillan.

Farh, Jiing-Lih, Anne S. Tsui, Katherine Xin, and Bor-Shiuan Cheng (1998). "The Influence of Relational Demography and *Guanxi*: The Chinese Case." *Organization Science* 9, no. 4: 471–88.

Fei, Xiaotong (1992 [1947]). *From the Soil: The Foundations of Chinese Society, A Translation of Fei Xiaotong's* Xiangtu Zhongguo, Tr. Gary G. Hamilton and Wang Zheng. Berkeley: University of California Press.

Fewsmith, Joseph (2001). "The Political and Social Implications of China's Accession to the WTO." *The China Quarterly*, no. 167: 573–91.

Fewsmith, Joseph (1988). "Agricultural Crisis in China." *Problems of Communism* 38, no. 6: 78–93.

Fligstein, Neil (1993). *The Transformation of Corporate Control* Cambridge, MA: Harvard University Press.

Frazier, Mark W. (2010). *Socialist Insecurity: Pensions and the Politics of Uneven Development in China*. Ithaca, NY: Cornell University Press.

French, John R. P., Jr., and Bertram H. Raven (1959). "The Bases of Social Power." Pp. 150–67, in Dorwin Cartwright, ed., *Studies in Social Power*. Ann Arbor, MI: Institute for Social Research.

Frye, Timothy, and Edward D. Mansfield (2003). "Fragmenting Protection: The Political Economy of Trade Policy in the Post-Communist World." *British Journal of Political Science* 33, no. 4: 635–57.

George, Alexander L., and Andrew Bennett (2005). *Case Studies and Theory Development in the Social Sciences*. Cambridge, MA: MIT Press.

Gewirtz, Julian (2017). *Unlikely Partners: Chinese Reformers, Western Economists, and the Making of Global China*. Cambridge, MA: Harvard University Press.

Ghosh, Madanmohan, and John Whalley (2008). "State-Owned Enterprises, Shirking, and Trade Liberalization." *Economic Modelling* 25, no. 6: 1206–15.

Goffman, Erving (1959). *Presentation of Self in Everyday Life*. Garden City, NY: Doubleday Anchor Books.

Gold, Thomas, Doug Guthrie, and David Wank, eds. (2002). *Social Connections in China: Institutions, Culture, and the Changing Nature of* Guanxi. Cambridge, UK: Cambridge University Press.

Gold, Thomas, William J. Hurst, Jaeyoun Won, and Qiang Li, eds. (2009). *Laid-off Workers in a Workers' State: Unemployment with Chinese Characteristics*. London: Palgrave Macmillan.

Gordon, Jeffrey N., and Curtis J. Milhaupt (2019). "China as a 'National Strategic Buyer': Toward a Multilateral Regime for Cross-Border M&A." *Columbia Business Law Review* 192, no. 1: 192–251.

Granrose, Cherlyn S., Qiang Huang, and Elena Reigadas (2000). "Changing Organizational Cultures in Chinese Firms." Pp. 483–96, in Neal M. Ashkanasy, Celeste Wilderom, and Mark F. Peterson, eds., *Handbook of Organizational Culture & Climate*. Thousand Oaks, CA: SAGE Publications.

Guth, William D., and Ian C. MacMillan (1986). "Strategy Implementation Versus Middle Management Self-Interest." *Strategic Management Journal* 7, no. 4: 313–27.

Guthrie, Douglas (1998). "The Declining Significance of *Guanxi* in China's Economic Transition." *The China Quarterly*, no. 154: 254–82.

Hafen, Susan (2004). "Organizational Gossip: A Revolving Door of Regulation and Resistance." *Southern Journal of Communication* 69, no. 3: 223–40.

Hambrick, Donald C., and Phyllis A. Mason (1984). "Upper Echelons: The Organization as a Reflection of Its Top Managers." *Academy of Management Review* 9, no. 2: 193–206.

Han, Yong, and Yochanan Altman (2009). "Supervisor and Subordinate *Guanxi*: A Grounded Investigation in the People's Republic of China." *Journal of Business Ethics* 88, no. Supp. 1: 91–104.

Hanser, Amy (2008). *Service Encounters: Class, Gender, and the Market for Social Distinction in Urban China*. Palo Alto, CA: Stanford University Press.

Hasmath, Reza, Jessica C. Teets, and Orion A. Lewis (2019). "The Innovative Personality? Policy Making and Experimentation in an Authoritarian Bureaucracy." *Public Administration and Development* 39, no. 3: 154–62.

Hay, Donald, Derek Morris, Guy Liu, and Shujie Yao (1994). *Economic Reform and State-Owned Enterprises in China, 1979–87*. Oxford: Oxford University Press.

Heilmann, Sebastian (2008a). "From Local Experiments to National Policy: The Origins of China's Distinctive Policy Process." *The China Journal*, no. 59: 1–30.

Heilmann, Sebastian (2008b). "Policy Experimentation in China's Economic Rise." *Studies in Comparative International Development* 43, no. 1: 1–26.

Heilmann, Sebastian, and Elizabeth J. Perry (2011). "Embracing Uncertainty: Guerrilla Policy Style and Adaptive Governance in China." Pp. 1–29, in Sebastian Heilmann, and Elizabeth J. Perry, eds., *Mao's Invisible Hand: The Political Foundations of Adaptive Governance in China*. Cambridge, MA: Harvard University Press.

Heilmann, Sebastian, and Lea Shih (2013). *The Rise of Industrial Policy in China, 1978–2012*. Cambridge, MA: Harvard-Yenching Institute Working Paper.

Hellman, Joel (1998). "Winners Take All: The Politics of Partial Reform in Postcommunist Transitions." *World Politics* 50, no. 2: 203–34.

Hersey, Paul, Kenneth H. Blanchard, and Dewey E. Johnson (1996). *Management of Organizational Behavior: Utilizing Human Resources*, 7th edn. Englewood Cliffs, NJ: Prentice Hall.

Hickman, Craig R. (1990). *Mind of a Manager, Soul of a Leader*. New York: John Wiley & Sons.

Hillman, Ben (2014). *Patronage and Power: Local State Networks and Party-State Resilience in Rural China*. Palo Alto, CA: Stanford University Press.

Hong, Hu [洪虎] (1999). 《国有经济改革与企业制度创新》 [*SOE Reform and Institutional Innovation*]. Beijing: Zhonggong zhongyang dangxiao chubanshe.

Horak, Sven, and Katja Restel (2016). "A Dynamic Typology of Informal Institutions: Learning from the Case of *Guanxi*." *Management and Organization Review* 12, no. 3: 525–46.

Horowitz, Michael C., Allan C. Stam, and Cali M. Ellis (2015). *Why Leaders Fight*. Cambridge, UK: Cambridge University Press.

Hou, Yue (2019). *The Private Sector in Public Office: Selective Property Rights in China*. Cambridge, UK: Cambridge University Press.

House, Robert J. (1996). "Path-Goal Theory of Leadership: Lessons, Legacy, and a Reformulated Theory." *The Leadership Quarterly* 7, no. 3: 323–52.

Hsieh, Chang-Tai, and Zheng (Michael) Song (2015). "Grasp the Large, Let Go of the Small: The Transformation of the State Sector in China." *Brookings Papers on Economic Activity*. Washington, DC: Brookings Institution.

Hsueh, Roselyn (2011). *China's Regulatory State: A New Strategy for Globalization*. Ithaca, NY: Cornell University Press.

Hsueh, Roselyn, Francesca R. Jensenius, and Akasemi Newsome (2014). "Fieldwork in Political Science: Encountering Challenges and Crafting Solutions: Introduction." *PS: Political Science & Politics* 47, no. 2: 391–93.

Hu, Angang [胡鞍钢] (2001).《腐败：中国最大的社会污染：对中国90年代后半期腐败经济损失的初步估计》 [Corruption: China's Largest Social Pollution, Preliminary Estimates of the Economic Losses Caused by Corruption in China in the Second Half of the 1990s].《领导文萃》 [*Leadership Compendium*], no. 9: 34–39.

Huang, Xu, Kan Shi, Zhijie Zhang, and Yat L. Cheung (2006). "The Impact of Participative Leadership Behavior on Psychological Empowerment and Organizational Commitment in Chinese State-Owned Enterprises: The Moderating Role of Organizational Tenure." *Asia Pacific Journal of Management* 23, no. 3: 345–67.

Huang, Yasheng (2003). *Selling China: Foreign Direct Investment during the Reform Era*. Cambridge, UK: Cambridge University Press.

Hurst, William (2009). *The Chinese Worker after Socialism*. Cambridge, UK: Cambridge University Press.

Jago, Arthur G. (1982). "Leadership: Perspectives in Theory and Research." *Management Science* 28, no. 3: 315–36.

Jaros, Kyle A. (2019). *China's Urban Champions: The Politics of Spatial Development*. Princeton, NJ: Princeton University Press.

Jefferson, Gary H., and Inderjit Singh, eds. (1999). *Enterprise Reform in China: Ownership, Transition, and Performance*. Oxford: Oxford University Press.

Jiang, Fuxiu, and Kenneth A. Kim (2020). "Corporate Governance in China: A Survey." *Review of Finance* 24, no. 4: 733–72.

Jiang, Fuxiu, and Kenneth A. Kim (2015). "Corporate Governance in China: A Modern Perspective." *Journal of Corporate Finance* 32: 190–216.

Jiang, Junyan, and Zhaotian Luo (2021). "Leadership Styles and Political Survival of Chinese Communist Party Elites." *The Journal of Politics* 83, no. 2: 777–82.

Jing, Runtian, and E. Patrick McDermott (2013). "Transformation of SOEs in China: A Strategic Action Model." *Management and Organization Review* 9, no. 1: 53–86.

Jing, Yijia (2017). "Creative Incrementalism: Governance Reforms in China Since 1978." *Chinese Political Science Review* 2, no. 1: 56–68.

Johnston, Hank, and Carol Mueller (2001). "Unobtrusive Practices of Contention in Leninist Regimes." *Sociological Perspectives* 44, no. 3: 351–75.

Jones, Benjamin F., and Benjamin A. Olken (2009). "Hit or Miss? The Effect of Assassinations on Institutions and War." *American Economic Journal: Macroeconomics* 1, no. 2: 55–87.

Kardon, Isaac B., and Wendy Leutert (2022). "Pier Competitor: China's Power Position in Global Ports." *International Security* 46, no. 4: 9–47.

Katzenstein, Peter J., and Lucia A. Seybert, eds. (2018). *Protean Power: Exploring the Uncertain and Unexpected in World Politics*. Cambridge, UK: Cambridge University Press.

Keister, Lisa A. (2000). *Chinese Business Groups: The Structure and Impact of Interfirm Relations During Economic Development*. Oxford: Oxford University Press.

Keister, Lisa A., and Randy Hodson (2009). "Ownership and Innovation during Economic Development: Corporate Ownership and Strategy Formation in China." Pp. 129–63, in Lisa A. Keister, ed., *Work and Organizations in China after Thirty Years of Transition*. Bingley, UK: Emerald.

Kingdon, John W. (1984). *Agendas, Alternatives and Public Policies*. Boston: Little, Brown.

Kipnis, David (1984). "The Use of Power in Organizations and in Interpersonal Settings." *Applied Social Psychology Annual*, no. 5: 179–210.

Klitgaard, Robert (1988). *Controlling Corruption*. Berkeley: University of California Press.

Knight, W. Andy (2009). "Distinguishing and Unifying Visionary Leadership and Mechanical Management." Pp. 135–47, in Joseph Masciulli, Mikhail A. Molchanov, and W. Andy Knight, eds., *The Ashgate Research Companion to Political Leadership*. Burlington, VT: Ashgate.

Köll, Elisabeth (2019). *Railroads and the Transformation of China*. Cambridge, MA: Harvard University Press.

Kollock, Peter (1994). "The Emergence of Exchange Structures: An Experimental Study of Uncertainty, Commitment, and Trust." *American Journal of Sociology* 100, no. 2: 313–45.

Koss, Daniel (2021). "Party Building as Institutional Bricolage: Asserting Authority at the Business Frontier." *The China Quarterly*, no. 248(S1): 222–43.

Kotter, John P. (1997). *Matsushita Leadership: Lessons from the 21st Century's Most Remarkable Entrepreneur*. New York: The Free Press.

Kowalski, Przemyslaw, Max Büge, Monika Sztajerowska, and Matias Egeland (2013). "State-Owned Enterprises: Trade Effects and Policy Implications." OECD Trade Policy Paper, no. 147.

Kowert, Paul A., and Margaret G. Hermann (1997). "Who Takes Risks? Daring and Caution in Foreign Policy Making." *Journal of Conflict Resolution* 41, no. 5: 611–37.

Lampton, David M. (2013). *Following the Leader: Ruling China, from Deng Xiaoping to Xi Jinping*. Berkeley: University of California Press.

Landry, Pierre F. (2008). *Decentralized Authoritarianism in China: The Communist Party's Control of Local Elites in the Post-Mao Era*. Cambridge, UK: Cambridge University Press.

Lant, Theresa K., Frances J. Milliken, and Bipin Batra (1992). "The Role of Managerial Learning and Interpretation in Strategic Persistence and Reorientation: An Empirical Exploration." *Strategic Management Journal* 13, no. 8: 585–608.

Lardy, Nicholas R. (2019). *The State Strikes Back: The End of Economic Reform in China?* Washington, DC: Peterson Institute for International Economics.

Lardy, Nicholas R. (2001). "Issues in China's WTO Accession." Testimony before the US-China Security Review Commission. www.brookings.edu/articles/issues-in-chinas-wto-accession/

Lee, Ching Kwan (2017). *The Specter of Global China: Politics, Labor, and Foreign Investment in Africa*. Chicago: University of Chicago Press.

Lee, Ching Kwan, ed. (2007). *Working in China: Ethnographies of Labor and Workplace Transformation*. London: Routledge.

Lee, Ching Kwan (1998). *Gender and the South China Miracle: Two Worlds of Factory Women*. Berkeley: University of California Press.

Lee, Hong Y. (1978). *The Politics of the Chinese Cultural Revolution: A Case Study*. Berkeley: University of California Press.

Leng, Ning, and Cai (Vera) Zuo (2022). "Tournament Style Bargaining within Boundaries: Setting Targets in China's Cadre Evaluation System." *Journal of Contemporary China* 31, no. 133: 116–35.

Leutert, Wendy (2022). "Sino-Japanese Engagement and the Making of China's National Champions." *New Political Economy* 27, no. 6: 929–43.

Leutert, Wendy (2018a). "The Political Mobility of China's Central SOE Leaders." *The China Quarterly*, no. 233: 1–21.

Leutert, Wendy (2018b). "Firm Control: Governing the State-Owned Economy Under Xi Jinping." *China Perspectives*, nos. 1/2: 27–36.

Leutert, Wendy, and Sarah Eaton (2021). "Deepening Not Departure: Xi Jinping's Governance of China's State-Owned Economy." *The China Quarterly*, no. 248(S1): 200–21.

Leutert, Wendy, Elizabeth Plantan, and Austin Strange (2023). "Puzzling Partnerships: Overseas Infrastructure Development by Chinese State-Owned Enterprises and Humanitarian Organizations." *Studies in Comparative International Development* 58, no. 2: 195–223.

Leutert, Wendy, and Samantha A. Vortherms (2021). "Personnel Power: Governing State-Owned Enterprises." *Business and Politics* 23, no. 3: 419–37.

Li, Anthony H. F. (2017). "E–commerce and Taobao Villages: A Promise for China's Rural Development?" *China Perspectives*, no. 3: 57–62.
Li, Chen (2016). "Holding 'China Inc.' Together: The CCP and the Rise of China's *Yangqi*." *The China Quarterly*, no. 228: 927–49.
Li, Chen (2014). *China's Centralized Industrial Order: Industrial Reform and the Rise of Centrally Controlled Big Business*. London: Routledge.
Li, Hongbin, and Li-An Zhou (2005). "Political Turnover and Economic Performance: The Incentive Role of Personnel Control in China." *Journal of Public Economics* 89, no. 9: 1743–62.
Li, Ju (2012). "Fight Silently: Everyday Resistance in Surviving State-Owned Enterprises in Contemporary China." *Global Labour Journal* 3, no. 2: 194–216.
Li, Lanqing (2009). *Breaking Through: The Birth of China's Opening-Up Policy*, Tr. Yuan Ling and Siying Zhang. Oxford: Oxford University Press.
Li, Lianjiang (2019). "The Cadre Resignation Tide in the Wake of the 18th Party Congress." *China: An International Journal* 17, no. 3: 188–99.
Li, Xiaojun, and Ka Zeng (2019). "To Join or Not to Join? State Ownership, Commercial Interests, and China's Belt and Road Initiative." *Pacific Affairs* 92, no. 1: 5–26.
Lieberthal, Kenneth G., and David M. Lampton, eds. (1992). *Bureaucracy, Politics, and Decision Making in Post-Mao China*. Berkeley: University of California Press.
Lieberthal, Kenneth, and Michel Oksenberg (1988). *Policy Making in China: Leaders, Structures, and Processes*. Princeton, NJ: Princeton University Press.
Lijphart, Arend (1992). "Democratization and Constitutional Choices in Czecho-Slovakia, Hungary and Poland 1989–91." *Journal of Theoretical Politics* 4, no. 2: 207–23.
Lin, Alex Yu-Ting, and Saori N. Katada (2022). "Striving for Greatness: Status Aspirations, Rhetorical Entrapment, and Domestic Reforms." *Review of International Political Economy* 29, no. 1: 175–201.
Lin, Lauren Yu-Hsin (2013b). "Do Social Ties Matter in Corporate Governance? The Missing Factor in Chinese Corporate Governance Reform." *George Mason Journal of International Commercial Law* 5, no. 1: 39–74.
Lin, Li-wen (2017). "Reforming China's State-Owned Enterprises: From Structure to People." *The China Quarterly*, no. 229: 107–29.
Lin, Li-wen (2013a). "State Ownership and Corporate Governance in China: An Executive Career Approach." *Columbia Business Law Review*, no. 3: 743–800.

Lin, Li-wen, and Curtis J. Milhaupt (2013). "We Are the (National) Champions: Understanding the Mechanisms of State Capitalism in China." *Stanford Law Review* 65, no. 4: 697–759.

Lin, Ling [林凌], ed. (1984). 《四川经济体制改革》 [*Sichuan Economic System Reform*]. Chengdu: Sichuansheng shehui kexue chubanshe.

Lin, Yi-min, and Tian Zhu (2001). "Ownership Restructuring in Chinese State Industry: An Analysis of Evidence on Initial Organizational Changes." *The China Quarterly*, no. 166: 305–41.

Lindstedt, Catharina, and Daniel Naurin (2010). "Transparency Is Not Enough: Making Transparency Effective in Reducing Corruption." *International Political Science Review* 31, no. 3: 301–22.

Liu, Xielin, Xiao Wang, and Yimei Hu (2021). *Catch-up and Radical Innovation in Chinese State-Owned Enterprises: Exploring Large Infrastructure Projects*. Northampton, MA: Edward Elgar.

Lü, Xiaobo (2000). *Cadres and Corruption: The Organizational Involution of the Chinese Communist Party*. Palo Alto, CA: Stanford University Press.

Lü, Xiaobo, and Elizabeth J. Perry, eds. (1997). Danwei: *The Changing Chinese Workplace in Historical and Comparative Perspective*. Armonk, NY: M. E. Sharpe.

Lutgen-Sandvik, Pamela (2006). "Take This Job and … :Quitting and Other Forms of Resistance to Workplace Bullying." *Communication Monographs* 73, no. 4: 406–33.

Lyons, Thomas P. (1990). "Planning and Interprovincial Co-ordination in Maoist China." *The China Quarterly*, no. 121: 36–60.

Ma, Dali (2011). "A Relational View of Organizational Restructuring: The Case of Transitional China." *Management and Organization Review* 8, no. 1: 51–75.

Manion, Melanie (1985). "The Cadre Management System, Post-Mao: The Appointment, Promotion, Transfer and Removal of Party and State Leaders." *The China Quarterly*, no. 102: 203–33.

Marinova, Svetla, John Child, and Marin Marinov (2011). "Evolution of Firm- and Country-Specific Advantages and Disadvantages in the Process of Chinese Firm Internationalization." Pp. 235–69, in Christian G. Asmussen, Pedersen Torben, M. Devinney Timothy, and Tihanyi Laszlo, eds., *Dynamics of Globalization: Location-Specific Advantages or Liabilities of Foreignness?* Bingley, UK: Emerald Group.

Marquis, Christopher, and Kunyuan Qiao (2020). "Waking from Mao's Dream: Communist Ideological Imprinting and the Internationalization of Entrepreneurial Ventures in China." *Administrative Science Quarterly* 65, no. 3: 795–830.

Marquis, Christopher, and András Tilcsik (2013). "Imprinting: Toward a Multilevel Theory." *Academy of Management Annals* 7, no. 1: 195–245.
McMillan, John, and Christopher Woodruff (1999). "Interfirm Relationships and Informal Credit in Vietnam." *Quarterly Journal of Economics* 114, no. 4: 1285–320.
Meier, Kenneth J., and Laurence J. O'Toole (2006). *Bureaucracy in a Democratic State: A Governance Perspective*. Baltimore, MD: Johns Hopkins University Press.
Mertha, Andrew C. (2009). "'Fragmented Authoritarianism 2.0': Political Pluralization in the Chinese Policy Process." *The China Quarterly*, no. 200: 995–1012.
Mertha, Andrew C. (2008). *China's Water Warriors: Citizen Action and Policy Change*. Ithaca, NY: Cornell University Press.
Milner, Helen V., and Keiko Kubota (2005). "Why the Move to Free Trade? Democracy and Trade Policy in the Developing Countries." *International Organization* 59, no. 1: 107–43.
Minzner, Carl (2018). *End of an Era: How China's Authoritarian Revival Is Undermining Its Rise*. Oxford: Oxford University Press.
Mohan, Giles, and May Tan-Mullins (2019). "The Geopolitics of South–South Infrastructure Development: Chinese-Financed Energy Projects in the Global South." *Urban Studies* 56, no. 7: 1368–85.
Morgan, Gareth (1993). "Organizations as Political Systems." Pp. 212–17, in Christopher Mabey, and Bill Mayon-White, eds., *Managing Change*, 2nd edn. London: Paul Chapman.
Muczyk, Jan P., and Bernard C. Reimann (1987). "The Case for Directive Leadership." *Academy of Management Perspectives* 1, no. 4: 301–11.
Mulder, Mauk, and Ad Stemerding (1963). "Threat, Attraction to Group, and Need for Strong Leadership: A Laboratory Experiment in a Natural Setting." *Human Relations* 16, no. 4: 317–34.
Mwase, Nkunde, and Yongzheng Yang (2012). "BRICs' Philosophies for Development Financing and Their Implications for LICs." International Monetary Fund Working Paper, No. WP/12/74.
Naughton, Barry (2019). "The Financialisation of the State Sector in China." *East Asian Policy* 11, no. 2: 46–60.
Naughton, Barry (1995). *Growing Out of the Plan: Chinese Economic Reform, 1978–1993*. Cambridge, UK: Cambridge University Press.
Nee, Victor, and Sonja Opper (2012). *Capitalism from Below: Markets and Institutional Change in China*. Cambridge, MA: Harvard University Press.
Nielsen, Richard A. (2016). "Case Selection via Matching." *Sociological Methods & Research* 45, no. 3: 569–97.

Nolan, Peter (2001). *China and the Global Economy: National Champions, Industrial Policy and the Big Business Revolution*. London: Palgrave Macmillan.

Nolan, Peter (1998). *Indigenous Large Firms in China's Economic Reform: The Case of Shougang Iron and Steel Corporation*. London: Contemporary China Institute, School of Oriental and African Studies, University of London.

North, Douglass C. (1990). *Institutions, Institutional Change and Economic Performance*. Cambridge, UK: Cambridge University Press.

Northouse, Peter G. (2019). *Leadership: Theory and Practice*, 8th edn. Thousand Oaks, CA: SAGE Publications.

O'Brien, Kevin J., and Lianjiang Li (1999). "Selective Policy Implementation in Rural China." *Comparative Politics* 31, no. 2: 167–86.

Oi, Jean C. (1999). *Rural China Takes Off: Institutional Foundations of Economic Reform*. Berkeley: University of California Press.

Oi, Jean C. (1992). "Fiscal Reform and the Economic Foundations of Local State Corporatism in China." *World Politics* 45, no. 1: 99–126.

Ozery, Tamar G. (2021). "Illiberal Governance and the Rise of China's Public Firms: An Oxymoron or China's Greatest Triumph?" *University of Pennsylvania Journal of International Law* 42, no. 4: 921–1004.

Paik, Wooyeal, and Richard Baum (2014). "Clientelism with Chinese Characteristics: Local Patronage Networks in Post-Reform China." *Political Science Quarterly* 129, no. 4: 675–702.

Pearce, Jone L., ed. (2011). *Status in Management and Organizations*. Cambridge, UK: Cambridge University Press.

Pearce, Jone L., Imre Branyiczki, and Gregory A. Bigley (2000). "Insufficient Bureaucracy: Trust and Commitment in Particularistic Organizations." *Organization Science* 11, no. 2: 148–62.

Pearson, Margaret M., Meg Rithmire, and Kellee S. Tsai (2022). "China's Party-State Capitalism and International Backlash: From Interdependence to Insecurity." *International Security* 47, no. 2: 135–76.

Pellegrini, Ekin K., and Terri A. Scandura (2008). "Paternalistic Leadership: A Review and Agenda for Future Research." *Journal of Management* 34, no. 3: 566–93.

Peng, Mike W. (2003). "Institutional Transitions and Strategic Choices." *Academy of Management Review* 28, no. 2: 275–96.

Peng, Qiang [彭强] (1993). 《全民所有制企业改组为国家独资有限公司的设想》 [Thoughts on Reorganization of Ownership by the Whole People into Wholly State-Owned Limited Liability Companies]. 《改革内参》 [*Internal Reference Materials on Reform*], no. 13: 18–19.

Pettigrew, Andrew M. (1987). "Context and Action in the Transformation of the Firm." *Journal of Management Studies* 24, no. 6: 649–70.

Podolny, Joel M., Rakesh Khurana, and Marya Hill-Popper (2004). "Revisiting the Meaning of Leadership." *Research in Organizational Behavior* 26: 1–36.

Politburo. CCP Central Committee (2015). 《中央管理企业负责人薪酬制度改革方案》 [Compensation Reform Plan for Heads of Enterprises Managed by the Center]. January 1.

Prakash, Aseem (2000). *Greening the Firm: The Politics of Corporate Environmentalism*. Cambridge, UK: Cambridge University Press.

Prasad, Pushkala, and Anshuman Prasad (2000). "Stretching the Iron Cage: The Constitution and Implications of Routine Workplace Resistance." *Organization Science* 11, no. 4: 387–403.

Przeworski, Adam (1991). *Democracy and the Market: Political and Economic Reforms in Eastern Europe and Latin America*. Cambridge, UK: Cambridge University Press.

Raines, Susan S., and Aseem Prakash (2005). "Leadership Matters: Policy Entrepreneurship in Corporate Environmental Policy Making." *Administration & Society* 37, no. 1: 3–22.

Ramamurti, Ravi (1987). "Leadership Styles in State-Owned Enterprises." *Journal of General Management* 13, no. 2: 44–55.

Raven, Bertram H. (2008). "The Bases of Power and the Power/Interaction Model of Interpersonal Influence" *Analyses of Social Issues and Public Policy* 8, no. 1: 1–22.

Raven, Bertram H. (1992). "A Power/Interaction Model of Interpersonal Influence: French and Raven Thirty Years Later." *Journal of Social Behavior and Personality* 7, no. 2: 217–44.

Raven, Bertram H. (1965). "Social Influence and Power." Pp. 371–82, in Ivan D. Steiner and Martin Fishbein, eds., *Current Studies in Social Psychology*. New York: Holt, Rinehart, and Winston.

Raynard, Mia, Fangmei Lu, and Runtian Jing (2020). "Reinventing the SOE? Negotiating Change during Profound Environmental Upheaval." *Academy of Management Journal* 63, no. 4: 1300–35.

Redding, Gordon (2013). *The Spirit of Chinese Capitalism*. Boston: De Gruyter.

Redding, Gordon (2002). "The Capitalist Business System of China and Its Rationale." *Asia Pacific Journal of Management* 19, nos. 2–3: 221–49.

Remmer, Karen L., and Erik Wibbels (2000). "The Subnational Politics of Economic Adjustment: Provincial Politics and Fiscal Performance in Argentina." *Comparative Political Studies* 33, no. 4: 419–51.

Rithmire, Meg E. (2023). *Precarious Ties: Business and the State in Authoritarian Asia*. Oxford: Oxford University Press.

Rithmire, Meg E., and Hao Chen (2021). "The Emergence of Mafia-Like Business Systems in China." *The China Quarterly*, no. 248: 1037–58.

Rose-Ackerman, Susan (1999). "Political Corruption and Democracy." *Connecticut Journal of International Law* 14, no. 2: 363–78.

Rosen, Daniel H. (2014). *Avoiding the Blind Alley: China's Economic Overhaul and Its Global Implications*. New York: Asia Society Policy Institute.

Rosen, Daniel H., Wendy Leutert, and Shan Guo (2018). "Missing Link: Corporate Governance in China's State Sector." San Francisco: Asia Society Special Report with Rhodium Group.

Rotberg, Robert I. (2017). *The Corruption Cure: How Citizens and Leaders Can Combat Graft*. Princeton, NJ: Princeton University Press.

Rui, Huaichuan (2005). *Globalization, Transition and Development in China: The Case of the Coal Industry*. London: Routledge.

Sabel, Charles F., and David Stark (1982). "Planning, Politics, and Shop-Floor Power: Hidden Forms of Bargaining in Soviet-Imposed State-Socialist Societies." *Politics & Society* 11, no. 4: 439–75.

Sarros, Joseph C., George A. Tanewski, Richard P. Winter, Joseph C. Santora, and Iain L. Densten (2002). "Work Alienation and Organizational Leadership." *British Journal of Management* 13, no. 4: 285–304.

SASAC (2017). 《中央企业投资监督管理法》 [Measures for the Supervision and Administration of Investment of Central SOEs] and 《中央企业境外投资监督管理办法》 [Measures for the Supervision and Administration of Overseas Investment of Central SOEs]. January 18. www.gov.cn/xinwen/2017-01/18/content_5160910.htm#1

SASAC (2012, 2013, 2014). 《中国国有资产监督管理年鉴》 [*State-Owned Assets Supervision and Management Yearbook*]. Beijing: Zhongguo jingji chubanshe.

SASAC (2009).《中央企业负责人经营业绩考核暂行办法》 [Interim Measures for Operational Performance Assessments of Central SOE Principals]. December 28. www.moj.gov.cn/pub/sfbgw/flfggz/flfggzbmgz/201004/t20100428_144810.html

SASAC, Research Office (2012).《探索与研究：国有资产监督管理和国有企业改革研究报告》 [*Exploration and Research: State-Owned Assets Supervision and Management and SOE Reform Research Report*]. Beijing: Jingji chubanshe.

Saunders, Elizabeth N. (2011). *Leaders at War: How Presidents Shape Military Interventions*. Ithaca, NY: Cornell University Press.

Scissors, Derek (2017). *Chinese Investment: Revenge of the State*. Washington, DC: American Enterprise Institute.

Scott, James C. (2008 [1987]). *Weapons of the Weak: Everyday Forms of Peasant Resistance*. New Haven, CT: Yale University Press.

Shamir, Boas, Robert J. House, and Michael B. Arthur (1993). "The Motivational Effects of Charismatic Leadership: A Self-Concept Based Theory." *Organization Science* 4, no. 4: 577–94.

Shao, Ning [邵宁] (2014).《国有企业改革实录, 1998–2008》 [*The Reform of State-Owned Enterprises in Memoir, 1998–2008*]. Beijing: Jingji kexue chubanshe.

Shen, Xiaoxiao, and Kellee S. Tsai (2016). "Institutional Adaptability in China: Local Developmental Models under Changing Economic Conditions." *World Development* 87: 107–27.

Shih, Victor C. (2008). *Factions and Finance in China: Elite Conflict and Inflation*. Cambridge, UK: Cambridge University.

Shirk, Susan L. (1993). *The Political Logic of Economic Reform in China*. Berkeley: University of California Press.

Silverthorne, Colin, and Ting-Hsin Wang (2001). "Situational Leadership Style as a Predictor of Success and Productivity among Taiwanese Business Organizations." *The Journal Psychology* 135, no. 4: 399–412.

Singh, Harbir, and Michael Useem (2016). *The Strategic Leader's Roadmap: 6 Steps for Integrating Leadership and Strategy*. Philadelphia, PA: Wharton Digital Press.

Skålnes, Tor (2016). *The Politics of Economic Reform in Zimbabwe: Continuity and Change in Development*. London: Palgrave Macmillan.

Slater, Robert (1999). *Jack Welch and the GE Way: Management Insights and Leadership Secrets of the Legendary CEO*. New York: McGraw Hill.

Smith, Mitchell P. (1997). "The Commission Made Me Do It: The European Commission as a Strategic Asset in Domestic Politics." Pp. 167–86, in Neill Nugent, ed., *At the Heart of the Union: Studies of the European Commission*. New York: St. Martin's.

Soifer, Hillel D. (2012). "The Causal Logic of Critical Junctures." *Comparative Political Studies* 45, no. 12: 1572–97.

Solinger, Dorothy (2009). "The Phase-Out of the Unfit: Keeping the Unworthy Out of Work." Pp. 307–36, in Lisa A. Keister, ed., *Work and Organizations in China after Thirty Years of Transition*. Bingley, UK: Emerald Group.

Sotirin, Patty, and Heidi Gottfried (1999). "The Ambivalent Dynamics of Secretarial 'Bitching': Control, Resistance, and the Construction of Identity." *Organization* 6, no. 1: 57–80.

Stark, David, and László Bruszt (1998). *Postsocialist Pathways: Transforming Politics and Property in East Central Europe*. Cambridge, UK: Cambridge University Press.

State Council (2017). 《国务院国资委以管资本为主推进智能转变方案》 [Plan for State Council State-Owned Assets Supervision and Administration Commission Promotes Functional Transformation Plans Focusing on Capital Management]. April 27. www.gov.cn/zhengce/content/2017-05/10/content_5192390.htm

State Council (2003). 《国务院办公厅关于公布国务院国有资产监督管理委员会履行出资人职责企业名单的通知》 [General Office of the State Council Notice Regarding the State-Owned Assets Supervision and Administration Commission Carrying Out Investor Responsibilities Enterprise List]. October 21. www.gov.cn/gongbao/content/2003/content_52517.htm

State Council (1992).《全民所有制工业企业转换经营机制条例》 [Regulations on the Transformation of the Operational Mechanisms of Industrial Enterprises Owned By the Whole People]. July 23. www.reformdata.org/1992/0723/21459.shtml

State Council (1983).《关于国营企业利改税试行办法》 [On the Trial Measures for the Tax Reform of SOEs]. April 24. www.gov.cn/gongbao/shuju/1983/gwyb198311.pdf

State Economic and Trade Commission (2000). 《国有企业改革与建立现代企业制度》 [State-Owned Enterprise Reform and Establishing a Modern Enterprise System]. Beijing: Falü chubanshe.

State Economic System Restructuring Commission (1992).《有限责任公司规范意见》 [Opinions on Standardizing Limited Liability Companies]. May 11. www.gov.cn/gongbao/shuju/1992/gwyb199216.pdf

State Economic System Restructuring Commission, Policy and Regulation Division (1992). 《关于制定《全民所有制工业企业换经营机制暂行条例》内部讨论情况》[Circumstances of the Internal Discussion on Drafting the "Regulations on Transformation of the Operational Mechanisms of Internal Enterprises Owned by the Whole People"]. 《内部参考》[Internal Reference Materials], no. 7: 18–24.

State Economic System Restructuring Commission, State Economic Commission, Ministry of Finance, People's Bank of China, State Council, Production Office (1992).《股份制企业试点办法》 [Pilot Measures for Joint-Stock Enterprises]. May 11.

State-Owned Assets Administration Bureau, State Planning Commission, Economic Structural Reform Commission, State Council Economic and Trade Office (1992). 《关于国家试点企业集团国有资产授权经营的实施办法（暂行）》[Interim Implementation Measures of the Authorized Operation of State-Owned Assets of National Pilot Enterprise Groups]. September 11. https://law.pkulaw.com/chinalaw/075a28c84c65ad8abdfb.html

Steinfeld, Edward S. (1998). *Forging Reform in China: The Fate of State-Owned Industry*. Cambridge, UK: Cambridge University Press.
Steinmo, Sven, Kathleen Thelen, and Frank Longstreth, eds. (1992). *Structuring Politics: Historical Institutionalism in Comparative Analysis*. Cambridge, UK: Cambridge University Press.
Suchman, Mark C. (1995). "Managing Legitimacy: Strategic and Institutional Approaches." *Academy of Management Review* 20, no. 3: 571–610.
Sutherland, Dylan (2003). *China's Large Enterprises and the Challenge of Late Industrialization*. London: Routledge.
Szakonyi, David, and Johannes Urpelainen (2014). "Who Benefits from Economic Reform? Firms and Distributive Politics." *The Journal of Politics* 76, no. 3: 841–58.
Tan, Yeling (2021). *Disaggregating China, Inc.: State Strategies in the Liberal Economic Order*. Ithaca, NY: Cornell University Press.
Tarrow, Sidney (2010). "The Strategy of Paired Comparison: Toward a Theory of Practice." *Comparative Political Studies* 43: 230–59.
Teiwes, Frederick C., and Warren Sun (2016). *Paradoxes of Post-Mao Rural Reform: Initial Steps Toward a New Chinese Countryside, 1976–1981*. London: Routledge.
Teiwes, Frederick C., with Warren Sun (1999). *China's Road to Disaster: Mao, Central Politicians, and Provincial Leaders in the Unfolding of the Great Leap Forward, 1955–1959*. Armonk, NY: M. E. Sharpe.
Thelen, Kathleen A., and James Conran (2016). "Institutional Change." Pp. 51–70, in Orfeo Fioretos, Tulia G. Falleti, and Adam Sheingate, eds., *The Oxford Handbook of Historical Institutionalism*. Oxford: Oxford University Press.
Thompson, James D. (1967). *Organizations in Action: Social Science Bases of Administrative Theory*. New York: McGraw-Hill.
Torigian, Joseph (2022). *Prestige, Manipulation, and Coercion: Elite Power Struggles in the Soviet Union and China after Stalin and Mao*. New Haven, CT: Yale University Press.
Truex, Rory (2016). *Making Autocracy Work: Representation and Responsiveness in Modern China*. Cambridge, UK: Cambridge University Press.
US Department of State (1999). Declassified Cable from Shenyang Consulate, February. Declassified in part on March 30, 2016, at the author's request.
US Embassy in Beijing (1999). Declassified Cable, June. Declassified in part on April 6, 2016, at the author's request.
Useem, Michael (2022). "Leading Corporations in the U.S. and Other National Settings: What Will Be Common to Their Leadership, and What

Will Be Different?" Pp. 159–73, in Gama Perruci, ed., *The Study and Practice of Global Leadership*. Bingley, UK: Emerald.

Useem, Michael, Harbir Singh, Neng Liang, and Peter Cappelli (2017). *Fortune Makers: The Leaders Creating China's Great Global Companies*. New York: Public Affairs.

Vachudová, Milada A. (2005). *Europe Undivided: Democracy, Leverage, and Integration after Communism*. Oxford: Oxford University Press.

Van Maanen, John (1979). "The Fact of Fiction in Organizational Ethnography." *Administrative Science Quarterly* 24, no. 4: 539–50.

Van Verseveld, Annemieke (2016). "Superior Orders." *Oxford Bibliographies* – International Law (online). www.oxfordbibliographies.com/display/document/obo-9780199796953/obo-9780199796953-0133.xml

Vortherms, Samantha A. (2019). "China's Missing Children: Political Barriers to Citizenship Through the Household Registration System." *The China Quarterly*, no. 238: 309–30.

Walder, Andrew G. (1995). "Local Governments as Industrial Firms: An Organizational Analysis of China's Transitional Economy." *American Journal of Sociology* 101, no. 2: 263–301.

Walder, Andrew G. (1991). "Workers, Managers and the State: The Reform Era and the Political Crisis of 1989." *The China Quarterly*, no. 127: 467–92.

Walder, Andrew G. (1986). *Communist Neo-Traditionalism: Work and Authority in Chinese Industry*. Berkeley: University of California Press.

Walder, Andrew G. (1983). "Organized Dependency and Cultures of Authority in Chinese Industry." *The Journal of Asian Studies* 43, no. 1: 51–76.

Wallace, Jeremy L. (2016). "Juking the Stats? Authoritarian Information Problems in China." *British Journal of Political Science* 46, no. 1: 11–29.

Walter, Carl, and Fraser J. T. Howie (2012). *Red Capitalism: The Fragile Financial Foundation of China's Extraordinary Rise*. Hoboken, NJ: Wiley.

Wang, Haibo [王海波], ed. (1986). 《工业经济史》[*History of Industrial Economics*]. Beijing: Jingji guanli chubanshe.

Wang, Junhao [王俊豪], Xiao Xingzhi [肖兴志], and Tang Yaojia [唐要家] (2008). 《中国垄断性产业管制机构的设立与运行机制》[*The Establishment and Operation of Regulatory Agencies in China's Monopoly Industries*]. Beijing: Shangwu yinshuguan.

Wang Mengkui [王梦奎], and Xing Junfang [邢俊芳] (1987). 《关于股份制问题》 [*On the Issue of Shareholding*]. Beijing: Zhongguo jingji chubanshe.

Wang, Shaoguang (1997). "China's 1994 Fiscal Reform: An Initial Assessment." *Asian Survey* 37, no. 9: 801–17.

Wang, Yijing, and Daniel Laufer (2020). "How Does Crisis Management in China Differ from the West? A Review of the Literature and Directions for Future Research." *Journal of International Management* 26, no. 1: 100708.

Weber, Isabella M. (2021). *How China Escaped Shock Therapy: The Market Reform Debate*. London: Routledge.

Weber, Max (1998 [1946]). "Bureaucracy." Pp. 196–244, in Hans H. Gerth, and C. Wright Mills, eds., *From Max Weber: Essays in Sociology*. London: Routledge.

Weldes, Jutta (1996). "Constructing National Interests." *European Journal of International Relations* 2, no. 3: 275–318.

Wilpert, Bernhard, and Sophia Y. Scharpf (1990). "Intercultural Management–Joint Ventures in the People's Republic of China." *International Journal of Psychology* 25, nos. 3–6: 643–56.

Wu, Bangguo [吴邦国] (1995). 《吴邦国同志在与参加国家试点企业集团工作会议代表座谈时的讲话》 [Speech by Comrade Wu Bangguo to Representatives Attending the Work Meeting on Enterprise Group National Pilots]. Pp. 1–7, in State Economic and Trade Commission, Enterprise Division, 《我国企业集团试点的政策与实践》 [Policies and Practice of China's Enterprise Group Pilots]. Beijing: Zhongguo jingji chubanshe.

Wu, Howei, and Bin Xu (2021). "Did State-Owned Enterprises Do Better during COVID-19? Evidence from a Survey of Company Executives in China." *Journal of Economics and Business* 115.

Wu, Jinglian [吴敬琏] (1993). 《大中型企业改革：建立现代企业制度》 [*Reform of Large and Medium-Sized Enterprises: Establishing a Modern Enterprise System*]. Tianjin: Tianjin renmin chubanshe.

Wu, Jinglian [吴敬琏], and Qian Yingyi [钱颖一] (1993). 《关于公司化》 [On Corporatization]. 《经济日报》 [*Economic Daily*]. August 24.

Wu, Jinglian, and Guochuan Ma (2016). *Whither China? Restarting the Reform Agenda*. Oxford: Oxford University Press.

Xin, Katherine R., and Jone L. Pearce (1996). "*Guanxi*: Connections as Substitutes for Formal Institutional Support." *Academy of Management Journal* 39, no. 6: 1641–58.

Xu, Xianxiang [徐现祥], Xianbin Wang [王贤彬], and Yuan Shu [舒元] (2007). 《地方官员与经济增长》 [Local Officials and Economic Growth]. 《经济研究》 [*Economic Research Journal*], no. 9: 18–31.

Xu, Yi-chong (2018). "China's Giant State-Owned Enterprises as Policy Advocates: The Case of the State Grid Corporation of China." *The China Journal*, no. 79: 21–39.

Xu, Yi-chong (2017). *Sinews of Power: The Politics of the State Grid Corporation of China*. Oxford: Oxford University Press.

Yang, Dali L. (1996). *Calamity and Reform in China: State, Rural Society, and Institutional Change Since the Great Leap Famine*. Palo Alto, CA: Stanford University Press.

Yang, Mayfair Mei-hui (1994). *Gifts, Favors, and Banquets: The Art of Social Relationships in China*. Ithaca, NY: Cornell University Press.

Yeung, Henry W.-C. (2016). *Strategic Coupling: East Asian Industrial Transformation in the New Global Economy*. Ithaca, NY: Cornell University Press.

Yuan, Baohua [袁宝华] (2019). 《扩权让利：国有企业改革的突破口》 [Expansion of Autonomy and Transfer of Profits: A Breakthrough in SOE Reform]. Pp. 52–67, in 曲青山 [Qu Qingshan] and 吴德刚 [Wu Degang], eds., 《改革开放四十年口述史》 [*Oral History of Forty Years of Reform and Opening*]. Beijing: Zhongguo renmin daxue chubanshe.

Yue, Qingtang [岳清唐] (2018).《中国国有企业改革发展史 (1978–2018)》 [*The History of the Reform and Development of China's State-Owned Enterprises (1978–2018)*]. Beijing: Shehui kexue wenxian chubanshe.

Yukl, Gary, and Cecilia M. Falbe (1991). "Importance of Different Power Sources in Downward and Lateral Relations." *Journal of Applied Psychology* 76, no. 3: 416–23.

Yukl, Gary, and William L. Gardner III (2019). *Leadership in Organizations, Global Edition*, 9th edn. Harlow, UK: Pearson.

Yukl, Gary, and J. Bruce Tracey (1992). "Consequences of Influence Tactics Used with Subordinates, Peers, and the Boss." *Journal of Applied Psychology* 77, no. 4: 525–35.

Zhang, Chunlin (2019). "*How Much Do SOEs Contribute to China's GDP and Employment?*" Washington, DC: World Bank.

Zhang, Delin (2008). "Reform of SOEs: A Three Year Disconnect from Difficulties Leads to System Innovation." Pp. 139–62, in Wang Mengkui, ed., *China in the Wake of Asia's Financial Crisis*. London: Routledge.

Zhang, Dicheng [章迪诚] (2006). 《中国国有企业改革编年史, 1978–2005》 [*Chronicle of China's SOE Reform, 1978–2005*]. Beijing: Zhongguo gongren chubanshe.

Zhang, Jianjun (2015). "From Market Despotism to Managerial Hegemony: The Rise of Indigenous Chinese Management." *Management and Organization Review* 11, no. 2: 205–10.

Zhang, Jin (2004). *Catch-Up and Competitiveness in China: The Case of Large Firms in the Oil Industry*. London: Routledge.

Zhang, Lu (2014). *Inside China's Automobile Factories: The Politics of Labor and Worker Resistance*. Cambridge, UK: Cambridge University Press.

Zhao, Jianping, and Yi-chong Xu (2012). "The Shenhua Group: A Giant Made in a Decade." Pp. 19–46, in Yi-chong Xu, ed., *The Political Economy of State-Owned Enterprises in China and India*. London: Palgrave Macmillan.

Zheng, Junwei, Xueqin Gou, Guangdong Wu, Xianbo Zhao, Hongyang Li, and Bingsheng Liu (2021). "The Ambidextrous and Differential Effects of Directive versus Empowering Leadership: A Study from Project Context." *Leadership and Organization Development Journal* 42, no. 3: 348–69.

Zhi, Qiang, and Margaret M. Pearson (2017). "China's Hybrid Adaptive Bureaucracy: The Case of the 863 Program for Science and Technology." *Governance* 30, no. 3: 407–24.

Zhou, Li-an [周黎安] (2018). 《'官场 + 市场'与中国增长故事》 ["Bureaucratic + Economic Markets" and China's Growth Story]. 《社会》 [*Society*] 38, no. 2: 1–45.

Zhou, Li-an [周黎安] (2014). 《行政发包制》 [Administrative Subcontracting]. 《社会》 [*Society*] 34, no. 6: 1–38.

Zhou, Li-an [周黎安] (2008). 《转型中的地方政府:官员激励与治理》 [*Local Government in Transition: Official Incentives and Governance*]. Shanghai: Gezhi chubanshe.

Zhou, Mingsheng [周明生] (1998). 《资本经营何以雷声大雨点小: 杨瑞龙教授访谈录》 [Operational Management of Capital: How the Thunder is Large and the Rain is Small – Record of Interview with Professor Yang Ruilong]. 《改革内参》 [*Internal Reference Materials on Reform*], no. 8: 13–15.

Zhu, Tianbiao (2002). "Developmental States and Threat Perceptions in Northeast Asia." *Conflict, Security & Development* 2, no. 1: 5–29.

Zhu, Xufeng (2018). "Executive Entrepreneurship, Career Mobility and the Transfer of Policy Paradigms." *Journal of Comparative Policy Analysis*, 20, no. 4: 354–69.

Zou Dongtao [邹东涛], and Zhang Xiaowen [张晓文] (1998). 《试点企业印证了改革的难度》 [Pilot Enterprises Prove the Difficulty of Reform]. 《改革内参》 [*Internal Reference Materials on Reform*], no. 24: 15–17.

Index

Locators in *italics* refer to tables and figures.

(continued from page ii)

LILIANA B. ANDONOVA *Governance Entrepreneurs: International Organizations and the Rise of Global Public-Private Partnerships*

NATHAN M. JENSEN and EDMUND J. MALESKY *Incentives to Pander: How Politicians Use Corporate Welfare for Political Gain*

RICHARD W. CARNEY *Authoritarian Capitalism Sovereign Wealth Funds and State-Owned Enterprises in East Asia and Beyond*

TIMOTHY WERNER *Public Forces and Private Politics in American Big Business*

CHRISTIAN R. THAUER *The Managerial Sources of Corporate Social Responsibility: The Spread of Global Standards*

MICHAEL P. VANDENBERG and JONATHAN M. GILLIGAN *Beyond Politics: The Private Governance Response to Climate Change*

JEROEN VAN DER HEIJDEN *Innovations in Urban Climate Governance: Voluntary Programs for Low Carbon Buildings and Cities*

KIYOTERU TSUTSUI and ALWYN LIM (Editors) *Corporate Social Responsibility in a Globalizing World*

LLEWELYN HUGHES *Globalizing Oil: Firms and Oil Market Governance in France, Japan, and the United States*

VICTOR MENALDO *The Institutions Curse: Natural Resources, Politics, and Development*

ASEEMA SINHA *Globalizing India: How Global Rules and Markets are Shaping India's Rise to Power*

HEVINA S. DASHWOOD *The Rise of Global Corporate Social Responsibility: Mining and the Spread of Global Norms*

EDWARD T. WALKER *Grassroots for Hire: Public Affairs Consultants in American Democracy*

Printed in the USA
CPSIA information can be obtained
at www.ICGtesting.com
CBHW050053151124
17337CB00015B/110

9 781009 48652